THE PREPARATION OF SERMONS

The
PREPARATION
of SERMONS

Andrew Watterson Blackwood

ABINGDON PRESS
New York ● *Nashville*

THE PREPARATION OF SERMONS

Copyright MCMXLVIII by Stone & Pierce

Library of Congress Catalog Card Number: 48-10392

K

SET UP, PRINTED, AND BOUND BY THE
PARTHENON PRESS, AT NASHVILLE,
TENNESSEE, UNITED STATES OF AMERICA

Dedicated
to
Those Who Guide
the
Ministers of Tomorrow
in
Learning How to Preach

Foreword

THIS BOOK seems to me the most important I have written. It shows what I have learned through the study of preaching, and how my thinking on the subject has changed. For ten years and more I approached homiletics as a science; through another decade or so I investigated preaching as an art; for about ten years I have been engaged in the study of sermons. Now I look on this last as most nearly ideal, because it combines the advantages of the other two approaches and avoids most of their weaknesses. It fixes attention on preparing for the pulpit, not on the theory of preaching or on the personality of the preacher.

Owing to the size of the field and the limits of space, I discuss how rather than what to preach. In our seminary, as elsewhere, other professors deal with what to preach; in the practical department we try to learn how. To us, that seems much more difficult; at least we can find less guidance in books. If anyone questions the difficulty, let him try to show or tell a group of ministerial students how to prepare and deliver a sermon. Here, then, we are to consider "the preacher's forgotten word, how."

As for the motive behind this book, I can echo a professor at Columbia University: "I began to write as a means of reaching the largest possible audience, or if you prefer, as a means of bringing the public into my classroom. I dare say I never wrote again for any other purpose." [1] The only "public" I now wish to reach consists of the best people I know: students for the ministry, pastors on the field, and missionaries beyond the seven seas. Under God these friends hold in their hands the future of the Church and the hope for the Kingdom, for they bring to men the evangel.

First in view come students of theology. From Plato's *Republic* they need to learn that "the direction in which education starts

[1] John Erskine, *The Memory of Certain Persons* (Philadelphia: J. B. Lippincott Co., 1947), p. 182.

a man will determine his lifework." In the seminary anyone who ought to become a minister can learn how to preach. From professors and books he can learn how to handle tools; in the spirit of prayer he can form habits of toil; in classroom and study he can set up ideals he will never need to change, though he may watch them soar. In short, every young preacher must work out his own salvation.

Next come pastors out on the field, including missionaries abroad, both men and women. Year after year a wise parish leader goes through a book or two about preaching, to check up on his pulpit work and lay plans for still better sermons. If any pastor at home or abroad will follow the trail he finds in this book, he can help to promote a revival of preaching—a revival that seems to have begun.

Whether mature or young, the student of preaching will deal with cases, in the form of sermons by the masters. According to John Dewey, "There can be no discovery of a method without cases to be studied. The method is derived from observation of what actually happens, with a view to seeing that it happens better the next time."[2] The value of such work depends a good deal on care in the selection of cases. For such uses I have prepared a volume of representative sermons by well-known preachers of yesterday and today.[3]

The student of preaching can learn still more by preparing and delivering sermons of his own. Like every other artist, the preacher learns best by doing, provided he always preaches as well as he can. So the friend in view needs to watch his step, especially as he draws near to middle age. Unless he takes care, he may begin to slip, and deliver weaker sermons at forty than at thirty. The preacher may not know that he has begun to go back, but the lay officers know. If he talked things over with a deacon or a steward "not too polite to tell the truth," the preacher might begin to mend his ways. He

[2] *Education and Democracy* (New York: The Macmillan Co., 1920), p. 197.
[3] See *The Protestant Pulpit* (New York and Nashville: Abingdon-Cokesbury Press, 1947).

8

would find that the fault lies in study, or in the lack of study and of a working method.

Amid his reading and study the parish minister ought to prepare and deliver sermons in a way all his own, and not like that of some pulpit giant, present or past. In our day few ministers can hope to become pulpit orators, but every man who ought to preach can learn how to prepare for his own pulpit, and in the preparation find many of earth's holiest joys.

If any pastor seeks first the kingdom of God, loves all sorts of people, studies the work of preaching, and prepares for effectiveness in the pulpit according to the ideals of this book, he can keep growing as a preacher year after year. Why then should any of God's heralds think of crossing the deadline before he dies? Who will resolve to prepare sermons week after week so as to promote a revival of preaching as the noblest work on earth? "God Almighty had only one Son, and He became a Preacher."

I wish to thank the following who have helped me with this book: Mrs. Blackwood and our ministerial sons; librarians and professors here and elsewhere; parish ministers and seminary students. These two have aided in reading proofs: John P. Amstutz and Harold E. Davenport. Countless others have also shown me kindnesses that I can never begin to repay.

ANDREW WATTERSON BLACKWOOD

Contents

Contents

CHAPTER I

The Work of the Preacher

PREACHING should rank as the noblest work on earth. The man called of God to proclaim the gospel ought to stand out as the most important man in the community, and all that he does for Christ and the Church should head up in his preaching. In the pulpit he can do much of his best work for time and eternity. As a rule we ought to employ superlatives sparingly, but not when we discuss the work of the preacher.

What do we understand by preaching? It means divine truth through personality or the truth of God voiced by a chosen personality to meet human needs. Divine truth comes largely from the Scriptures but it also comes from other sources. Human needs spring mainly from sin but also from other roots. The man in the pulpit looks on himself as called of God to use these truths in meeting those needs one by one. Such a way of thinking goes back to Phillips Brooks. In the best series of Lyman Beecher Lectures so far,[1] he described preaching as "the bringing of truth through personality," and as "the communication of truth by man to men." Everywhere in those Lectures, and in his ten volumes of sermons, the Boston pastor showed that he wished to help the friends who filled the pews of Trinity Church.

From another point of view preaching calls for the interpretation of life today in light that comes from God today, largely through the Scriptures. This way of approaching the subject accords with the ideals of John Bunyan, who has taught us to think of the minister as dwelling in "the house of the interpreter." There he learns to employ the truths of God in meeting the needs of men. Both up in the pulpit and out in the parish he strives to interpret the will of God for the friends who look to him for guidance.

---

[1] See *Lectures on Preaching* (New York: E. P. Dutton & Co., 1898), chap. I.

Why do we regard such an interpreter as the most important man in any community and his preaching as the most important part of his lifework? For the answer we turn to the history of the Church. Unfortunately, we can only glance at a few of God's heralds from age to age, but we can see enough to make the point clear. If any man wishes to become a master in the realm of preaching, he should engage in a study of Church history, with special emphasis on representative sermons.

THE HISTORY OF PREACHING

In the Old Testament the prophets stood out head and shoulders above other men. When Sargent painted his frieze of the prophets at the Public Library in Boston, he presented a group of men unsurpassed for strength of personality and power of utterance. Think of Isaiah and Amos, Hosea and Micah, Jeremiah and Ezekiel, and other seers not well known today. Those men spoke at different times, but they all belong together, for they show the meaning of "truth through personality." Every one of them looked on himself first of all as an interpreter of God's truth in order to meet the needs of men in that day. Hence we sing at the ordination of a minister:

> God of the prophets, bless the prophets' sons;
>
> . . . .
>
> Anoint them prophets! Make their ears attent
> To Thy divinest speech; their hearts awake
> To human need; their lips make eloquent
> To gird the right and every evil break.

In the New Testament a study of preaching begins with John the Baptist, an evangelistic herald second only to our Lord. The roll of preachers includes Peter, Paul, and the author of the Epistle to the Hebrews. In fact, the New Testament consists largely of apostolic preaching as reported through the Early Church.[2] These men have lived in history mainly because they served as preachers

[2] See C. H. Dodd, *The Apostolic Preaching and Its Developments* (London: Hodder & Stoughton, 1936).

of the gospel. Before they entered on that lifework the future apostles lived with the Master Teacher, and learned from Him how to preach. In the days of His flesh our Lord spent much of His active ministry in "the training of the twelve." [3] Why? Doubtless because He wished the Church from the beginning to exalt the work of the preacher.

The history of the Early Church teaches much the same lesson, both positively and negatively. In those early days, whenever the tides of spiritual life and power rose high, preaching stood first in the thinking of the leaders. For example, turn to Chrysostom, Augustine, and Ambrose. Those men excelled in other ways, but each of them stood out first of all as a preacher. Every one of them has lived in history mainly because of his preaching. On the other hand, whenever the Early Church permitted something else to usurp the place of the pulpit, the spirituality of God's people suffered a decline. [4]

Throughout the Middle Ages two men above all others endeared themselves to the people of God. Those two did not live at exactly the same time, but they came close enough together to mark the golden era of the Middle Ages. Like the apostles and the Early Church fathers, Bernard of Clairvaux and Francis of Assisi excelled in other respects, but each of them regarded himself first of all as a preacher. With voice and pen each interpreted the will of God to meet the needs of his day. Largely for that reason they live now in the hearts of all who love the preaching of the Word.

At the Reformation the work of the preacher stood out still more strongly. If anyone had asked Martin Luther what he counted first in his life and work, he would have replied in terms of preaching. So would John Calvin, John Knox, and the other leaders of the Reformation, with only an exception here and there. Those men served God and the Church in various other capacities. Luther, for instance, translated the Bible into German that still sings its way into Christian hearts. He did much to start the Protestant Church toward hymns

[3] Under this title see the work by A. B. Bruce (New York: Geo. H. Doran Co., 1908).

[4] See Kenneth S. Latourette, *A History of the Expansion of Christianity* (New York: Harper & Bros., 1937), Vol. I.

of high literary and musical quality, in the language of the common people. Calvin excelled as a commentator and a theologian. But first of all those men stood out as preachers.

In the Counter Reformation the Roman Church began again to exalt the work of the preacher. Partly because of what the Protestant Reformers had done, the leaders of the "Mother Church" started a movement that produced the French Catholic preachers of the seventeenth century. Never since the days of Chrysostom has the Christian Church listened to sacred oratory such as came from Bossuet and Bourdaloue, Massillon and Fénelon. Today many of us prefer other types of preaching, but when we think of pulpit oratory in its upper reaches we must give the palm to those Frenchmen, who showed the brilliance of the spoken word.

Over in England a little later, John Wesley and George White-field led in a revival of the Christian Church. According to Lecky and other historians, the Wesleyan Movement did much to avert in Britain a counterpart of the French Revolution. While Wesley displayed various other gifts, he regarded himself first of all as a preacher, and as a promoter of the Kingdom through other preachers. Whitefield, also, stood out as a herald of the gospel. From that time to this, wherever the Wesleyan Movement has spread throughout the world, the cause has prevailed largely because of preaching.

As for other churches in Great Britain, time does not permit even a passing glance. But a study of the facts would show that wherever the Church has prospered spiritually, stress has fallen upon the work of the pulpit. During the latter part of the Victorian era, for instance, a lover of preaching faced an embarrassment of riches whenever he went to London or Edinburgh. Which of the various pulpit masters should he single out, and which ones should he fail to hear? If England during the time of Queen Elizabeth had sounded like a nest of singing birds, either of those cities two hundred years afterwards had become the home of pulpit masters.

Here in the United States the spiritual welfare of the Church has varied, and so has the emphasis on the ministry of preaching. At times in the past, such a city as Brooklyn or Boston could have adopted the motto of a Scottish city in olden days: "Let Glasgow Flourish through the Preaching of the Word." As for the pulpit masters who have brought luster to the American Church, many of their names will appear in the chapters that follow. Meanwhile every young preacher should rejoice because he follows in the succession of mighty men who spoke for God with passion and with power.

THE DECLINE OF THE PULPIT

More recently the pulpit seems to have lost much of its prestige. Over in Scotland businessmen have shortened that motto to read: "Let Glasgow Flourish!" On our side of the water few ministers of the gospel seem able to influence civic life and action through sermons. Many of our pastors have let other aspects of the work loom larger than their preaching, but the men and women who come to church believe in the primacy of the pulpit. Any bishop or pulpit committee will testify that when a pulpit becomes vacant, the leaders of the local church ask for a minister who can preach.

The causes of the decline include many factors, such as the increase of secularism, the prevalence of immorality, and the spirit of distraction. The climate of our time does not encourage the young man who wishes to write beautiful poetry or preach spiritual sermons. Many of our lay friends live on their nerves, and their spirit of being busy and troubled about many things may extend to the pastor. In time he may begin to act like the manager of a merry-go-round, or the chief actor in a three-ring circus, and not as an ambassador from the King of Kings. All the while, down in his heart, the dear man wishes that he knew how to put the first thing first.

The lack of proper training also helps to account for the plight of many a preacher today. More than a few local ministers have never learned how to preach, or else they have forgotten what they once knew. At the seminary a student may "pass" a number of courses but never really master homiletics and public speaking, and out in the parish he may continue to flounder as a preacher. If so, he ought to study the life of Henry Ward Beecher, or of Thomas Chalmers,

17

each of whom tried to preach for a number of years before he learned how. Meanwhile, what happens to the flock? As Milton said, "The hungry sheep look up, and are not fed."

Any such case will yield to the right sort of treatment. Paderewski had reached the age of twenty-four ere he quit merely "playing the piano," and commenced to master his art, a discipline to which he gave the rest of his life. So did young Beecher have to learn his main business the hard way, in the midst of parish duties. When the Brooklyn pastor later spoke to ministerial students he must have been echoing his early experiences at Indianapolis:

You have not begun your education yet. You are but getting ready to study when you begin to preach. If you preach for five years, and find that your work is slow, and much of it obscure, and does not produce the results aimed at, do not be discouraged. The work is so great that you need not be ashamed, after working for years, if you find that you are still an apprentice and not a journeyman.[5]

THE THREE METHODS OF STUDY

The man who would learn how to preach may approach the subject in one of three ways, all of which appear in a well-known definition: "Homiletics is the science of which preaching is the art and the sermon is the finished product." The three methods have to do, respectively, with the science of homiletics, the art of preaching, and the study of sermons. Naturally these divisions overlap, for facts do not fit systems. Still, we can think of the three methods as good, better, best. If each of them has its pitfalls, so has everything else on earth. In this book we shall pay some attention to the science of homiletics, more to the art of preaching, and most to the preparation of sermons.

The science of homiletics calls for emphasis on what a minister ought to know about preaching. The method leads to definition of terms and classification of types. In some of the older books the system became as complicated as a medical textbook on anatomy. That way

[5] *Yale Lectures on Preaching*, first series (New York: J. B. Ford Co., 1872), pp. 61-62.

of approach to the work of the preacher made little appeal to his imagination. At times the task of preparing for the pulpit has threatened to become little more than the assembling of enough dry bones to show the skeleton of a truth that died long ago. If such an account seems severe, ask many an elderly minister what he derived from the study of homiletics.

In the wrong hands the teaching of homiletics as a science has contributed to the low estate of the pulpit. Many who have tried to master the terminology of the science have emerged with a set of molds, or forms, into which they have poured materials for sermons. Through no fault of their own these young men have thought about "sermonizing" in terms of rules, and not life. They have never learned to enjoy the work of the study or the delivery of sermons. When shall professors of homiletics learn to set forth "the romance of preaching"? [6]

The art of preaching goes far to remedy these defects. In the study of an art a young man seeks to enjoy beauty as well as learn truth. A sculptor must know the anatomy of the body before he can make a statue of a man, but amid all this knowledge a young artist cherishes a sense of life and motion, with much of warmth and color. In the study of preaching as an art the future minister learns to use imagination. In time he begins to see why Horace Bushnell wrote about "Our Gospel a Gift to the Imagination." [7]

This way of looking at preaching as an art does not meet with favor everywhere. Certain evangelical ministers like to quote Phillips Brooks: "A sermon is a piece of bread to be eaten, and not a work of art to be enjoyed." These dissenters ask how we can think about art when we listen to Amos or John the Baptist, Charles H. Spurgeon or Dwight L. Moody. Surely Isaiah and the apostle Paul, or Chrysostom and Francis of Assisi, never thought of sermons as works of art!

Without going all the way with these critics we can see the pitfalls

[6] See the book of this name by C. S. Horne (New York: F. H. Revell Co., 1914).

[7] Horace Bushnell, *Building Eras in Religion* (New York: Charles Scribner's Sons. 1909), chap. VIII.

in the study of preaching as an art. Unless a minister keeps close to God, he may let the sermon become an end in itself, and not a means of grace. But that holds true in every other art, such as music or poetry. The higher the realm into which human beings soar, the larger the possibility of falling below the ideal. On the other hand, when we sit spellbound as the preacher guides us up to the mountaintop, some of us find it hard to think of a sermon as a "piece of bread to be eaten." But why should we quarrel about labels? Can we not find a third method that will combine the strength of homiletics with the sweetness of artistic study, and then add something all its own?

The study of sermons provides a third method. At times this way of approach runs parallel with the other two, but only for a while. Ideally every minister ought to know something about homiletics and more about the art of preaching, but he should think most of all about the sermon. He ought to look on himself not as a scientist with a mass of knowledge, or as an artist with a gift of appreciation, but as a preacher with ability to prepare all sorts of sermons. In order to do such work again and again, he ought to study the sermons of other men and then form habits all his own.

From this point on we shall think about the sermon, both in its parts and as a whole. We shall assume that the work of preaching affords the most attractive opportunity for usefulness on earth today, and that the sermon constitutes the chief product of the minister's labors from week to week. We shall also take for granted that he seeks and follows the guidance of the Holy Spirit in answer to prayer.

Suggested Readings

Broadus, John A. *On the Preparation and Delivery of Sermons,* 1870. Revised by J. B. Weatherspoon. New York: Harper & Bros., 1942.

Brooks, Phillips. *Lectures on Preaching.* New York: E. P. Dutton & Co., 1877.

Dargan, Edwin C. *The History of Preaching.* New York: Hodder & Stoughton, 1905, 1912. Two vols.

Garvie, Alfred E. *The Christian Preacher.* New York: Charles Scribner's Sons, 1921.

Jefferson, Charles E. *The Building of the Church*. New York: The Macmillan Co., 1910.

Luccock, Halford E. *In the Minister's Workshop*. New York and Nashville: Abingdon-Cokesbury Press, 1944.

Pattison, T. Harwood. *The Making of the Sermon*, 1898. Revised 1946. Philadelphia: Judson Press.

CHAPTER II

The Sense of Human Needs

OW DOES THE MAN in the study determine what to preach? The pastor may pray as though everything depended on God and work as though everything depended on the preacher. If he has a teaching mind, he may look on the sermon for the next Sunday morning as part of the year's pulpit work.[1] So he does well to think in terms of the Christian Year with its onward movement, but he himself must never be far from the central Sun. The pastor across the street may regard himself as a physician of souls, and deal with each sermon as a case study more or less by itself. Such an account oversimplifies the facts, for many a preacher follows neither plan. Whatever his method, the wise man begins with some human need, and meets that need with divine truth.

Sometimes we talk about meeting human needs as though we had discovered an eighth wonder in the world. We may employ new labels, some of them fancy, but when we go to Isaiah and Hosea, or Peter and Paul, we find that they have done what we now attempt. Who ever heard of a prophetic or apostolic message delivered at random or in a vacuum? The same principle has governed preaching throughout the history of the Church. Whenever an oral discourse has deserved to be called a sermon, it has met the needs of the hearers. The truth in hand may have concerned world missions, world brotherhood, or world peace, but only as that truth related to the friends in view.

How then does the minister determine what human needs to meet next Sunday morning? Must he go over the whole ground every time before he decides what to preach? No. If he wishes to make the most of the hours in the study, he settles all of these matters in advance, but still he keeps the windows of his soul open for new light. At first

---

[1] See A. W. Blackwood, *Planning a Year's Pulpit Work* (New York and Nashville: Abingdon-Cokesbury Press, 1942).

the novice may feel that the whole business looks mechanical, but soon he will find that the sense of human need makes his heart burn.

THE THREE ASPECTS OF THE SUBJECT

Three factors enter into the equation, all on the human level. The first has to do with the world today; the second, with the home community; the third, with the preacher himself. Consciously or unconsciously, he lets these factors influence every decision about the content and the form of a sermon. Herein he finds no small part of the fascination and the difficulty in preaching today.

1. *The state of the times* affects the substance and the tone color of every sermon. "Today is not yesterday." The interpreter of God's truth makes ready to utter what the auditors most need to hear. Hence he must shift the emphasis from time to time, though never so as to ignore basic truths. For example, turn to the book of Isaiah, and note how the tone color of chapters 1-12 differs from that of chapters 40 through 55. In each case the "forthteller" was speaking to the condition of those whom he addressed. In our own country sermons during easy days of prosperity have differed from those in the same pulpit during hard times of depression.

Let no one construe this as a plea for sweeping surveys which cover everything in general and touch nothing in particular. Only a statesman in the kingdom of God can rise to heights where he surveys heaven and earth, and a man of this type can bring forth only a few surveys each year. But every parish minister needs to sense the meaning and force of *Weltanshauung* and *Weltschmertz*. Whenever people suffer in a burning, fiery furnace, "in all their afflictions he is afflicted." If not, how can he hope to speak for the God of all mercy and comfort? In the sanctuary a minister's view of the world as a whole and his sense of its anguish at heart may appear in his choice of hymns and in the spirit of his prayers more than in sermon topics and in subject matter. But woe be to the parish whose minister does not know the world of his day and the spirit of his age.

2. *The needs of the home community* enter into the equation more directly. Each congregation has needs all its own, and these the pastor

23

must sense before he can do his best work as the local interpreter of God's truth. For example, in 1869, when Phillips Brooks went to Trinity Church, Boston, at the age of thirty-three, he knew much about the condition of our land during those years of reconstruction. But before he decided how to carry on the work of pulpit and parish, he made a careful study of the field, and then he made ready for a change of tactics. In Philadelphia, for ten years, "he had appeared almost a reformer and agitator, with a work to do outside the pulpit." But in Boston "he gave himself to his parish, and exclusively to the preacher's task." [2]

In the war against sin pulpit tactics from week to week depend on parish strategy, and that varies according to the needs of the community. In a certain field a minister found the people concerned about the doctrines of Christianity but scarcely awake to the necessity of applying them in the community. In the next parish he found concern about the application of Christian truths to local needs but little understanding of the doctrines themselves. Consequently, in the first field he began to stress what the apostle Paul wrote in the latter parts of his epistles, whereas in the other field the pastor emphasized the doctrines in the earlier portions of those letters.

The incoming coach of a varsity football team follows much the same course. During the winter he becomes acquainted with the other members of the staff, winning their friendship and consulting with them daily about team strategy. With the beginning of spring practice he starts to size up his squad, both as a whole and man by man. During the summer he makes plans for the work in the fall. At the opening of the season he knows what he wants to do, and he makes every move count. One year he must strengthen the backfield; the next season he must concentrate on the linemen. All of this has a bearing on a minister's work outside the pulpit, but those other activities do not concern us now. Let us conclude that a preacher's tactics from week to week depend on his strategy for the work of the pulpit.

3. *The personality of the preacher* also influences the decisions about

[2] A. V. G. Allen, *Life and Letters of Phillips Brooks* (New York: E. P. Dutton & Co., 1907), II, 134-35.

what to do in the pulpit. Since preaching calls for "truth through personality," every minister ought to know what he can do and what he can not, at least not now. Young David must not sally forth in the armor of King Saul. During the first year out on the field the young minister may feel that the situation calls for a course of sermons about the doctrines of our faith, or about the duties. If the preacher can prepare only one message of a certain kind, and then must wait a month before he attempts another, let him work that way. If he learns about metropolitan preachers who excel in preparing special series, let him rejoice in the liberty of serving God in his own way.

"Son of man, stand upon thy feet, and I will speak unto thee." In terms of our day this may mean: "Young minister at Cream Ridge, dare to be yourself! Preach the gospel in your own fashion and not in that of some giant!" You may not agree with Karl Barth in certain other respects, but you can accept what he says about preaching. The Swiss theologian insists that God makes Himself known in three ways: supremely in Christ, largely through the Bible, and also through the preacher today.[3] At Cream Ridge He wishes to speak through the man whom He has chosen as pastor. So be yourself, young man, your best self!

This working principle helps a man decide about requests for sermons on difficult subjects. He may feel flattered when friends ask for messages about the unpardonable sin and the valley of dry bones, but soon he will see the wisdom of Charles H. Spurgeon. When a young minister asked the London preacher what to do with such a request, the older man advised a polite refusal:

As a rule, never! If there must be exceptions, let them be few. You do not keep a shop to which customers may come and give their orders. When a friend suggests a topic, think it over, consider whether it be appropriate, and see whether it comes to you with power. Receive the request courteously, but if the Lord whom you serve does not cast His light upon the text, do not preach upon it, let who may persuade you.[4]

[3] See Karl Barth, *The Word of God and the Word of Man* (Boston: The Pilgrim Press, 1928), chaps. IV, VI.
[4] *Lectures to My Students*, first series (London, 1875), p. 101.

A glance over the last few pages will show why a student in the seminary may dread the ordeal of preaching in class. Especially during the first year, how can a young man sense the needs of a world full of confusion, size up the situation in a parish that exists only in dreamland, and appraise personal resources that seem elusive? In view of such difficulties, who can wonder that some student sermons seem unreal? In fact, certain writers in our field agree with Fénelon that we should not subject students to such an ordeal.

We who hear many sermons by students believe in these ministers of tomorrow. Some of us listen to eight or ten, even twelve, week after week. Only once in a while do we wonder whether or not the young man ought to preach, but we often wish we could impart a strong sense of human needs today. Only God can do that, and He does much of it after a man goes out to his first parish. Meanwhile He wishes every young preacher to employ imagination as he prepares for some hypothetical field.

Student preaching during the summer goes far to remedy this defect. For three or four months a young man lives among friends in a local church, and on each Lord's Day strives to meet the needs he has discovered there. Better still, after two years at the seminary he may go out for an "internship." There for fifteen months he labors under a mature pastor who knows how to guide the young man in preparing for both pulpit and parish. After such an internship the student comes back to the divinity school and completes his training. He has tasted the joys of the parish ministry, discovered the limitations of his equipment, and resolved to work as never before. Why do we not require more young men to act as interns?

The mature pastor also ought to remember these working principles. What man of middle age does not need to cultivate a world view, know his parish well, and work within his limits? But if a minister wishes to keep growing as a preacher, he must extend those limits week after week. In preparing for the pulpit he ought to remember the counsel of William Carey: "Expect great things from God; attempt great things for God." Whatever the world scene, the local situation, and the ministerial handicaps, no interpreter of God's truth ought to engage in Lilliputian preaching. The work of the pulpit in our time calls for faith and courage, with a spirit of prophetic adventure and apostolic optimism. What then will such a man prepare to preach?

THE MEANING OF SERMONIC LABELS

The man with a sense of human needs prepares different kinds of sermons. From this point onward various types of pulpit work will appear under certain labels. What do they mean? Before we turn to the answers, let us give heed to Brooks:

> The ordinary classifications of sermons are of little consequence. We hear of expository preaching and topical sermons, of practical sermons, of hortatory discourses, each separate species seeming to stand by itself. It seems as if the preacher were expected to determine each week what kind of sermon the next Sunday was to enjoy and set himself deliberately to produce it. . . . To my mind the sermon seems a unit and . . . no sermon seems complete that does not include all these elements. . . . Every sermon must have a solid rest on Scripture, and the pointedness which comes of a clear subject, and the conviction which belongs to well-thought argument, and the warmth that proceeds from earnest appeal.[5]

To all of that every lover of preaching must say amen. But when we turn to the ten volumes of sermons from Brooks himself we find all sorts of emphases, for one sermon differs from others as one star differs from all the rest. However, when we look closely we see that Brooks tended to preach in one of two ways. In about half of the two hundred published sermons he addressed the seeker after God; and in the other half, the person who had found Him. In his sixty-three volumes of sermons Spurgeon followed much the same course. Half of them he addressed primarily to the unsaved or the unchurched; the rest he spoke mainly to those who loved the Lord. While those two pulpit masters differed from each other in many respects, they held much the same theory about their pulpit work as pastoral evangelists.

The evangelistic emphasis marks the preaching of the minister who

[5] *Lectures on Preaching*, pp. 129-31.

accepts the ideals of the New Testament. According to C. H. Dodd of Cambridge University, whenever the writers of the New Testament employ the word "preaching," they refer to what we know as evangelism.[6] They also give room to other sorts of pulpit work, but not under the name of "preaching." In our day, fortunately, almost every branch of the Christian Church stresses evangelistic preaching, though sometimes under a different name.

In this realm a pastor finds it hard to keep the balance, for he may run to either of two extremes. On one hand he may stress evangelistic preaching so much that he neglects what Horace Bushnell terms "Christian nurture."[7] In recent years only an occasional parish minister has gone to this extreme, but many a preacher has dealt with other subjects so continuously as not to tell any seeker how to find the Saviour. In a congregation that styles itself evangelical a seeker after God can attend divine services for a year without learning how to find Him. Elsewhere a believer in the Lord can attend for twelve months without learning how to live as a Christian today. What a lack of balance, and what a need for strategy!

The evangelistic sermon brings the hearer face to face with Christ as the Son of God, and moves the hearer to accept Him as Saviour and Lord. Strange as the fact seems to a man who has never preached, this kind of pulpit work appeals to saints who have loved the Lord for years. It shows them the pit from which they have been dug, and encourages them to do personal work among their friends, whether unsaved or unchurched. According to pastors now at work all over the land, hosts of men and women today are waiting for an introduction to the Saviour. Fulton J. Sheen insists that in the United States ten million adults walk our streets groping after God. In how many of our churches could one of them be sure to find Him next Sunday morning or evening?

At certain seasons of the year the evangelistic appeal comes with special force. During both Advent and the Lenten season the good

[6] C. H. Dodd, *op. cit.,* pp. 7-8.
[7] See his book of this name (1847). New edition with introduction by L. A. Weigle (New Haven: Yale University Press, 1947).

news from God accords with the aspirations of men and women seeking a way of escape from their baser selves. In fact the period between Thanksgiving and Easter may well become the harvest season of the Christian Year. Especially in late winter, when the weather becomes worst and sickness abounds, when deaths often follow, the evangel brings out to church more men and women than at any other season. So the wise man keeps sounding the evangelistic note, often at the morning service. At other seasons, too, he presents the claims of Christ on the allegiance of everyone for whom He died and in whose life He yearns to rule.[8]

The doctrinal emphasis likewise marks preaching that helps men and women today. Indeed, Christian doctrine forms the core of almost every sermon that appeals to both head and heart. For example, in almost every evangelistic sermon worthy of the name some Christian truth provides the basis of an appeal to accept Christ.[9] But from time to time a minister ought to prepare sermons directly doctrinal. This kind of sermon means the pulpit interpretation of a Christian truth for a practical purpose. In the heart of Boston, then strongly Unitarian, Brooks often preached directly about the doctrine of the Trinity. At other times he set forth Christian teachings about the Incarnation and the glory of God as Light. On the basis of his experience he told young ministers what every pastor ought to know by heart and often repeat:

No preaching ever had any strong power that was not the preaching of doctrine. . . . Preach doctrine, preach all the doctrine that you know, and learn forever more and more; but preach it always, not that men may believe it, but that men may be saved by believing it.[10]

Young people today need doctrinal sermons even more than in Brooks's time, and they need such pulpit work in thought-forms of their own day. At university centers pastors find that young women have as many doubts as young men, and respond to the right sort

[8] See Rev. 3:20, where Christ appeals to one man in a worldly church.
[9] See A. W. Blackwood, *Evangelism in the Home Church* (New York and Nashville: Abingdon-Cokesbury Press, 1942), chap. IV.
[10] *Lectures on Preaching*, p. 129.

of doctrinal preaching. In university chapels many students regard Reinhold Niebuhr as their favorite preacher, because he encourages everyone to bring his brains to church and keep them busy there. When these young men and women go back home some of them wonder why the pastor does not deal with such doctrinal subjects as "The Workings of God's Providence Today" (Rom. 8:28), and "The Gospel of the Sovereignty" (Ps. 97:1).

On the other hand young people who think for themselves protest against doctrinal preaching that consists in "the unilluminating discussion of unreal problems in unintelligible language." During World War I, when Joseph Fort Newton preached at the City Temple, he went down to a London theater one night to conduct an aftermeeting. Since he had not heard the sermon that the assembled soldiers wished to discuss, he began by asking the "Tommies" what the speaker had said about the subject, "The Grace of God." One of them spoke out: "The preacher told us that the grace of God is plentiful, sufficient for all our needs, and near at hand. But he did not tell us what the grace of God is. Perhaps you, sir, will be good enough to do that!" Newton felt nonplussed; he had been preaching for years, and he had often touched on divine grace, but he had never tried to tell lay friends what the word meant.[11]

In a world full of wars and rumors of wars, men and women, old and young, feel grateful for the right sort of preaching about "The Last Things," though not under that heading. For example, in the Apostles' Creed and in the hymnal they find more than a little about the "communion of saints," but they do not know what the truth means in terms of today. One Sunday afternoon at the Fifth Avenue Presbyterian Church in New York City, a throng listened eagerly to John S. Bonnell as he told the meaning of these mystic words. Ever since that hour many of those hearers have rejoiced anew in the assurance that they can hold fellowship with the children of God everywhere, both on earth and in heaven. Especially at the celebration of the Lord's Supper Christians ought to give thanks because they can

---

[11] J. F. Newton, *The New Preaching* (Nashville: Cokesbury Press, 1930), p. 120.

enter into fellowship with those whose faces they shall behold no more on earth.

The evening service may lend itself to doctrinal preaching, and so may vespers. In three different parishes, as diverse as fields can be in our homeland, a certain minister often preached directly about doctrine at the evening service. In each congregation he heard from the lay officers that they had despaired of getting people to attend church after dark, but he found many persons eager to learn about the basic truths of Christianity. He also found that if he wished to address a throng of seekers after truth, he must study theology. He enjoyed theology all the more because he could use it all in the pulpit, as he strove to meet the needs of men.

The ethical emphasis resembles the doctrinal, except that one relates ⌐ to duty whereas the other concerns truth. The Bible consists of both elements, and little else: "The Scriptures principally teach what man is to believe concerning God, and what duty God requires of man." So if any minister has been neglecting the pulpit interpretation of doctrine or duty for practical ends, how has he been meeting the needs of the friends in his parish? Do they not need to learn the will of God about "The Forgiveness of Wrongs," and "The Christian Cure for Race Prejudice"?

Young people especially ought to hear luminous interpretations of how to live in a world cursed with wars and preparations for war. Many of them feel perplexed about personal living and overwhelmed by problems of wider scope. They wonder how they can cling to moral standards and keep themselves "unspotted from the world." In more than a few fields the young folk respond to ethical sermons which show what the Bible teaches about Christian duty, and how to make that teaching bear on life today. But they want ethical teaching to come from a friend with a large heart, and not from a critic with a big stick.

In a sense every message from the sacred desk ought to move in an ethical atmosphere. But some ministers rely on atmosphere as a sub-stitute for ethical teaching that would make Christian duty clear. By all means saturate your sermons with the spirit of the New Testament, but from time to time preach directly on "What Jesus Says about Marriage," or "How to Keep Sunday." Does not the future welfare of our civilization, under God, depend largely on the maintenance of the Christian home and on the observance of the Lord's Day?

The young minister, however, may have to wait awhile before he can prepare sermons mainly ethical, as he will find it easier to make ready for almost any other kind of pulpit work. Soon after one future professor of homiletics first came to the divinity school, he had to preach before the class. Not knowing any better, he chose to speak on an ethical subject: "A Strong Man's Declaration of Dependence." Starting with the Apostle's words about eating food that had been sacrificed to idols (I Cor. 8:13), the sermon dealt with (1) Things always right—do them, though the heavens fall. (2) Things always wrong—do them not, though the neighbors sneer. (3) Things neither right nor wrong—do them or do them not, according to the conscience of your weaker brother; when in doubt, don't. At the end of that discourse the teacher in charge told the class: "The young man has presented the most difficult kind of pulpit work, an ethical sermon."

A mature pastor may shy away from delicate issues for the sake of prudence, since he knows that some lay officers and their wives do not care for ethical sermons. They want to hear the Word; they wish him to preach the gospel and nothing but the gospel. By this they mean comforts and warnings that have to do with salvation. God forbid that any of His messengers make light of these friends and their desire for evangelistic sermons. May He also forbid that fears deflect a man from declaring "the whole counsel of God." In our day the minister who dodges the pulpit interpretation of duty ought to regard himself as a coward, if not a false prophet. On the other hand, a wise man bases his ethical teachings squarely on the Bible. "Thus saith the Lord!"

Many such fears prove to be groundless. Often they originate in the study, and not in the pew. If a pastor toils over one of the Lord's parables about money, and then tells the people what the parable means in terms of today, they receive what he brings straight from the Book. Gradually he finds that many people object to man-made labels, but not to God-given messages. The same often holds true with people who insist that they will not listen to evangelistic sermons, or doctrinal discourses. Very well! Let them have their say. Keep on smiling. Remember that these labels belong in the study, and not elsewhere. In the pulpit never call attention to how you preach, but lay the stress on why you preach. If you prepare and speak aright, the majority of the people will respond.

What if they rebel? Sometimes, alas, they will not accept the teaching of God's Word, usually because of its ethical demands. Did not people stone William Booth, largely because of ethical utterances; and before him, John Wesley? Think of Savonarola and Chrysostom, each of whom lost his life because he had told people about their duties to God. What else did our Saviour warn His disciples to expect when they rebuked people because of sin? "If any man will come after me, let him deny himself, and take up his cross daily, and follow me" (Luke 9:23). In the Greek, note the strong verb "will"—determination. These words tell the cost of being a Christian, a cost that every preacher of truth and duty must stand ready to pay, for he must speak in a world where Christ Himself went to the Cross, and that largely because of His ethical teachings.

Fortunately, a pastor need not deal with delicate issues all the time. Sermons with *a pastoral emphasis* seldom make church folk angry. Over in Liverpool, John Watson (Ian Maclaren) became known as a pastor second to none, and as a preacher of helpful sermons. He excelled in strengthening and cheering men and women who had begun to feel jaded, wondering whether life could be worth what it cost. In the words of a friend who heard him twice every Lord's Day, "Our minister always puts heart into you for the coming week." Indeed, he kept on bringing people hope and cheer long after he had gone home to God.

The pastoral sermon is one that strengthens and cheers the believer in Christ, especially anyone who finds the going hard. Sometimes this sort of pulpit work goes under the name of "devotional," or "inspirational." Examples of such preaching appear everywhere in the published sermons of George H. Morrison—for example *Flood Tide* and *The Return of the Angels*—and also in the writings of John Henry Jowett—for example, *Apostolic Optimism* and *Brooks by the Traveler's Way*. Now and again critics used to speak of Jowett's pulpit work as "weak and thin," but hosts of intelligent people thronged to hear his uplifting sermons, and came away as from a mountaintop. Today many of us feel the need for more of a teaching ministry, but we ought also to hear the call for binding up the broken heart. "Comfort ye, comfort ye my people!" (Isa. 40:1.)

Other labels will meet us as we go along. Some of these titles, such as "the life-situation sermon," may seem new and strange, and so will the form of the messages. But when we go to the Scriptures we find that the prophets and the apostles, like their Lord, repeatedly dealt with life situations, and in a sense they never did anything else. So let us not shy away from any homiletical label because it seems "new."

But what about the old labels? With all of the inventions and discoveries in other fields, why must the preacher bother about "the topical sermon," "the textual sermon," and "the expository message"? For much the same reason that a lover of poetry uses such old labels as narrative and lyric, and a farmer refers to a dairy cow, a beef animal, and grade stock. Why should a man discard labels that have come down from other days? On the other hand, no one need fall down and worship them. With sermon labels, as with names of dairy stock, judge each case on its merits.

In a sense a single label will do for all the sermons any minister ought to preach: "messages from God for the needs of men." So form the habit of asking each coming sermon this question: "Will you enable me to meet some human need?" If a certain type of message will insure a truth of God to meet the needs of your people now, prepare that sermon. If any pulpit work does not measure up to this standard, do not let such stuff usurp the place of a message from God. As for labels, if you employ them rightly, you can keep from feeding the household the same sort of fare week after week. In short, use divine truth in meeting human needs today—all kinds of truths for all sorts of needs.

Suggested Readings

Baxter, Batsell B. *The Heart of the Yale Lectures*. New York: The Macmillan Co., 1947.

Beecher, Henry Ward. *Yale Lectures on Preaching*, Series I-III, 1872-74.

Buttrick, George A. *Jesus Came Preaching*. New York: Charles Scribner's Sons, 1932.

Farmer, Herbert H. *The Servant of the Word*. New York: Charles Scribner's Sons, 1942.

Gossip, Arthur J. *In Christ's Stead*. New York: Geo. H. Doran Co., 1925.

Jowett, John Henry. *The Preacher, His Life and Work*. New York: Geo. H. Doran Co., 1912.

Scherer, Paul E. *For We Have This Treasure*. New York: Harper & Bros., 1944.

Stewart, James S. *Heralds of God*. New York: Charles Scribner's Sons, 1946.

CHAPTER III

The Beginnings of a Sermon

NO MINISTER can tell how he starts to prepare a sermon. The whole matter belongs under "the mystery of preaching." What the Lord Jesus taught about the birth of a soul may apply to the beginnings of a sermon: "The wind blows where it wills, and you hear the sound of it, but you do not know whence it comes or whither it goes; so it is with every one who is born of the Spirit" (John 3:8 R.S.V.). As the Apostle writes, "Where the Spirit of the Lord is, there is freedom" (II Cor. 3:17*b* R.S.V.).

Hence every interpreter ought to prepare messages in ways all his own. From time to time his methods ought to differ according to his aims and his materials. But he should lay down one rule, with never an exception: "Start, continue, and end with prayer." Before he puts anything down on paper, he should look up to the One who knows all the needs of human hearts and all the resources of divine grace. In the spirit of the upward look the minister can go to work, and form the habit of "watchful waiting." Sooner or later he will begin to see the way to start a message for the people.

Away then with ideas about a "system" for making sermons! No minister can learn from a professor or a guidebook how to start work on a message for a given congregation. Who on the outside can tell what the people ought to hear, and how the man in the study ought to proceed? All of that must rest with the preacher and his Lord, but a few suggestions may help a young man get his bearings.

THE SEED-THOUGHTS OF SERMONS

1. The impulse that leads to a sermon may come to the pastor when *outside the study.* During a round of pastoral calls, or while on a visit to the hospital, the minister sees the need for a certain message. Without revealing the secrets of any confiding soul, the man with a shepherd heart can bring the truth of God to bear on the sense of fear,

worry, or despondency. The minister needs to know how laymen respond to the world situation, how a father's heart quivers when he thinks of what will await his teen-age boy round the next few turns in life's pathway. Again and again the minister with open eyes may sense the call for preaching about "God's Providence Today."

The seed-thought of the sermon may emerge during contacts with a layman at his work. Whenever Thomas Chalmers journeyed on a stagecoach, he liked to sit with the driver up on the box. Without interfering with the management of the four-horse team the minister could learn much about horses and men. One day at a bend in the road he saw that the coachman flicked one of the horses with his whip. A little later, when Chalmers asked why, the friend on the box explained that the horse shied at a place along the road, and that he needed something to divert his attention. Out of that incident, after long musing, Chalmers evolved the best-known sermon a Presbyterian has ever preached, "The Expulsive Power of a New Affection."

Spurgeon, too, formed the habit of finding in unexpected places the germ-thoughts of future messages. One day, as he walked down by the sea, he looked out over ships with their sails unfurled. Then he saw the beginnings of a sermon, "There Go the Ships." What he made out of that subject depended on the way his imagination kept working. Beecher used to find seed-thoughts as he crossed the river on a ferry boat, and as he walked about on his farm up the Hudson. Like many a city pastor today Beecher found that his hearers enjoyed two sorts of messages. They wanted to learn something strange about a thing they could see every day, and something familiar about a thing remote from their daily experience. In order to interest such people, a man must live; he must know how to see, how to feel, and how to share.

Here the preacher's work resembles that of the poet. In 1911, at the age of thirty-seven, John Masefield began to write long narrative poems. One evening in May when he took a walk in the country, as he was going through a hedge between the beech wood and ordinary land, he said to himself: "I will write a poem about a blackguard who becomes converted." That evening he made the first draft of "The

Everlasting Mercy," and on it he worked for the next three weeks. In like fashion, during a fishing expedition in Wales, where he caught no fish, he thought to himself that he must "show how a good woman is made wretched through no fault of her own." After another three weeks of toil this idea led to "The Widow in the Bye Street."[1] To the present hour these two poems by Masefield keep suggesting sermons.

— 2. Again, the impulse that leads to a sermon may come *while a man works in the study*. The idea may grip him while reading a book of the Bible, perhaps in the original tongue or in one of the recent translations. He may know by heart what James Denney of Glasgow termed the classic New Testament chapter about the death of Christ. But one morning the pastor sees in the midst of the passage something new and strange: "The love of Christ controls us" (II Cor. 5:14, R.S.V.). The Apostle here refers to Christ's love for us, and that on the Cross. When His love controls heart and life, His grace begins to transform. What good news for the friend in the pew, and for the world today! Where else can either the layman or the world find power to control and transform?

Once more, the idea may spring out of a passage not so familiar. For instance, take Ezek. 47:1-12, about the healing waters that flow from the Temple. The minister has been thinking about the world's need of God, because he has been going through *A History of the Expansion of Christianity*, by Kenneth S. Latourette. In the vision of the seer the pastor finds what he needs for a message about the will of God for the world today. As the healing waters issued from the Temple and soon became a river mighty enough to cleanse the Dead Sea, so the "blest river of salvation" flows from the Church, bringing life to every part of the world that lies under the shadow of death. Much the same truth, in a different form, appears in Ezek. 37:1-10, about the coming of life into a valley full of dead men's bones. In dealing with either passage the man who would preach must first be able to see and feel.

No pastor, however, can expect an illuminating flash every time

[1] See *Poems* (New York: The Macmillan Co., 1936), pp. viii-ix.

he starts to prepare a sermon. The metropolitan preacher who urges a young minister always to start with a problem crying out for solution may have to prepare only twenty-five or thirty messages a year. What if he served in a parish where he spoke to some of the same people more than a hundred times between August and August? How could he find seed-thoughts for that many sermons? Perhaps by setting apart in the study a place for a homiletical garden. Why did Brooks never run out of something to preach? Indeed, why did he wish he could preach oftener? Because he had formed the habit of letting sermons grow from seedlings. So had Spurgeon and Beecher and many another who seemed to speak extempore.

3. The idea for a sermon may come out of *the minister's private seed plot*. The old-fashioned method called for the use of notebooks, one after another. During three years at the seminary Brooks spent most of his time reading and seeing and thinking. In his notebooks he wrote out all sorts of suggestions that he afterwards used in sermons. In a far different fashion Beecher used to store away for future use ideas on which he wanted to preach. In the final stages Beecher's message assumed its form quickly, but the seed-thought had been growing for months, or even years. Psychologically, this way of letting sermons mature shows the fructifying power of "unconscious incubation."

Any such method accords with the experience of masters in other fields that call for the use of imagination. For instance, turn to painting. In the studio Titian used to keep at work on several projects, because he planned not to finish a painting soon after he had begun. Like many a poet such as Milton, Titian must have learned that a conception lives in the hearts of men according to the length of time it has taken to mature in the soul of the artist. So the value of a sermon may depend on the number of weeks, months, or even years it has taken to grow in the heart of the preacher.

4. Many of the ideas for sermons come out of *the Christian Year*. During one summer vacation Oscar F. Blackwelder, of Washington, D. C., spent a part of every morning in preparation for the coming year's pulpit work. As a Lutheran he was planning to follow the course

of the Church Year, though not slavishly. When the rush started again in September, he would have on his desk a general plan for the coming year, with a more detailed program for the time leading up through Advent to Christmas. He might not know exactly what he would preach early in January, twelve weeks later, but he knew the field in which he would be working, and he would have something growing in that part of his homiletical garden. In a busy parish a wise minister never runs out of something to preach twice every Lord's Day.[2] In churches not liturgical pastors may preach according to a homemade Christian Year, as we shall see in due time.

THE STATEMENT OF PURPOSE

Whatever the genesis of the sermon, the hour comes for the minister to decide about the purpose. "The man without a goal seldom gets anywhere," said Charles E. Jefferson. "Laymen frequently stand nonplussed at the close of a sermon, not knowing what they ought to think or what they ought to do." [3]

At the end of the hour in church a deacon may whisper to his wife, "I don't know what the parson was driving at, do you?"

Then she may reply, "No, and I don't think he knew, either!"

Laymen feel that preachers fail here more often than anywhere else. As a safeguard against aimlessness, the man in the study does well to write down his purpose, and then keep the statement in view throughout the week before he delivers the sermon.

"As a marksman aims at his target and its bull's-eye, and at nothing else, so the preacher must have *a definite point* before him, which he has to hit." These words from John Henry Newman relate to the needs of the hearer:

The preacher aims at the divine glory, not in any vague and general way, but definitely by the enunciation of some article or principle of the revealed Word. So, further, he enunciates it, not for the instruction of the whole world, but for the sake of the very persons before him. . . . A hearer,

[2] See A. W. Blackwood, *Planning a Year's Pulpit Work*.
[3] See *Quiet Hints to Growing Preachers* (New York: T. Y. Crowell Co., 1901), p. 87.

then, is included in the very idea of preaching, and we cannot determine how in detail we ought to preach until we know whom we are to address.[4]

The purpose has to do with moving the will of the hearer to action,] * which may be only within the heart. There the Spirit of God does what the fathers called His "office work," both for time and for eternity. The preacher may address five hundred men and women, or a thousand. Even so, he moves them Godward one by one. If he holds forth about the forgiveness of sins, he wishes the friend in the pew to deal with his own transgressions, here and now. Near the close of a message about the forgiveness of injuries the hearer should resolve by the grace of God to forgive the one who has done him wrong. If the hearer himself has injured any person, he should determine to make amends and bring about a reconciliation. After such a feeling arises in the heart, the action may involve a man's entire being. The sermon that moves the hearer rightly leads him to do the will of God with all his powers.

After a minister has set down his purpose, he can use it to guide and restrain in all he does with the sermon. Near the beginning of his labors he may decide about the text, or he may start with the text if it grips him and moves him to supply a certain need. Whatever the order of purpose and text, the aim ought to govern everything that follows. The purpose guides in accumulating materials and in] determining what to retain. Some of them he finds in the passage, and others elsewhere. Amid all the various sources he uses the purpose as a sort of magnet. This kind of study goes far to relieve a man from drudgery, and to insure hours full of adventure. But first a man must learn how to use that magnet.

No one illustration can set forth all the truth about the making of a sermon, but the building of a bridge affords a good comparison. Prior to World War I, the people on the North Side in Pittsburgh used to journey up the river, cross over a bridge, and travel down into the city. In order to shorten that route an engineer planned for a bridge straight across the river into the heart of the city. After a while he saw

---

[4] *The Idea of a University*, part II, chap. VI.

the structure complete, with a single exception: the new bridge lacked an approach. Month after month there stood the massive structure, full of beauty and strength, all unused. How like a sermon without a purpose that has to do with human needs today!

If a minister could plan to make sermons as an engineer plans a bridge and its approaches, writers of books could lay down rules. For example, begin with the conclusion, and end with the introduction. This, of course, refers to the planning and not to the writing, which ought to proceed from the beginning, through the middle, and on to the end. Once a friend asked O. Henry about the secret of planning a short story. "It's simple," he answered with a smile. "Just think of your ending and plan your story up to that ending." But when a young preacher tries to carry out such a rule, he finds the way far from clear; his mind does not follow the pattern the mentor points out. Of one thing, however, the novice may feel sure: the purpose ought to govern the growth of every sermon. Before an engineer can begin to plan a bridge, he must know the purpose of that structure. When he has completed the work, including the approaches, the people can begin to use the bridge.

From this point on we shall think about various stages in the development of a sermon as it grows to completion in the study, and then as it sounds from the pulpit. We shall assume that the minister lives among his people and knows what they need when they come to the sanctuary. We shall think of that ideal city into which he wishes to lead them as a group and one by one; and we shall keep our eyes open for a vision of the King whom they are to meet in the heart of the city. We shall hope that the friend in the study will find almost as much joy in preparing to preach as in delivering his sermon. If so, he will understand why George Matheson sang: "O Joy that seekest me through pain."

The young minister who still feels confused may wish to follow a work sheet, but he must not regard it as fixed and final, like the laws of the Medes and Persians. Neither should he look on the preparation of a sermon as complicated and bewildering. When he once gets his bearings he will find that the chief difficulties have to do with determining what to preach and with deciding about the plan, for habit takes care of many other things. Consciously or unconsciously, however, a thoughtful minister goes through certain stages like these that follow, though often in a different order.

1. Allow abundance of *time* for the sermon to grow.
2. Set up a lofty *goal*, in writing.
3. Choose a *text* in line with the purpose.
4. Embody the purpose in a *conclusion*.
5. Start to *assemble* all sorts of *materials*.
6. Let the whole matter *incubate* for a while.
7. Begin to think about the *topic* of the sermon.
8. Gradually *arrange* the *materials* according to the aim.
9. Begin to think also about *illustrations*.
10. Decide about the *introduction*, or the approach.
11. *Write out* the sermon as a whole, at one sitting.
12. The next day *revise* the manuscript with care.
13. Prepare to *deliver* the message from God.
14. In the pulpit *forget* about the preparation.
15. *Trust God* to bless the preaching of His Word (Isa. 55:10, 11).

Suggested Readings

Black, James. *The Mystery of Preaching.* New York: F. H. Revell Co., 1924.

Brastow, Lewis O. *The Work of the Preacher.* Boston: Pilgrim Press, 1914.

Breed, David R. *Preparing to Preach.* New York: Geo. H. Doran Co., 1911.

Davis, Ozora S. *The Principles of Preaching.* Chicago: University of Chicago Press, 1924.

Jowett, John Henry. *The Preacher, His Life and Work.* New York: Geo. H. Doran Co., 1912.

CHAPTER IV

The Custom of Using a Text

WHERE DOES THE MINISTER find the truth of God to meet the needs of men today? First of all, in the Bible. When he starts to prepare a sermon, he chooses a passage of scripture. If he follows the custom of the fathers, he uses a text with every sermon, and in the delivery of the message he starts by repeating the text. After he has spoken, he wishes the illuminated text to keep shining in the heart of every hearer. So the pastor looks on the text as the biblical source of the sermon, the fountainhead from which he derives the central message. Would that all of this might prove as simple as it sounds!

THE ADVANTAGES TO THE PREACHER

The advantages to the minister are not so great as those to the people, but still we may begin with him as he works in the study. At present we shall take for granted that he knows how to choose a text, and how to deal with it in preparing a sermon.

1. This way of preaching goes far to assure the speaker *a message from God,* for in the Scriptures he finds truth that comes from God today. So he sets himself to discover such a truth, and then share it with his friends. In the pulpit he ought to speak with assurance. As a lawyer pleading before the Supreme Court bases his argument on the Constitution, so the advocate at the bar of reason depends upon the Bible. In either case a man has to do his own thinking, and not merely quote at random.

2. Again, the proper use of a text encourages the minister to set up *a goal for every sermon.* If he chooses to speak about the Holy Spirit, he may have difficulty in making the subject clear and luminous for men and women who think in other terms. But if he singles out a text, preferably short, he can focus attention on a single aspect of the truth about the Holy Spirit. For instance, let him start with these words from our Lord with reference to the Spirit: "He will guide you into

all the truth" (John 16:13a, R.S.V.). When the minister sets himself to prepare a sermon about "The Holy Spirit, Our Teacher," he need not fear to bring his subject out into the open. He will find that people who come to church, however little they know, wish to learn about the Spirit of God. At least they can understand what it means for Him to teach and for them to learn His will today.

3. The use of a text for a sermon also *leads the man in the study to pray*, for the Scriptures and prayer go together as inseparably as the light and the heat of the sun. When he starts to brood over a text in its background, he finds it natural to look up for guidance. If he keeps thinking about the Holy Spirit as Teacher, the interpreter can enter at once into the meaning and atmosphere of his text. When the Spirit shines upon the open page and brings the truth to light in the face of the Lord Jesus, the pastor can speak out of his own experience, not merely about something that happened far away and long ago. All of this Raymond Calkins must have had in view when he wrote *The Eloquence of Christian Experience*.[1]

4. All the while *the minister must work*. When he prays for guidance, and prays without ceasing, he discovers that the guidance comes through the use of all his God-given powers. Why should anyone wish the Lord to do for him what he can do for the Lord? If a man expects to comprehend a passage in its setting, he must read and think as well as pray. Though he starts with the Bible, he should consult other books, including commentaries, but under God he must rely mainly on his own thinking. In the completed sermon he may not employ all he has learned about the passage and the subject, but he can feel the glow that comes to the man who has done his best work for Christ and the home church.

5. Through the mastery of texts and contexts week after week a pastor can keep *growing in knowledge and in power*. Whenever he prepares a sermon, he can fix attention on a truth or a duty outside himself, something large and high. During the eleven months between summer holidays he can deal with various portions of the Bible, and in

---

[1] New York: The Macmillan Co., 1927.

different ways. If he plans wisely, he charts a course that will require him to master one Bible book after another. Week after week, in the study alone with his Lord, the parish minister can take a sort of postgraduate course in the Bible. So he plans to work like a bee, which gathers nectar from field and flower, and not like a spider, which spins a web out of its own inner self.

The young pastor who begins to look on preaching from the Bible as a godsend will appreciate what James Black, of Free St. George's Church in Edinburgh, has written about his early days in the ministry:

> I had a dreadful experience during my first few months as a minister. . . . Like most young men, I knew very little about the business of preaching. . . . Here is what I said to myself each week. "Go to, Sir! thou shalt write a sermon on Temptation." Which I did, dealing with it, in a young man's large way, as comprehensively as I could. I then found a text for it, and tagged it on like a label. And after that, I had absolutely nothing more to say about Temptation.
>
> Next week, I said, "Go to, Sir! thou shalt write a sermon on Providence." Which I did, again exhausting the subject as thoroughly as I could. And after that I had nothing more to say about Providence! . . . At the end of three months, I thought I had exhausted all available truth: and certainly I had exhausted myself. I remember wondering whether I could slink away decently, or whether there should be a public exposure in Presbytery!
>
> Then I made a remarkable discovery, . . . that if I were only content to preach from a definite text or passage . . . I could preach on temptation this morning, and temptation the next morning, and temptation the third morning. For I discovered that if I stuck to my passage and dealt with the phase of truth enshrined in it, I could take a dozen texts . . . and yet be fresh on each one of them. In attempting to crush a whole subject into one sermon, I was only attempting the impossible, spoiling the subject by unnatural compression . . . and ruining my own peace of nerves.[2]

This master of pulpit speech voices the feelings of many able preachers in Britain. They insist that preaching today, as in the past, calls for the use of the Bible at the heart of a sermon. Sometimes they irritate us in the United States by finding fault with our sermons. They tell us that our pulpit work would prove more interesting and

[2] *The Mystery of Preaching* (New York: F. H. Revell Co., 1924), pp. 152-53.

helpful if every young minister formed the habit of working from a text that he chose to meet some human need today. These observers from abroad forget how little time many a parish leader over here leaves for study after he has done everything else throughout the week. Who can wonder that in the pulpit the distracted man "goes everywhere preaching the gospel," and that some of the people give the sanctuary "absent treatment"?

THE ADVANTAGES TO THE PEOPLE

The advantages to the people outweigh those to the minister, because preaching exists for them more than for him.

1. When they come to church, they expect *a message from God* in response to the needs of their hearts today. Few of them could put into words any theory about revelation and inspiration, but then the minister himself cannot begin to comprehend the spell that the Scriptures cast over the spirits of men and women. The lay friends feel themselves in the presence of a mystery they do not understand, but they can tell when the living Christ speaks through His servant in the pulpit. On the way home they say one to another: "Did not our heart burn within us, while he talked with us by the way, and while he opened to us the scriptures?" (Luke 24:32.)

2. This kind of pulpit work *meets the needs of the hearer.* For an object lesson turn to Frederick William Robertson.[3] Every Sunday morning that young clergyman preached from a text; at the second service he spoke from a longer passage. Whatever the portion of scripture in hand, Robertson did not content himself with explaining a passage. He preached from the Bible as a means of grace, the best of such means, but never as an end in itself. Largely for this reason he endeared himself to poor and rich, from servantgirls and workingmen to lovers of the King's English and mystical seekers after God. What a range of human interests!

3. Preaching from texts enables the people to *grow in understanding*

---

[3] See *Sermons Preached at Brighton*, one vol. ed. (New York: Harper & Bros., n.d.). Also, James R. Blackwood, *The Soul of Frederick W. Robertson* (New York: Harper & Bros., 1947).

and in grace. After a year or more in which the minister has unfolded one text after another, and has shown the bearing on the hearer's life today, the layman enjoys recalling each text from which his friend in the pulpit has drawn the water of life. In the hour of temptation the churchgoer finds in one of those illuminated texts a way to escape without sin. In the time of sorrow, also, he finds "the peace of God, which passes all understanding." At a tuberculosis hospital a university student lay hour after hour, unable to read. One day he told the pastor of a church near the campus: "I can repeat every text from which you preached last year, and give you the substance of every sermon. I thank God for something good to think about night after night."

So much for the ideal, but what about the facts on the other side? Everyone can think of popular preachers, such as John Haynes Holmes, who do not work from texts, and of mechanical pulpiteers whose hearers sometimes wish they had never heard of texts. Evidently this way of preaching does not work like a machine, for no method can prove effective in the hands of a bungler. Not every minister knows how to choose a text and how to deal with it in preparing a message. Unfortunately no teacher or book can show a young man how to choose a text—or a wife—for in either case the young pastor may discover that he has been chosen. Whenever a text makes a man's heart burn, he can use it in causing other hearts to burn. According to an old seaman, "Preaching means taking out of your heart something hot, and then thrusting it into my heart."

THE CHOICE OF THE TEXT

A few suggestions may help the novice.

1. *Begin with your aim.* If you think of fear today as "public enemy number one," you will find in the Book countless texts about faith as the victory over fear.

2. Watch the seasons of *the Christian Year.* In the months leading up to Advent, think of how God dealt with men, one by one, in Old Testament days. In the record about Daniel in the lions' den you will find the sort of faith that conquers fear (Dan. 6:16*b*). Before Christmas deal with the fears of people today (Luke 2:10). After New

48

Year's Day, when people think about the earthly life of our Lord, preach about the stilling of the waves and of human fears (Mark 4:40). After Pentecost, if the lay friends care for Paul, show how he vanquished fears amid a storm at sea (Acts 27:24). But do not attempt all of this in any one year; seek after variety.

3. Be sure that *the text belongs in the Bible*. Do the words appear in the Revised Standard Version of the New Testament? If you preach a missionary sermon from Mark 16:15, you may have to answer embarrassing questions. So with the tale about the woman taken in adultery (John 8:1-11), or the words of the eunuch to Philip (Acts 8:37). A skillful preacher can use that passage from the Fourth Gospel as the heart of the message about "The Tenderness of Jesus," "Jesus as a Gentleman," or "A Sermon in the Dust." But if you attempt anything of the sort, be frank; tell the people that these words do not appear in the oldest manuscripts of the New Testament, and that you employ them because you think they tell the truth about our Lord. All the while study the latest modern versions; better still, begin with the Greek or the Hebrew.

4. Choose *a text that makes sense*. Only a sleight-of-hand performer would talk for twenty-five minutes about "This is that" (Acts 2:16). In the context these words from the Apostle at Pentecost come to us charged with meaning and power, and for this very reason the text of the sermon ought to embody a message. Not every passage, however, needs to seem clear at first glance. Why not preach about the old proverb: "The fathers have eaten sour grapes, and the children's teeth are set on edge" (Ezek. 18:2b)? This adage tells about the workings of God's providence and grace through what we know as heredity and environment, especially in the home.

Out of grief in a family circle has come the best-known sermon of our generation, "But When Life Tumbles In, What Then?"[4] When A. J. Gossip first preached after the death of his wife, he turned to a text that must have made every hearer wonder (Jer. 12:5), for this passage told about footmen and horses, and the swelling of

[4] A. W. Blackwood, *The Protestant Pulpit*, sermon 24.

the Jordan. But the message itself more than justified the choice of the text. Who that has read the sermon can ever forget both topic and text, or refrain from giving thanks for the strength and assurance the man with the bleeding heart drew from such unfamiliar words?

5. As a rule give the preference to *a positive rather than a negative text*. In the first psalm deal with the fruitful tree rather than the worthless chaff. Better still, paint the two contrasting pictures, as in the psalm itself, but stress the good more than the bad. In the Sermon on the Mount preach about the house on the rock, which stood, rather than the house on sand, which fell. Here again, if only for variety, the rule permits exceptions. But if a man wishes to interpret the Scriptures he ought to make clear that they stress Carlyle's "Everlasting Yea" more than his "Everlasting No." [5]

6. Give the right of way to a text that *appeals to the imagination,* bringing out something to see, to feel, and to do. Go through the two hundred sermons by Brooks, and note how he almost always began with a text that showed either a person in action or a picture for the eye. Remember that the layman in our day excels in seeing rather than in thinking. Almost every person born since the beginning of World War I has been educated imaginatively rather than logically. Hence the churchgoer wants the preacher to see what he says; not to argue, but to paint scenes like those in the parables.

7. As a rule give the preference to *the short text*. In the sermon the minister can repeat a short text often, and the layman can remember it easily. In a book of radio addresses [6] Ralph W. Sockman uses a variety of texts, all of them short. He would agree with Beecher that a preacher ought to use a text as a gateway into a field; and not waste time swinging on the gate. Look at these texts in Sockman's volume: "Choose life"; "I will fear no evil: for thou art with me"; "This is the way, walk ye in it"; "Sirs, what must I do to be saved?" "Arise, and be not afraid"; "We are saved by hope."

8. As a rule have *only one text for a sermon*, and make that one glow. Such a mature preacher as James S. Stewart can start with more

[5] See *Sartor Resartus*, bk. II, chaps. 7, 9.
[6] *Now to Live* (New York and Nashville: Abingdon-Cokesbury Press, 1946).

texts than one, but as a young minister, when you have not time enough to make a single text clear and luminous, why double the difficulty? You may notice the contrast between the words of Jacob, "All these things are against me" (Gen. 42:36c), and those of the Apostle, "We know that all things work together for good to them that love God" (Rom. 8:28a). Or take the contrast between two other texts: "Moses knew not that the skin of his face shone" (Exod. 34:29b, A.S.V.); and Samson "knew not that [the Lord] was departed from him" (Judg. 16:20c, A.S.V.). In each case why not prepare two contrasting sermons? Why add to the layman's feeling of biblical confusion by scrambling what the Book keeps separate?

9. From week to week choose a *variety of texts*. Be like the Master's householder, who brings out of his treasure store things new and old. Set forth the new in an old, familiar light; the old in a new and pleasing light. "Old" and "new" here mean what the layman knows, and what he does not. Among all these suggestions about choosing texts, this one may prove the most important and the most exacting. Unconsciously a preacher may fall into a rut; since he has enjoyed preparing and preaching from a text of a certain kind, he tries another of the same sort, and then a third. Soon his work begins to suffer from sameness. May the Lord deliver any local interpreter from making the Holy Scriptures seem insipid! "My soul, be on thy guard!"

THE TASK OF INTERPRETATION

Still less can any book or professor lay down laws about the interpretation of a text. That must depend on various factors, including the background and tone color of the text, the personality and seeing eye of the preacher, the knowledge and interests of the hearers. What the young man sees must depend on what the sacred author wrote, on what the interpreter finds, and on what he wishes the friend in the pew to see. Theoretically all of this may sound formidable, but practically it proves to be fascinating. When a man loves the Book and loves the people, he finds joy in using all his God-given powers to meet their needs. As for the way, here are a few suggestions.

1. Allow *abundance of time*. Like Beecher, have all sorts of future

sermons growing in your homiletical garden. Let each of them remain there until it has become ready for use. After you have preached a sermon, you will find that people remember it approximately as long as you thought about the message before the delivery. For much the same reason the part of a plant or shade tree beneath the surface may bulk as large as what appears to the eye. So if you wish to prepare sermons that will live, allow each of them time to grow.

2. Find out *what the text meant* to the man who wrote it. Go back to the book in which the words appear. Remember that a verse in the Gospel according to John differs from a passage in Judges, and that words from Ecclesiastes differ from those in Esther. Herein lies much of the value in knowing the Scriptures as they were written, book by book. If Spurgeon had thought about the contents and tone color of Judges, he would not have preached a sermon about Samson as an object lesson of consecration. On the other hand, the minister who knows the Book of Judges can find in it a wealth of preaching materials. In Samson as the ancient world's strongest man the interpreter can see the need of religion for a young athlete's body.

The text itself calls for exegesis, which signifies "drawing out" the meaning of the words, one by one and as a whole. Beginning with the Hebrew or the Greek—if a man knows the original tongues—he can find out the thought content and emotional spirit of the text. Such work calls for exegetical commentaries, many of which deal with the original tongues. The volumes of the *Moffatt New Testament Commentary* require no such knowledge. As for "homiletical commentaries," which provide plans for ready-made sermons, they may prove helpful to a lay preacher, but they deserve no place on the shelves of a man with college and seminary training. An educated minister needs an exegetical commentary or two on every major book of the Bible, with other standard books that show the meaning of Holy Writ.[7]

3. Gradually formulate the practical *message in terms of today*, so as to preach here and now. You will find that what James Denney,

[7] For a list see A. W. Blackwood, *Preaching from the Bible* (New York and Nashville: Abingdon-Cokesbury Press, 1941), pp. 227-39.

the Scottish theologian, wrote about the Gospels holds true everywhere else in the Bible:

> When we preach from the gospels, and see what Jesus was, and said,
> and did, and suffered, let us remember to make the application in the
> present tense. Never preach about the historical Christ; preach about the
> living, sovereign Christ. . . . It is not because He lived, but because He lives,
> that we have life also; it is not because the historical imagination is highly
> developed, so that we can make the evangelists' pages vivid, and be affected
> as by a fine scene in a drama—not for this reason, but because we confess
> with our mouth and believe in our heart that God raised Him from the
> dead, that we are saved. Faith always has its object here and now, and
> without faith there is no religion.[8]

4. The time will come to decide about *the form of the sermon.*
Into all of that we need not enter here, but we ought to note one fact:
the ability to use a text in meeting a human need today depends on an
understanding of both the text and the need. A wise man, as we have
already seen, does not start with a wooden form, and then go to the
Bible or elsewhere for materials to fill up the mold. He senses the
need, and then finds in the Book a truth to meet that need. Only after
he understands both the need and the passage can he begin to think
clearly about the ultimate form of the sermon.

All of this may sound mechanical, but so would an account of
preliminary work by any artist. A biography[9] tells about the young
sculptor who designed and fashioned the statue of the Minute Man,
at Concord. Before Daniel C. French entered this competition and
won the prize, he had never made a statue, but as a son of Concord
he knew why people there wanted to celebrate the centennial of
1776. After he had reviewed the facts in the case he decided on the
conception of the Minute Man. At the age of twenty-four he
completed the statue that embodied the ideals of the Revolutionary
fathers and of their descendants a hundred years later. The biography tells how young French used both eye and hand in helping

[8] See *Studies in Theology* (New York: A. C. Armstrong & Son, 1897) p. 154.
[9] See Margaret French Cresson, *Journey into Fame, The Life of Daniel Chester
French* (Cambridge:Harvard University Press, 1947), pp. 63-84.

others see what he had learned about the meaning of American history.

"Preachers need the artist's way of seeing universal truth, and not until the modern pulpit is willing to take the trouble to understand how poets, painters, musicians work, will the art of preaching come again into its own." [10]

Suggested Readings

Brown, Charles R. *The Art of Preaching*. New York: The Macmillan Co., 1922.

Phelps, Austin. *The Theory of Preaching*. Revised by F. D. Whitesell. Grand Rapids: Eerdman's, 1947.

Vinet, Alexandre. *Homiletics*, Edinburgh, 1858.

[10] Willard L. Sperry, *Reality in Worship* (New York: The Macmillan Co., 1925), p. 248.

CHAPTER V

The Value of Textual Sermons

WHEN young Daniel French had decided what he wished to do in making a statue for Concord Common, he began to make all sorts of blackboard sketches and clay models. At last he showed the other members of the household four of those models, and to his delight he found that they all preferred the one he liked best. That one he used in making the statue of the Minute Man. If young French had been learning how to preach, he might have worked out various plans for dealing with the truth in a certain text. Among other ways he would have thought about a textual sermon.

A textual sermon is one whose structure corresponds with the order of the parts in the text. In a sermon, as in a statue, much depends on the strength and the grace of the structure. Whether or not the structure calls attention to itself, it has as much to do with the message as the bony framework has to do with a man's body. If at present we think about the textual way of dealing with the results of exegesis, let us remember that other methods have also commended themselves to pulpit masters of yesterday and today; indeed, the textual method has largely fallen out of use.

For examples of textual preaching turn to Frederick Robertson. At the morning service he would preach from a text with two contrasting truths. When he dealt with Matt. 5:48, "Be ye therefore perfect," he would bring out two aspects of the subject, and only two. First he discussed "The Christian Aim—Perfection." Then he took up "The Christian Motive—because it is right and Godlike to be perfect." When he started with John 8:32, "Ye shall know the truth and the truth shall make you free," he dealt first with "The Truth That Liberates," and then with "The Liberty That Truth Gives." For numerous examples of his work see *The Sermons Preached at Brighton.* Other men, of course, employ the textual method in far different ways.

THE ADVANTAGES OF THE METHOD

1. This kind of pulpit work *fixes attention on one part of the Scriptures*. Instead of confusing the layman by flitting hither and thither, the minister settles down to make clear a few words that he can illuminate. For instance, he may deal with the text that George Adam Smith regarded as the noblest in the Old Testament: "What doth the Lord require of thee, but to do justly, and to love mercy, and to walk humbly with thy God?" (Mic. 6:8). From this text the preacher may draw the subject "The Meaning of a Man's Religion." Then the introduction may deal with the problem that appears in the verses preceding the text. All of that has to do with the query, "What doth the Lord require of thee?"

The answer comes from the parts of the text itself. Whatever the wording, these have to do with justice, kindness, and humility—in this order. At the foundation of a good man's life stands justice; he must do it, and keep on doing it, day after day. More important still, he should love kindness; in it he should live and move and have his being, as in the home where he dwells. Last of all, and best of all, comes walking with God in humility. In the verse as a whole see how the stress falls on the three infinitives. Do you wonder that this verse appears as the chief motto in the Alcove of Religion at the Library of Congress? How could you make this threefold truth stand out more strongly than through a textual sermon?

2. The beginner will find this sort of message comparatively *easy to prepare*. He may not think so while he delves into the meaning of the passage, but he should do that in any case. After he knows what it means in its own setting he should encounter few obstacles in helping the layman see the form of the text. Of course, this will hold true only if he has chosen a passage that makes the divisions of thought stand out. For example, in a sermon from Isa. 40:31 William P. Merrill uses the topic "The Practical Value of Religion."[1] First, according to the custom in our day, he discusses the problem. Another

[1] See C. W. Ferguson, *The Great Themes of the Christian Faith* (New York: R. R. Smith, 1930), pp. 107-15.

introduction might deal with the text in its three parts, which seem to come in the wrong order. Why not transpose them so as to secure a climax? Consider the matter, and then you will follow the order in the text!

After the approach, Dr. Merrill's sermon consists of three parts: (1) "They shall mount up . . . as eagles"—strength for keeping up ideals; (2) "They shall run, and not be weary"—strength for meeting crises; and (3) "They shall walk, and not faint"—strength for the daily routine. To another interpreter, less exact, the three parts might suggest the visions of youth, the achievements of middle life, and the serenity of old age. In still other hands the facts would lead to a three-part message concerning (1) the hours of vision—they come seldom and do not tarry; (2) the days of progress—they come more often, and hope burns high; and (3) the years of drudgery—they fill up most of life and bring the most exacting tests. With a man, as with an automobile, the chief test may come in low gear. What a text for a baccalaureate sermon!

3. If the man in the pulpit knows his business, *the hearer can follow* the textual sermon with ease and satisfaction. As the message unfolds, he can see the various stages. When he follows the trail in Mic. 6:8, he can begin to appraise his own heart and life. Better still, he can remember the text and the interpretation for days and years to come, largely because this text appeals to the imagination. If he commits to memory the thirty-two words, he can see in them a bird's-eye view of his own career on earth. What an illuminated text!

4. This kind of preaching *brings the hearer close to the heart of the Bible*. Not every such sermon grows out of a royal text, but still this way of preaching does call attention to many a bright star in the sky. When a man teaches Shakespeare, he wishes the student to become familiar with the noblest passages. At Harvard each year G. L. Kittredge required every man in the Shakespeare class to know by heart eight hundred of the choicest lines. In the pulpit the pastor can make no such demands, but he can encourage the layman to see the glory of God as it shines out in many a golden text.

The man who seldom preaches textually may shy away from the

supreme passages, lest his treatment of John 3:16 or Rom. 8:28 fall short of the text. But the friends who listen to his sermons do not feel that way; they do not expect anyone now to live on the heights of the Fourth Gospel or the Epistle to the Romans. They feel glad when the pastor takes up a passage that they love, and shows them why they love it. For the same reason university students of Shakespeare wish to deal with the supreme plays. And yet the library of a seminary professor, with thousands of printed sermons, contains only one real message about John 3:16, and none about Rom. 8:28. That one about "the golden text of the Bible" shows how to make the truth stand out. In preaching on "Love in Four Dimensions," William M. Clow points to the breadth—"God so loved the world"; the length—"that he gave his only begotten Son"; the depth—"that whosoever believeth in him should not perish"; the height—"but have everlasting life." [2]

THE OBJECTIONS TO THE METHOD

In view of these advantages, and others like them, why has the textual sermon fallen out of favor? As we shall see later, in the history of preaching almost every famous sermon has been topical rather than textual.[3] Advocates of such pulpit work sometimes overstate their case. Some of them make the reader feel that he ought always to preach this way instead of resorting at times to other methods. Wherein lie the objections to the textual method?

No one could object to the right sort of textual sermons. The fault lies not in the label but in the contents. With an exception here and there the friends who hear the pastor's messages know little and care less about technical terms. But they begin to grow restless if the pastor's discourses from week to week all seem alike, each one less inviting than the last. If people absent themselves from the sanctuary, they may do so in part because they have grown weary of boardinghouse hash. And yet their pastor may feel that he has been carrying out the

[2] See *The Cross in Christian Experience* (New York: Geo. H. Doran Co., 1911), pp. 52-64.

[3] When I made a collection of thirty-nine representative sermons, past and present, I chose them for other reasons. When I had the list complete for that book, *The Protestant Pulpit*, I found I had included few textual sermons.

injunctions of the seminary professor who encouraged preaching from the Bible! So let us think about the other side of the case.

1. The textual method *does not lend itself to every passage* that calls for a sermon. Here and there the textual-minded pastor meets with difficulty in dividing his passage. He finds it like the Master's seamless dress, all in one piece. For instance, how could anyone separate into its elements John 19:5*b*, "Behold the man!" or I John 4:16*b*, "God is love"? From the first of these texts he may wish to preach about "Christ as the Ideal Man," and from the second, "The Best Thing About God." If so, let him proceed topically, or in some other fashion, thanking the Lord that the value of pulpit work depends far more upon the message than the method.

An extreme example may show how the textual method leads to mechanical sermonizing. An old-time divine began with the Latin form of Psalm 55:6. In their own setting those words might have led to a sermon about "The Restfulness of a Man's Religion." But the anatomist divided the short text into five parts—three too many. This fashion of reading into a text what it does not teach has become known as eisegesis. In the present case the sermon spoiled a picture, and turned poetry into prose.

1. "Who will give me"—Christian humility
2. "Give me wings"—prudent celerity
3. "Like a dove"—innocent simplicity
4. "Then would I fly away"—devout sublimity
5. "And be at rest"—permanent security [4]

2. A text may *contain more ideas than a minister can make clear* and luminous in twenty-five minutes. As an example take I Cor. 10:13, which begins this way: "No temptation has overtaken you that is not common to man" (R.S.V.). Only a preacher with talent could lead a congregation through all the windings of thought in that one verse. But anyone with an eye for a present-day message can lead the hearer

[4] See Marvin R. Vincent, *The Expositor in the Pulpit* (New York: Randolph Co., 1884), pp. 9-10.

to see truth about God's making a man strong enough to bear up under any temptation that ever can come.

Think of the matter in terms of engineering. When John Roebling and his son planned the Brooklyn Bridge, they computed the utmost strain the structure would ever have to endure, and then they built that bridge to stand, as it has stood for more than sixty years. Where did those engineers get the wisdom and skill that enabled them to plan and erect such a bridge? From the God about whom the Apostle writes in I Cor. 10:13. What an opening for a sermon, even if the words do not readily lend themselves to textual treatment!

3. This method often *leads to artificial sermons*. Unless a man studies the background of the text and the words themselves, he may draw out lessons the passage does not teach. For instance, a pulpit orator once held forth about "The Investment of the Years." He began with a text about the passing of our days on earth: "We spend our years as a tale that is told" (Ps. 90:9*b*). He drew the subject from the word "spend," which in the Hebrew means literally to "consume," and not to "invest," or anything else about money. Unintentionally, the would-be interpreter practiced eisegesis, which he might have avoided if he had consulted the American Standard Version, and back of that, the Hebrew.

Worse still, his message broke in two at the middle. First the pulpit orator dealt with "Life as a Fortune to Be Spent": everyone must decide whether to live as a miser, a spendthrift, or an investor. Thus far the treatment, though not textual, held together. But then the photographer shifted his camera. The preacher began to look at "Life as a Tale to Be Told": everyone may determine whether his days on earth shall constitute a love romance, a mystery tale, or a gospel story. This latter part of the sermon came largely out of the text as it stood in the King James, but the discourse as a whole lacked unity. It followed two separate patterns, either of which might have provided the framework for a helpful message.

4. Unlike that example, textual sermons often *lack human interest*. Even Spurgeon sometimes failed to show how his passage related to the needs of his hearers. At his best he excelled in textual preaching,

but once he dealt with Mark 10:45 in a mechanical fashion. If he had spoken about "The Spirit of Christian Service," he could have brought out the two main ideas in the text; but he chose to discuss five truths, with as little apparent connection as five islands in an archipelago. No one of the five parts came close to the spirit of the text in its setting, which had to do with the worldly ambitions of ministerial students in "The College of the Apostles":

1. "The Son of Man"—humanity
2. "Came"—antecedent existence
3. "Not to be ministered unto"—vicarious life
4. "But to . . . give his life a ransom"—vicarious death
5. "For many"—amplitude

5. Last of all and worst of all, textual sermons *may not prove helpful*. In extreme cases such pulpit work may do more harm than good. Efforts of this sort misrepresent the God of the Bible and repel men with common sense. The examples that follow do not concern textual preaching worthy of the name, since they show the folly of substituting human cleverness for biblical truth. They also make clear how a sacred text may seem farcical when the person in the pulpit lacks a feeling of reverence and a sense of humor.

Over in England such an old-time dominie dealt with that text about the desire for wings: "David did not desire wings like a grasshopper to hop from flower to flower, as those hasty souls do who leap in religion but do not run with perseverance; nor like an ostrich, which keeps to the earth though it be a bird, as hypocrites do who never mount towards heavenly things."

Nearer home, a backwoods exhorter descanted about Gen. 5:24— "Enoch walked with God: and he was not; for God took him." The speaker might have dealt with the meaning of a man's religion as "A Deepening Friendship with God," a friendship that brings joy and radiance to life here and now, with fullness and glory in the world beyond. But the exhorter chose to blaze a trail all his own; in textual fashion he talked first about Enoch's walk with God, and then about the words, "He was not": "Enoch was not an Episcopalian, for he walked; he did not dance. Enoch was not a Baptist, for he walked;

he did not swim. Enoch was not a Presbyterian, for he walked with God. Enoch was a Methodist, for God took him."

THE PATH OF WISDOM TODAY

In view of such vagaries, wherein lies the path of wisdom? The discussion here will concern the young man who has just begun to form habits for his lifework.

1. Let him choose *a text for every sermon.* He will find that a message never suffers from the right sort of connection with a worthy passage. When he rises to preach, he should wait for silence, and then begin with the text. By doing that he will save time, and put the best thing first. Apart from the benediction nothing in the last thirty minutes of public worship bulks so large and high as the text.

During the Bicentennial Celebration at Princeton, the Archbishop of Canterbury came across the Atlantic to bring greetings from the Established Church. When he rose to preach in the university chapel, he began with a text. Since he spoke not long after the close of World War II, these words from the Apostle carried all the more weight: "The earnest expectation of the creature waiteth for the manifestation of the sons of God" (Rom. 8:19). How else could the primate have begun so memorably? What save words from Holy Writ can match such an hour, or any other when every hearer expects a word from the throne of the Most High?

2. Let the minister resolve that whenever he announces a text he will *deal with it honestly.* He will know what it means and preach what it says. He will neither ill-treat it, misuse it, nor ignore it. Within proper limits he will feel free to set forth its truth and duty as the Spirit may direct. If the words from the Book lend themselves to a textual arrangement, he may determine to follow that trail; but if not, he can blaze a pathway of his own. A man who loves the Lord and knows the Book soon begins to develop an "exegetical conscience." Otherwise he might manhandle what he ought to count holy.

3. Realize the *value of each method.* No one system can suit all ministers and all occasions. Some of the fathers preached textual

sermons too exclusively, so that their pulpit work lacked variety and human interest. Many of the sons do not resort to this method often enough, so that their sermons may fall short in the way of freshness and helpfulness. Why should not fathers and sons meet on middle ground? Then the fathers would experiment with newer ways of presenting old truths and duties, and the sons would taste the satisfactions that come from dealing with texts according to their structure. Surely no one generation of preachers can claim a monopoly of the best ways to use divine truths in meeting human needs.

A word to the young reader: whether or not you employ the textual method, resolve that whenever you preach you will leave in the hearer's soul another illuminated text.

CHAPTER VI

The Need for Expository Work

PASTORS everywhere are becoming concerned about expository
preaching. An expository sermon here means one that grows
out of a Bible passage longer than two or three verses. Theoretically,
such a sermon differs from a textual one chiefly in the length of the
scripture units; practically, the two terms often overlap. For example, in a sermon you bring out the meaning and spiritual values of
Matt. 11:28-30; would you label the message expository or textual?
Probably the former, but either term would fit fairly well. Ap-
parently, then, an expository sermon means a textual treatment
of a fairly long passage, and a textual sermon means an expository
treatment of a shorter passage.

The two ways of preaching differ also in the treatment of the
passages. The shorter the unit of Holy Writ, the more fully you can
deal with the results of exegesis; the longer the unit, the more you
must select and omit, or else pass over lightly. Otherwise you might
not preach a sermon, but merely give a catalogue of facts with no more
unifying purpose or inner light than a page from a dictionary. In
expository preaching, therefore, put the emphasis on preaching, and
not on exposition. Go into the pulpit each time to meet a human
need, and not to explain a passage.

Expository work differs from textual also in being more difficult
to prepare. After a man has learned how to deal with a text, as we
have already seen, he may not find a textual sermon hard to prepare;
but when he tries to explain and illuminate a paragraph, a chapter,
or a Bible book, he may encounter all sorts of obstacles. In full view
of such difficulties many pastors these days wish to become proficient
in this kind of preaching. Since the Bible was written by books, and
the books by paragraphs,[1] they wish to deal with the Bible according

[1] In Psalms, however, the chapter affords the unit; in much of Proverbs, the verse.

to its character and its purpose. What else would you expect from men "learned in the Scriptures"?

How then should a young pastor start? By preparing an expository message occasionally, perhaps once a month. Such a working schedule, quite elastic, allows him time for careful preparation, and gives the people time to become accustomed to this new sort of pulpit fare— new at least to them. After six months or so the preacher can begin using such sermons more frequently, and after a year or two he may decide on one each Lord's Day, provided he has more than one service on Sunday. Only a man of unusual talent for this method, such as G. Campbell Morgan, would confine himself exclusively to this sort of pulpit work. As Henry Sloane Coffin insists, be sure at each service to make the pulpit fare differ from that of other services the same week. Then each time you enter the pulpit you will meet a different kind of human need.

THE CHOICE OF THE PASSAGE

At the beginning of his expository work a minister does well to single out a passage with few difficulties, giving the preference to a short paragraph rather than a long chapter. If he feels at home in Old Testament history, he may start with a passage from Genesis. In the career of Joseph, for instance, any lover of drama can find scenes full of life, motion, and color. In scene after scene action leads to conflict, conflict causes suspense, suspense brings tension, and tension reaches a climax; but the sacred writer never lets us down or sends us away from the scene unsatisfied,

The facts about young Joseph cause far less difficulty than those about such a man as Job, because the record about Job plumbs earth's lowest depths. But the young expositor need not hesitate to use his imagination in a sermon about some moving scene in the life of Joseph.[2] If a pastor wishes to interest young men and their girl friends, together with their fathers and mothers, he may speak on

[2] See Thomas Mann, *Joseph and His Brothers, Young Joseph, Joseph in Egypt,* and *Joseph the Provider* (New York: Alfred A. Knopf, 1934-44).

"How to Rise Above Temptation." The facts for the sermon come out of the passage that enshrines the text: "How then can I do this great wickedness, and sin against God?" What an appeal to the imagination of anyone who cares about "the white flower of a blameless life"!

Another minister finds it easier to start with a short psalm, such as Ps. 121. In the study he should learn much that he will not take into the pulpit; for example, what scholars say about this "song of degrees," or more correctly, this "song of ascents." In view of such findings he may think in terms of a song that Hebrew pilgrims used on the way up to Jerusalem for one of the yearly feasts. Little by little he develops a sermon under the heading "A Psalm for Vacation Time," or in another community, "A Psalm for the Railroad Man." As a keynote for the message he may begin with these climactic words: "The Lord shall preserve thy going out and thy coming in from this time forth, and even for evermore."

The psalm as a whole sings about the providence of God, not in terms scholastic and dull, but in doctrine set to music. The stress throughout falls on the word "keep," which rings forth six times, though in the King James the Hebrew verb appears three times as "preserve." In showing how the Lord keeps the pilgrim on life's pathway, the psalmist paints four word-pictures, which provide abundant materials for a sermon. If the preacher asks the hearers to keep their Bibles open at this psalm or else use this part of the responsive readings in the hymnal, he can point out the four parts, equal in length and rising towards a climax at the close. If the man in the pulpit has the soul of a poet, he can let this truth about God's Providence sing its way into the soul of everyone present, so that no one will ever forget the psalm of the traveler on his way home to God.

1. The God of the waiting hills—vss. 1-2
2. The God of the sleepless watch—vss. 3-4
3. The God of the friendly shade—vss. 5-6
4. The God of the winding road—vss. 7-8

In such expository work the structure of the sermon follows that of the passage. In the pulpit a man holds up in turn each of the parts of the psalm, showing what that part means in terms of today and with reference to the psalm as a whole. If he preaches well, he makes it easy for the hearer to remember the fourfold truth in connection with the four-part psalm, and vice versa. If the message calls for an illustration he may find one in the life of David Livingstone, who year after year in Africa drew comfort and peace from this and other psalms. David's sister tells about the young missionary doctor's going out from his boyhood home in a cottage at Blantyre:

"On the morning of 17th November we got up at five o'clock. My mother made coffee. David read the 121st and 135th Psalms, and prayed. My father and he walked to Glasgow to catch the Liverpool steamer." On the Broomielaw [the old-time dock on the Clyde], father and son looked for the last time on earth on each other's faces. The old man walked back slowly to Blantyre, with a lonely heart no doubt, yet praising God. David's face was now set toward the Dark Continent.[3]

In preparing a sermon about another psalm, such as the ninety-first, you may find no prominent structure, for the outpouring of a heart that overflows does not always run according to a careful pattern. You may have come to love the ninety-first psalm through reading Daniel Defoe's *Journal*, where that realistic novelist uses the psalm as a beacon light amid the London Plague of 1665. Now, several hundred years later, at a time when sickness and death stalk the streets of your city, preach from this psalm a message of peace and cheer: "Help from God in Days of Sickness." [4] Draw the ideas mainly from the passage, and put them together in a framework of your own. In the pulpit start with the words that Defoe put into the mouth of a saddler who went through the London Plague unscathed, and kept rendering succor to persons in distress: "Thou shalt not be afraid for the terror by night; nor for the arrow that flieth by day; nor for the pestilence that walketh in darkness; nor for the destruction that wasteth at noonday" (vss. 5-6).

[3] W. Garden Blaikie, *The Personal Life of David Livingstone* (New York: F. H. Revell Co., 1917), p. 52.
[4] For such local color see R. E. Prothero, *The Psalms in Human Life* (New York: E. P. Dutton & Co., 1909).

The pulpit expositor finds the going harder when he tries to interpret a prophetic passage, but after a young man has learned how to do this kind of pulpit work, he may dare to speak from Isa. 6:1-8 —"When a Young Man Comes to Church," or "A Young Man at Worship." In that experience of young Isaiah at the Temple a preacher can find a message for a college chapel. Such a case study would also interest the friends at the home church, where many of them feel concerned about the young man who has begun to worship God on the Lord's Day and may now devote his life to the service of men. In such a sermon be sure to preach positively, in the spirit of the passage, and throw no stones at young people today.

When a young man comes to church, he ought to behold a vision of God, high and lifted up; with a vision of himself and others as they appear in the eyes of God. In the resulting words of confession the young worshiper begins with himself, as he should, but he soon includes the people whom he loves. Then he receives the assurance of pardon, cleansing, and peace, all of which come through fire and through blood, for that burning coal from off the sacrificial altar tells of peace through pain. Last of all in the present sermon comes the young man's enlistment for service. Such a recital of the facts may seem tame, especially to a minister who has often read the passage, but if he uses imagination in making the facts live in terms of today, the sermon will glow with light from above, and the heart of many a hearer will burn with a new resolve to make God supreme in all of life. Here again the structure comes directly from the passage:

1. A young man's vision of God
2. A young man's vision of sin
3. A young man's vision of cleansing
4. A young man's vision of service

An older expositor may dare to preach from such a difficult prophecy as Isa. 52:13—53:12—"The Cross in the Old Testament," or "The Sufferings of Our Saviour." Here the minister looks on his passage not as a Jewish rabbi but in the light of the New Testament, after the fashion of Philip, who began with these words and preached about Jesus (Acts 8:35). In the poem from Isaiah the expositor sees five parts, or strophes, each in the Hebrew slightly longer than the one preceding. Out of these five divisions he can make a sermon about Christ, in terms of service, suffering, sacrifice, substitution, and satisfaction. This last refers to satisfaction that comes through suffering for others according to the will of God. Owing to the difficulty of making all this material luminous, why not prepare five sermons from the successive strophes, and have a series for Holy Week?

In the four Gospels almost every paragraph affords materials for an expository sermon which need not prove hard to prepare. Especially do the parables lend themselves to such uses, for every one of them shows inspired imagination at work among facts of life. The parables in the First Gospel differ from the ones in the Third: those in Matthew deal mainly with the kingdom of heaven; those in Luke have more to do with God's grace. Many who love the parables in Luke even more than the others find it easier to preach from those in the First Gospel. Who could not prepare a sermon from that parable about the four kinds of soil, under the heading "The Gospel from the Garden," or "The Gospel from the Farm" (Matt. 13:3-23)? Especially during spring and early summer the local color for the sermon would come from gardens or farms near at hand.

The narratives in the Book of Acts afford opportunities for all kinds of expository sermons, many of them not hard to prepare. For example, a pastor who wishes to encourage soul winning by laymen prepares a case study about Philip and the eunuch (Acts 8:26-40): "Introducing a Man to Christ." If the times call for a message about "The Christian Attitude Towards Race Prejudice," the sermon may grow out of facts in the tenth chapter, where Jewish Peter goes to be a guest in the home of Roman Cornelius. The same problem, in a much different form, appears in a novel by Sholem Asch, *East River*. According to that tale, Jews, Catholics, and Protestants once lived together in the district of New York City later given over to the building for the United Nations.

Parts of the epistles may cause the expositor difficulty. I and II Corinthians may not prove hard to expound, but portions of Ephesians and Colossians, or Romans and Galatians, yield more readily to textual or topical treatment than to expository uses. In addressing university students, however, Reinhold Niebuhr once spoke about "The Battle in a Man's Soul," taking his materials from the latter part of the seventh chapter of Romans, where good and evil contend for the mastery of a man's soul. In an expository sermon from the epistles a man does well to begin with such a passage, for it appeals to the imagination. However, unless he wishes to work hard, he will find less difficulty in many a narrative portion of Holy Writ.

The same principle applies in dealing with the Apocalypse. The Letters to the Seven Churches in the second and third chapters cause little difficulty, but in the book elsewhere a young minister finds passages too difficult to expound at present. With James Denney at Glasgow, the young expositor may look on "The Revelation to John" as the most Christian book in the Bible, but a wise man learns to find his way among hills and valleys before he attempts to scale the Alps. In short, young man, go slow!

THE LENGTH OF THE PASSAGE

In almost every book of the Bible the paragraph forms the unit of thought, and lends itself readily to expository treatment. These paragraph divisions appear prominently in the Revised Standard Version and in other modern translations of the New Testament; also in the American Standard Version and other modern renderings of the Old Testament. Every minister ought to have at hand a number of these translations, and use them in learning to think of the paragraph as the unit of thought. Gradually a man should form the habit of going to the paragraph for materials that will enter into the warp of the sermon.[5]

From time to time a chapter from the Bible leads to an expository message. First Corinthians thirteen led Henry Drummond to prepare the best-known sermon of its kind, "The Greatest Thing in the World."[6] In that message he pointed out three divisions of thought

[5] For an example see A. W. Blackwood, *The Protestant Pulpit*, sermon 11.
[6] See *Addresses* (New York: H. M. Caldwell Co., n.d.), pp. 9-44.

in the chapter and then dealt with each in turn, showing how they concerned love as the best thing on earth and in heaven. This kind of pulpit work calls for the use of imagination, which means in part ability to synthesize. The popular expositor must know how to put things together so as to form a single picture.

Once in a while the pastor may give a bird's-eye view of a whole book in the Bible. Between Christmas and Easter he may wish to preach every Sunday morning from the gospel according to Mark. If so, the sermon on the Lord's Day after Christmas may deal with "The Gospel for Busy People," or "The Gospel in Motion Pictures." Through this kind of sermon a man tries to get the hearer so interested in a Bible book that he will read it again and again, preferably as a whole. If the preacher merely dissected the book and displayed the skeleton, he might defeat his own purpose, for no layman enjoys looking at a skeleton, even though it shows the bony framework of a beautiful body. Here again the expositor must call on his imagination to make the book live.

One summer at the evening service a pastor gave a short series of book sermons from the Bible. In that university community he wished to reach high-school teachers and others who attended the summer school. He deliberately chose difficult books because he wished to test a theory that busy people would come to church at night, even in midsummer, if they got something to help them in daily living and thinking. Throughout that series he addressed more people than he had dared to expect, including teachers from elsewhere in the state and members of the home church. But he does not recommend such a series for a beginner in expository work.

> Job—"Why Must a Good Man Suffer?"
> Psalms—"How to Enjoy These Songs"
> Proverbs—"How a Young Man Should Live"
> Ecclesiastes—"What Is Best in Life Today?"

A mature pastor may even venture to preach a sermon about the Bible as a whole. Why do we put all sixty-six parts together and then call them "The Book"? Should we not think of them as "the divine library"? Such matters perplex many a thoughtful layman, and need attention from the pulpit. In any such sermon the preacher must know how to select and how to omit, so as to make a few things stand out. He may begin with Heb. 1:1, which tells about what we call the Old Testament and the New. Under the heading "Our Bible as One World" the preacher can tell about two hemispheres, each with three grand divisions. The Old Testament shows how God made ready for the coming of the Redeemer, and the New Testament exists to make Him known.

Whether the unit of scripture be short or long, the expository message should qualify as a sermon, not merely as an explanation of a passage. In the hands of such a master as Robertson or Alexander Maclaren this kind of pulpit work often resembled many another message that led people to think, feel, and act. In an expository sermon Maclaren would start with a brief text which he used as a gateway into the passage, where he found the bulk of the materials for a sermon. Then he gave the message a name, which must have guided him in completing the preparation and delivering the sermon. In collecting and arranging his materials he took from the passage as much as he needed and no more, feeling free also to use facts from the life of his day. As for structure, he planned to make a few truths stand out boldly. In the delivery also he strove after clarity and human interest. In brief, he used imagination, the *sine qua non* of the expositor, or any other preacher to common people.

THE ADVANTAGES OF EXPOSITORY WORK

1. This kind of preaching *honors the Scriptures*. It deals with them as they were written, with the book as the larger unit and the paragraph as the smaller one. In any case the passage may seem large or small, difficult or easy, but always the interpreter strives to do the same thing: he wishes to show what this part of the Bible means, and what difference the truth should make today. In any such undertaking, if he works in the spirit of prayer, he can rest in the assurance that the Book will do its own work in the hearts of God's children. Not

through magic and legerdemain, but like seeds that fall into prepared ground, the truths of Scripture bring their own harvest.[7]

2. Expository work *follows the noblest traditions of the Christian Church*. In apostolic days the preachers of the gospel tried to interpret the Hebrew Scriptures; whenever one of the apostles faced a group of people who knew the Old Testament, he would preach from their Bible. As we can learn from the reports of their sermons,[8] Peter and Paul looked on themselves as interpreters of the Book. In the Early Church at its best Chrysostom and Augustine, Ambrose and other leaders strove to interpret Holy Scripture. Those fathers used preaching methods different from our own, but still such a man as Chrysostom can show anyone today how to make the Bible live and glow:

> We have two qualities in Chrysostom which in their combination make him unique—he is a *Man of the Word and a Man of the World*. . . . Chrysostom himself is saturated with the Scripture, and is determined that his audience shall be taught to base their lives upon the principles of Holy Writ. . . . The Homilies of Chrysostom are not the expositions of a *lecturer*, but . . . the expositions of a *preacher*. . . . There is much force in the modern appeal for more expository preaching. I only submit that it must be *preaching*. The class-room is one place, the pulpit is another.[9]

At the Reformation, also, the leaders regarded themselves as expositors. Whenever Luther or Calvin arose to preach, he tried to interpret some portion of Holy Writ, one portion in a sermon. Luther would expound and enforce the lesson for the day, whereas Calvin would "lecture" through a book of the Bible, day after day, passage after passage. From that time to this, wherever the spirit of the reformers has prevailed, the local pulpit has given a place of honor to the exposition of Scripture. But if we of today hold true to the spirit of the reformers, we need not follow their methods slavishly. As they strove to interpret the written Word in thought-forms of their time,

[7] With reference to preaching study Matt. 13:23; Isa. 55:10-11.

[8] See R. B. Rackham, *The Acts of the Apostles* (New York: Edwin S. Gorham, 1901).

[9] C. S. Horne, *The Romance of Preaching* (New York, Fleming H. Revell Co.), pp. 144-46.

so ought we to set forth God's truth in ways that will appeal to people now.

3. Expository work of the right sort *feeds the people*. The apostles, the early fathers, and the reformers preached from the Bible as the surest means of helping people grow into the likeness of their Lord. So today the man who knows how to choose a passage and how to deal with it in thought-forms of his day can use it in promoting any cause for the Kingdom, or in dealing with any moral problem in the community. If he works intelligently and in faith, he can feed the people so well that they will keep spiritually strong and active; then they will not succumb to diseases of the soul, however prevalent round-about. Laymen who enjoy the right sort of biblical fare week after week love to work for Christ and His Kingdom; they also love the home church and its pastor. For an example of such a flock and such a shepherd, look for a parish church where a good man has fed the people from the Bible for the past ten years.

4. This kind of pulpit work enables the pastor to *keep growing year after year*. It obliges him to work, and leads him to pray. As the community interpreter of the Book he must find out what it means, and that calls for the use of all his intellectual muscles, which grow strong and supple through constant exercise. Day after day, while he makes ready to feed others, he can nourish his own soul. Except in midsummer he need not hie away to ministerial assemblies for the recharging of his worn-out batteries. For many such reasons, almost every minister who has given the expository method a fair trial over a number of years has come to believe in it with all his heart. This method works! Try it!

THE OBJECTIONS TO EXPOSITORY WORK

Why then has such preaching largely disappeared from many a pulpit? Partly because of imperfections in working methods.

1. Many a pastor today *does not know how* to prepare an expository sermon. The fault may lie with the seminary, where someone has failed to teach young men how to select a passage and what to leave out of the sermon, how to deal with the materials so as to make them

shine, how to use them in meeting the needs of the hearers today, how to preach a sermon that will help and not dangle a skeleton that will repel. In some cases the students do not elect such courses. As a consequence a good deal of expository work, so called, deserves the name of "work"; it shows lack of imagination. What a pity to send out men who cannot correctly represent God and His Book!

2. A certain type of expository work, so called, betrays *lack of preparation*. The "exposition" consists of running comments about successive parts of a passage that seems long and loose. In the hands of Spurgeon, almost a genius, such a Bible reading often proved helpful, but among other men running comments never reach any goal other than boredom. In expository preaching, as in other sorts of pulpit work, a sermon may prove to be worth as much or as little as it has cost in time, attention, and prayer.

3. Expository preaching of the wrong sort *does not interest the hearer*.[10] It makes him long to cry out: "All of that took place long ago and far away! What practical difference does it make to me, a businessman, here and now?" While he may not put the idea into words, he wishes the expositor to interpret life today. If laymen absent themselves from a sanctuary where the minister prides himself on "expounding the Word," they may do so not because they object to the materials but because they do not like the cooking and the service. They think that the pastor ought to set a good table every Lord's Day.

4. Pseudoexpository sermons *do not prove helpful*. These four objections may seem much alike, for they all stem from the same root: the would-be expositor has never learned how to prepare this kind of sermon. His fault may lie partly in the lack of a purpose, for if he began with a need out in the parish, he could find a passage to help him meet that need, and then he could prepare a message to embody his purpose. That is, he could if he knew how. Fortunately any man who ought to preach expository sermons can learn how. Let him begin by setting up this goal: "I am making ready to preach a sermon, and not merely explain a passage. If I start in time, work hard, and use

[10] See H. S. Coffin, *What to Preach* (New York: Geo H. Doran Co., 1926), pp. 33-38.

imagination, all in the spirit of prayer, I can prepare any expository sermon that my lay friends need to hear."

Suggested Readings

Blackwood, A. W. *Preaching from the Bible.* New York and Nashville: Abingdon-Cokesbury Press, 1941. Especially chaps. VII, XII.

Knott, H. E. *How to Prepare an Expository Sermon.* Cincinnati: Standard Publishing Co., 1930.

Patton, Carl S. *The Use of the Bible in Preaching.* Chicago: Willett, Clark & Co., 1936.

Taylor, W. M. *The Ministry of the Word.* New York: Randolph & Co., 1883.

CHAPTER VII

The Call for Other Materials

WE HAVE BEEN thinking about preaching as the interpretation of life today in light that comes from God today, largely through the Scriptures. Largely, but not altogether! A sermon that consisted wholly of materials from the Book of Books might lack human interest. As in everything else about the ministry today, a man has to keep his balance here. Many a young minister has tried to employ materials from almost every source except the Bible, and some older divines have ignored the ways in which God makes Himself known today. The path of wisdom lies between the two extremes. Why not take the warp of the sermon from Holy Scripture and the woof from life today, including books?

BOOKS DIRECTLY RELIGIOUS

Gradually the young minister ought to secure all kinds of books relating to the Bible. Among them he will value most the church hymnal, in which he finds all sorts of leads for sermons. If he is thinking about "The Gospel in the Rainbow," his mind turns to part of George Matheson's hymn: "I trace the rainbow through the rain." In this hymn, "O Love That Wilt Not Let Me Go," the preacher finds other suggestions for the coming sermon. If the message has to do with the Master's cure of the woman who touched the hem of His robe, the thought goes to the words of Whittier:

> The healing of His seamless dress
> Is by our beds of pain.

Those first six words may provide the topic for the sermon, and the phrase about "life's throng and press" may lead to a contrast between those who jostled about Him with curiosity and the one who touched Him with faith. In this respect the sermon will follow the text rather than the hymn. Then will come the message about Him and the one who touches Him here and now to find healing and peace. "If I touch even his garments, I shall be made well" (Mark 5:28, R.S.V.).

Again, the sermon may have to do with "How God Leads Today." At once the mind goes to the old Welsh hymn "Guide Me, O Thou Great Jehovah." Or one may think about the familiar words of Newman's hymn "Lead, Kindly Light":

> . . . I do not ask to see
> The distant scene,—one step enough for me.

Then the mind goes racing on to new vistas of truth and duty. In the resulting sermon the pastor need not quote often from hymns, or from anything else. In his study of sermons by the masters he does not find strings of quotations, but if he can throw light on the trail by quoting a few lines from a well-known song, he ought to welcome that light. He may even preach a sermon occasionally on a classic hymn, such as "When I Survey the Wondrous Cross."

From books about archaeology the pastor can glean facts for use in sermons. He may be thinking about "The Quietness of True Religion," and his mind turns to I Kings 6:7b, which tells about the building of the Temple without the sound of hammer or ax. When he turns to books he learns about the quarries of Solomon, which the pastor may have visited during a trip to the Holy Land. In any case he should know that they lie beneath the northern part of the Holy City, and that they once contained stone enough to build a city twice the size of Jerusalem within the walls. When that stone lies exposed to sunshine, wind, and rain, the masons find it hard to cut. So they used to "work" it down in the quarry, where they found the stone soft and easy to cut. All of these facts make a special appeal to members of the Masonic order, who alone know why.

The pastor who reads and thinks can draw materials from church history. There he can see how the God of the prophets and the apostles has revealed Himself to men and women in every age. He finds that people welcome facts from other days and other lands, if their friend in the pulpit can make the facts clear and show how

78

they bear on life today. During the past autumn the minister of a downtown city church announced a series of evening messages about the Protestant reformers, though not under that heading. Let us supply the name "The Faith of Our Fathers." These discourses came during the period before Advent, and helped to prepare the hearts of men for the truth of the Incarnation. Since the pastor knew how to deal with church history, he made each of those sermons as Christ-centered as though he had started with a passage from the Gospels.

In that series the first message had to do with John Huss, "The Morning Star of the Reformation." The second concerned John Wycliffe, "The Champion of the Common People." The third dealt with Martin Luther, "The Creator of a New World." The fourth presented John Calvin, "The Man with a Flaming Heart." The fifth introduced John Knox, "The Founder of the Presbyterian Church." A sixth might have rounded out the series with John Wesley, "The Man Who Averted a Revolution." Another local interpreter of Christian history might have selected other heroes and presented them in various ways. But he too would have found satisfaction in drawing sermonic materials from a source that most preachers ignore.[1]

The field of missions proves equally fruitful and far less difficult. The facts lie at hand in biographies that every pastor ought to read, if only to keep up with the women in the missionary society. He may start with heroes and heroines in his own branch of the ecumenical Church, and then go out to those of other denominations. In a few years a young minister can become acquainted with the lives of workers in the various fields, such as China and India. Before long he will find that he can neither preach nor pray without turning the thoughts of people towards the ends of the earth for which the Redeemer died. Soon he will discover that more than a few of his laymen have begun to read the lives of missionaries such as Wilfred Grenfell and Albert Schweitzer.

After Easter a pastor's love of missionary biography may lead to a series of evening sermons. If people's hearts often turn to the Pacific Ocean and the workers out that way, he may introduce

[1] See A. W. Blackwood, *Planning a Year's Pulpit Work*, chap. IX.

his friends to some of his heroes, such as John G. Paton of the New Hebrides, James Chalmers of New Guinea, John C. Patteson of Melanesia, Robert Morrison of China, and Guido Verbeck or Toyohiko Kagawa of Japan. Here again a minister's choice of subjects will depend on many factors. If he enters into the spirit of each hero, the resulting sermon will make clear the transforming power of the gospel.[2]

In the devotional classics, also, the preacher can find materials that will seem new and strange to people who have attended church for years. For the sake of his own inner health every parish minister needs to know and love the devotional classics, from Augustine's *Confessions* or *City of God*, to Austin Phelps's *Still Hour* or Andrew Murray's *With Christ in the School of Prayer*. For a while the pastor may live with the prose works of John Bunyan, especially *Grace Abounding, The Pilgrim's Progress, The Holy War,* and *The Jerusalem Sinner Saved.* Erelong the interpreter's thoughts and dreams will have to do with the Slough of Despond, the Hill Difficulty, and the Celestial City. After a man begins to feel at home in this mountain country, he can preach a series of evening sermons about "The Gospel According to Bunyan."

BOOKS NOT DIRECTLY RELIGIOUS

Next only to the Bible and the hymnal the pastor may love books of poetry. At Brighton, Robertson once wrote that a minister's choice of a favorite poet served as a sort of "nilometer," showing the depth or the shallowness of his soul. One pastor singles out Robert Browning, with all of his obscurity—often due to his leaps in logic. Other ministers prefer Tennyson, Wordsworth, Milton, or Dante. Robertson chose Dante, and knew his poetry almost by heart. Among recent bards the interpreter can find help in the works of Edwin Arlington Robinson, Emily Dickinson, and John Masefield. Thus far opinions differ, but all of us agree about Shakespeare. So give him the place of honor; year after year read a dozen or more

[2] See Henry P. Van Dusen, *They Found the Church There* (New York: Charles Scribner's Sons, 1945).

80

of this man's plays, including *Henry the Fourth*, in two parts, and *Henry the Fifth; A Midsummer-Night's Dream, Much Ado about Nothing, The Merchant of Venice, As You Like It, Twelfth Night, The Winter's Tale,* and *The Tempest; Romeo and Juliet, Julius Caesar, Hamlet, Othello, Macbeth, King Lear,* and *Antony and Cleopatra.*

Side by side with the poets may stand works of fiction. Many college and university graduates these days have become educated by reading the classics, and they expect the pastor to know the contents of what university professors consider the world's best books. Among them in fiction stand Thackeray's *Vanity Fair,* Scott's *The Heart of Midlothian,* Dickens' *David Copperfield,* George Eliot's *Adam Bede,* Thomas Hardy's *The Return of the Native,* Victor Hugo's *Les Misérables,* and Dostoevsky's *The Brothers Karamazov.*

As with poetry, the results of such excursions may not appear on the surface of a man's pulpit work, because few ministers can excel as "literary preachers." Usually the masters of the pulpit have employed few quotations. Both Robertson and Brooks read widely in world literature, but neither of them used such materials freely in the pulpit. Indirectly, however, such an interpreter draws continually from the world's best literature. In classic works of fiction, as in epic poems and in dramas, he finds moving interpretations of men and life here on earth.

Among current books of fiction no one can begin to keep up with the procession of "best sellers," but after a novel has lived and thrived for a year or two, the parish minister ought to know that book. One man's list for summer reading included *East River* by Sholem Asch, *The Robe* by Lloyd Douglas, *The Keys of the Kingdom* by A. J. Cronin, and *The Bishop's Mantle* by Agnes Sligh Turnbull. Hence the reader visited in turn with a Hebrew writer, a Congregational minister, a Roman Catholic doctor, and an Episcopalian gentlewoman, each of them with a message for our day. To this reading list some of us would add a few adventure tales by John Buchan, notably *Mountain Meadow.* Such reading helps a man to interpret the life of his day, and also influences his choice of words. "My nature is subdued to what it works in, like the dyer's hand."

Many of us derive still more help from biography. Every minister ought to know the standard lives of his favorite preachers, such as Chalmers, Robertson, and Alexander Whyte; or Bushnell, Beecher, and Brooks. In the way of materials for sermons, however, the pastor will derive more from books about men and women in other fields. Everyone ought to read Boswell's *Life of Johnson*, John G. Lockhart's *Sir Walter Scott*, Douglas S. Freeman's *Robert E. Lee*, and Carl Sandburg's *Abraham Lincoln*, both the *Prairie Years* and the *War Years*, especially the latter. What an easy way to become familiar with the main trends of history!

As for other books of biography, where can we draw the line? Some of us read everything of the sort we can get. For example, the son of a horse-and-buggy doctor takes delight in learning about the lives of physicians and surgeons, seen in such books as *The Life of Sir William Osler*, by Harvey Cushing; *Harvey Cushing*, by John F. Fulton; Victor G. Heiser's *An American Doctor's Odyssey;* the autobiographies of E. L. Trudeau, John M. T. Finney, and others from the galaxy at Johns Hopkins Medical School. Such a hobby in reading tends to keep a minister out of the rut, for when he looks at human beings through the eyes of experts in medicine, he knows human nature as it must have appeared to our Lord, the Beloved Physician.

Time would fail us to glance at books in other fields, such as science. Opinions differ concerning the amount of time a pastor should devote to magazines and newspapers, but surely he ought to know something about what his people read. Fortunately, he can single out the best newspapers, such as the *New York Times* or the *Christian Science Monitor*, where he can follow the main trends of the day. The same holds true of such a periodical as the *Atlantic Monthly* or *Harper's Magazine;* but many of us ought to spend less time in ephemeral reading and more in mastering books that open up permanent treasures. One pastor makes it a rule never to sit down while going through the morning paper; another not to pick it up until he goes home for lunch.

FACTS FROM OBSERVATION

Now we come to the chief source of sermonic materials, except the Bible. Like the prophet Amos and our Lord Himself, the pulpit masters of every age have drawn their facts from life rather than books. If the statement seems extreme, make a list of your favorite book preachers, both of yesterday and today, and then go through a volume of sermons by each man. Apart from the Scriptures, where did each of them secure his facts? Think of Chalmers and Whyte, Robertson and H. P. Liddon, John Bunyan and Richard Baxter. In our own day turn to J. S. Stewart or L. D. Weatherhead, H. E. Fosdick or C. E. Macartney, R. W. Sockman or Norman V. Peale. As a rule these men have read widely, but every one of them has drawn materials from the world about him more than from books in the study.

In our time the ablest preachers, like their predecessors, excel in the use of facts. "Three-fourths of preaching well consists in giving definite, well-chosen facts, and plenty of them. The other fourth doesn't matter." That sounds extreme, but still it calls attention to one difference between pulpit work that attracts and sermonizing that does not. In a single radio address such a preacher as J. S. Bonnell or O. F. Blackwelder uses more facts than another minister would employ in a month. At first glance the speaker may seem to be employing many illustrations, but on closer view the facts appear as building blocks to carry out the plan of the architect.

If he wishes to use facts from life, a man must be able to see. See what?

> Tongues in trees, books in the running brooks,
> Sermons in stones, and good in everything.

Where did Hosea or Paul find his facts? In life! The same held true even more in the reports of preaching by our Lord. In the "Teaching from the Hill," as in the parables, He drew much of the local color from nature as it came from the hand of God. But our Lord never referred to nature apart from persons, human and divine; He used it as the backgound for word pictures about God's dealings with His children. For some such reasons a seminary professor often prays silently for a young preacher: "Lord, I pray thee, open his eyes, that he may see" (II Kings 6:17).

In the life and work of farm and garden the interpreter can find all sorts of materials for sermons. He may preach in a city pulpit, but even there many of the people yearn for the wide, open spaces. Hence every pastor ought to know about seedtime and harvest, summer and winter, heat and cold, as they affect the lives of men and women today. When he addresses friends who have been cooped up all week, he can engage in "the open-air treatment of souls," and help them see what Henry Drummond styled "the natural law in the spiritual world."

For an example of a city pastor who often preached in terms of the open country, turn to a volume or two by George H. Morrison, of Glasgow. In a book of evening sermons, *Flood Tide*, you will find these subjects: "The Unreaped Corner"; "The Land of Hills and Valleys"; "The Choked Wells"; "The Message of the Rainbow"; "The Day of the East Wind"; and "The Wandering Bird." From these messages you will receive uplift rather than teaching, the sort of uplift that comes from a trip into the mountains, with an air of increased visibility. In the sermon about hills and valleys you will hear about the goodness of God in affording His children variety. All the while you will see how the man in the pulpit deals with the providence of God. To do that in terms of the world outdoors a man needs the heart and the eye of a poet.

The minister with tact and skill can secure preaching materials also from women's work in the home. Our Lord used such facts again and again; He spoke of the woman sweeping her room, the neighbor coming to borrow bread, and the housewife entertaining a guest at dinner. He told about children at play, a woman kneading her dough, and a mourner bewailing her dead. With Terence, He might have said: "Nothing human is foreign to me." In teaching and in preaching He spoke to people about things they could see and handle every day. So today when pulpit work becomes concrete and factual, in the way of the Master, the revival of preaching has already begun.

Business, too, affords materials for sermons. Among the parables fifty per cent have to do with business, directly or otherwise. The majority of these allusions concern money, doubtless because our Lord wished to reach men, and men have always thought much about money. He taught them how to use it as an asset, not a liability; so He referred to money in teaching about the kingdom of God. In much the same fashion George W. Truett often spoke to cattlemen in West Texas, showing them how to use money in doing the will of God, and not as an end in itself. When he preached about what they thought the *summum bonum*, he led them to seek first the kingdom of God.

Science also deserves attention from the pulpit. The man who preaches does not know all that savants have learned about the quantum theory and atomic energy. If he tried to explain the meaning of relativity, he might lead the hearers out into the deep, but he can make clear what all of us need to remember—that modern discoveries have altered life on the surface, but that they cannot transform the souls of men or set men free from fear. Where the Master told about the plow and the yoke, the interpreter now can speak of the combine in the harvest field and the airplane in the sky. Often he can preach about religion and life in terms of sickness and health,[3] ascribing thanks to God for the disappearance of typhoid fever and smallpox, and praying for the doing away with cancer.

Near commencement time, or else in the fall, the parish minister thinks much about school and college. From the study of medicine and law he has learned to use the case method. In the Gospels and elsewhere in the Book he can find case after case. For example, in the healing of the paralytic he can study a case about the meaning of forgiveness as the healing of the soul (Mark 2:10). In the school

[3] W. M. Mackay, *The Disease and Remedy of Sin* (New York: Geo. H. Doran Co., 1919).

experiences of boys and girls, also, he can see how to interpret life today as it appears in the eyes of God.

Indirectly the minister can encourage boys and girls, with their fathers and mothers, to appreciate the fine arts. He must feel sure about his facts, and not try to appear "superficially omniscient." Still he can promote the love of music, and see in it the handmaiden of religion. He can do much the same with other fine arts, especially painting, sculpture, and architecture. He can use in the pulpit facts about Raphael and Michelangelo, or Christopher Wren and Ralph Adams Cram. What a privilege to feel at home amid all the "holiness of beauty"!

The popular preacher makes still larger use of facts about sports. In baseball and football, tennis and golf, as in minor sports, anyone who knows his facts can do what Paul did with the foot race and the boxing match. In terms of the athletic field the minister can bring out the need of self-discipline, the call for team work, and the meaning of a "sacrifice hit." Such an interpreter appeals to men and boys, with many of their womenfolks. He also makes clear that the "old-time religion" concerns every nook and cranny of life here and now.

Does all this sound like going far afield? Of course, the man in the pulpit might become so much concerned about materials as to forget his purpose, but he must also guard against trying to reach the goal without using facts. How did Paul and other preachers in Bible days make clear and luminous the truths about God and the Kingdom? A British scholar has shown that the Apostle drew local color mainly from athletics and architecture, farming and military life,—all of them masculine.[4] Today, however, a man ought to think twice before he says much about war. Though he may believe in the justice of certain defensive wars in the past, he dare not encourage war itself. Rather should he uphold the Christian ideal, in the spirit of Milton's verse:

> . . . Peace hath her victories
> No less renown'd than war.

[4] See J. S. Howson, *The Metaphors of St. Paul* (London, 1862).

We might glance at still other fields, but we have gone far enough to make the idea clear. The man who wishes to interpret life today needs to send out a decree that his whole world shall be taxed. He ought to know the Bible as well as though he planned to use nothing else, and learn all he can about life as it appears elsewhere, both in books and in the world. However much this prospect may appall a young preacher, he will find that the pulpit masters of yesterday and today have excelled in the use of facts, for the glory of the One whom L. D. Weatherhead calls "the God of detail."

THE NEED OF A STOREHOUSE

Erelong the young minister will sense the need of a storehouse in which he can put the results of his reading and thinking, with the reports of what he sees and hears out in the world. For all of this an occasional pastor may rely on his memory, much as young Robertson, at Brighton, stored his mind with Scripture, poetry, and facts from many other sources. He kept filling that mental storehouse as long as he lived, so that whenever he took up a subject he could bring out from the inner treasure room biblical truths and recollections of what he had seen in a walking tour through the Alps. If any reader possesses such a memory and such ability to lay his finger on what he needs, he may pass by the next few pages.

Often in the study a young pastor runs short of facts. He finds it hard to discuss a truth or a duty concretely because he has not learned to think about God and men in terms of life today. If he lays plans for a homemade storehouse, he will find himself in first-class company. For example, think of the philosopher Hegel. As a growing lad Hegel showed few signs of brilliance, but he learned how to see and how to dig. At the age of seventeen he had begun to collect and classify all sorts of facts; through the years he kept putting away excerpts from his readings in classical literature and current periodicals, together with the results of observation and thinking. Gradually he began to use those raw materials for the making of articles and books.

Young Brooks followed much the same course, though his methods differed in detail. During three years at the divinity school he did not engage in what we term field work, but gave himself largely to the reading of books and the observation of life. He read widely, especially among the fathers of the Early Church, saw much, and thought hard. The results he put down in notebooks which he used as long as he lived:

> These note-books indicate that in his reading he kept his eye upon one incidental object, the accumulation of ideas, of pithy phrases, or epigrammatic statements, and above all of similes and comparisons. These he put down in condensed form, as so much material for future use. The rich and graceful style, the literary wealth and suggestiveness, the abounding metaphors,—these features which marked his writings came by the hard effort of years of preparation. He had indeed a native gift in this direction, but it had been cultivated to the utmost of his ability. There are many hundreds of similes collected here, which afterwards reappeared in his preaching.[5]

Another example comes from one of the wisest men in his time, Louis D. Brandeis, former Justice of the Supreme Court, who in his mature years accomplished an amount of work that seemed staggering.

He applied scientific management to his own life and work. His day ran according to a steady routine, in which hours, even minutes, were carefully scheduled. By planning, personal efficiency could be doubled or trebled. "Between what we do, and what we are capable of doing, there is a difference of one hundred per cent."[6]

As Arnold Bennett once put the idea, Brandeis learned how to live on twenty-four hours a day.

The self-discipline began early in life. Before Brandeis went to Europe for study at the age of sixteen, he had acquired a copy of John Todd's *Index Rerum*, in which he found a blank index for collecting and storing materials. "Let a young man when he begins life be in the habit of making an index of all that he reads which is

[5] A. V. G. Allen, *Life and Letters*, I, 181. Copyright 1907 by E. P. Dutton & Co.
[6] A. T. Mason, *Brandeis, A Free Man's Life* (New York: Viking Press, 1946), pp. 38, 432.

truly valuable (and he ought to read nothing else), and at the age of thirty-five or forty he has something of his own, which no price can purchase." In keeping with these words from the editor of the *Index*, the young student made his first notation: "The value of reading a book comes through concentration during the reading and in thinking about it afterwards."

All of this discussion points to a single conclusion: young man, organize your work. Form the habit of remembering what you read, what you see, and what you think. Unless you have powers approaching genius, you will remember such things more clearly and correctly if you write them out and put them away, one by one; but be sure to keep the storehouse simple.[7] Then you can turn to it for all kinds of preaching materials. Whatever the method in detail, remember that preaching in our day calls for the use of facts, facts, facts.

Suggested Readings

Good Reading. Committee on College Reading. New York: Penguin Press, 1947.

Luccock, Halford E., and Brentano, Frances. *The Questing Spirit.* New York: Coward-McCann, 1948.

McCall, Oswald W. S. *The Uses of Literature in the Pulpit.* New York: Harper & Bros., 1932.

[7] See A. W. Blackwood, *Planning a Year's Pulpit Work,* pp. 225-31.

CHAPTER VIII

The Choice of a Sermon Topic

SOONER or later all of these facts call for a name. In the preparation of a sermon the topic may come to view early or late. As
soon as a man catches a glimpse of his goal he may see what to call
his sermon. Some other time he may have to gather his materials
and start putting them together before he knows what to name them.
Whichever way his mind works, the preacher should have the topic
clearly in view before he starts to write out the message. Otherwise
he may prepare two or three sermons in lieu of one. Many a
preacher could improve all his pulpit work if he paid more attention
to sermon topics.

The "topic" refers to the name of the sermon, or the subject.
The "title" means the name of a book, or a series of sermons. The
"theme," or the "proposition," refers to a key sentence containing
the substance of the discourse. These terms appear in some books
interchangeably, but in the present work each of them stands apart.
As for the topic, every sermon ought to have a name that fits, and
every topic should lead to a sermon that glows. What an ideal!

THE IMPORTANCE OF THE TOPIC

Why attach importance to the name? Must every message from
God have a topic that appears in the Saturday newspapers? No!
Neither custom nor prudence makes such a demand. In a church that
stresses liturgical forms the rector may never announce the subject
of a sermon, whereas around the corner a pastor may advertise all
his topics. This custom has become more common in the United
States than in Britain, but on both sides of the Atlantic master
preachers have refrained from announcing topics; for example,
Marcus Dods and G. Campbell Morgan, Joseph Fort Newton and
George A. Buttrick have not usually announced their subjects.

The wise minister conforms to the traditions of his parish. If he announces topics, he finds them more effective for the second service than for the first. The preacher who attracts throngs at night or at vespers announces sermon topics. Then, too, the necessity of mailing subjects to the newspapers on Wednesday or Thursday acts as a spur for the man who tends to procrastinate. On the whole some of us favor the announcement of topics, especially for the evening service.

The real question, however, concerns the value of the topic in preparing and delivering a sermon. When the child of a man's heart comes to birth, he gives the offspring a name, and keeps that name in view throughout all the "Christian nurture." In Chicago, Frank W. Gunsaulus once preached on "Christ at the Disciples' Feet" (John 13:15). Gunsaulus had studied the record about Christ's washing the disciples' feet, and in the topic he had found a focal point to guide in preparing the message. In the pulpit he used the topic to let every hearer see the central truth and understand the details. To the present hour that topic has helped many a layman recall the message and then live in its light.

What do hearers remember about a sermon? Often the topic! In the history of preaching almost every message that has lived has done so partly because of its name. If the statement seems farfetched, make a list of published sermons that have lived a decade or more, and a list of other messages that you remember with satisfaction a year or so after the reading or hearing. In either group what do you recall most clearly? The topics! So the wise preacher takes advantage of the way the memory works. If the layman is to remember your next sermon, he will associate it with a subject. Why not give it a name that he will recall with ease?

So much for the theory; what of the facts? Look over the sermon topics in next Saturday's paper. Note how the topics of one minister compare favorably with headlines in the *New York Times*, while other sermon subjects suffer from sameness, tameness, lameness—sameness from week to week, tameness through lack of appeal, lameness through absence of religion. No layman who respects himself would cross the street to hear the sort of stuff that some topics set forth. One of the sermons may consist of truths from the Bible, with a bearing on the needs of our day. If so, why not give such a message the right sort of name? Why misrepresent God with a topic that makes Him seem devoid of interest and appeal? If these questions seem bootless, look again at the list in the Saturday paper!

THE TESTS OF A SERMON TOPIC

While you sit in the study, how can you size up a topic before you see it in print? By asking six questions.

1. "Is my subject *interesting but not sensational?*" Interesting to whom? To the man you wish to reach. As a rule, appeal to men rather than women, for if men come to church, women will not remain at home; if men keep coming, they will bring other men. The men in view come to find help in doing the will of God day after day. If they keep coming in numbers equal to the women, you know how to prepare and deliver sermons of interest and value to men.

Why not ascertain the kind of topics that appeal to the men you wish to reach? In a Bible class of a hundred laymen a young pastor handed out a list of fifty sermon topics. He wished to increase attendance at the evening service, and he asked those friends to select eight subjects on which they would like to hear sermons. The majority of them responded by handing in lists, and later by coming to hear the sermons. They had not been attending the second service, but soon they started bringing their friends. The men who filled out the lists helped the preacher still more by opening his eyes to the need of using topics they could understand. Among the eight on the composite list these stood at the top: "The Meaning of a Man's Religion," "What Is Faith?" and "What Is Life Everlasting?"

Up to that time he had relied largely on subjects that did not appeal to men; for example, "The Suburbs of the Soul." That topic had come to him in a dream, but without any Joseph or Daniel to explain what it meant, so he never preached that sermon. After he found that those laymen did not care for fleecy abstractions, he began to preach doctrine, and he strove to make it bear on the lives of men day after day. In another congregation such a poll may lead to a different kind of pulpit work. The fact remains that whenever a minister announces a subject or a series, he should feel sure of its appeal to the men he wishes to reach. In short, be interesting!

Interesting, but not sensational! A sensational topic calls attention to itself and the preacher, not to Christ and His gospel. A lurid subject may attract a throng of curiosity-seekers, but what of the effect on the person the preacher most wishes to help? Why repel him by "smartness"? "No man can bear witness to Christ and himself at the same time." Fortunately sensationalism has largely disappeared from the pulpit today, for sermons and subjects may seem dry and dull but seldom unseemly. Perhaps because of global wars and their aftermath a spirit of humility and awe has guided and restrained almost every man who has dared to preach.

The following examples, however, come to mind. A young fellow who afterwards resigned the ministry held forth about "The Sex Life of Samson." An older man spoke about "A Night with the Witch of Endor." A third "preached" about John the Baptist as "The Man Who Lost His Head at a Dance." A fourth perpetrated a pun about his home town: "Putting the Ill in Clarksville," and again drew a crowd to laugh about "The Middle-Age Spread." And yet we wonder why thoughtful laymen quit coming to church!

2. Again, is the topic *clear but not revelatory?* For examples of clear topics look at these: "The Comfort in Handel's Messiah," "The Cross in Terms of Healing," and "The Christian Secret of Radiance." Or take these from Gossip: "What Christ Does for a Soul," "The Message of Jesus the Layman," and "The Gospel According to Christ's Enemies." Such a topic shows the layman what the minister plans to do, but does not tell what to expect in detail. This kind of subject goes with a teaching sermon or a teaching book. When a man wishes to instruct, he writes a volume about preaching from the Bible, not one about the need for a different kind of pulpit work today.

Must a preacher always use topics clear as crystal? The Lord forbid! After a man has learned to use imagination for the glory of the God from whom it comes, he may preach on "The Gospel in the Snow" (Isa. 1:18), "The Sermon in the Supper" (I Cor.

11:26, in the Greek), or "A Text for the New Year" (Matt. 6:33). Gossip often preaches on topics such as these: "The Crowning Attribute of God," "What Christ Hates Most," and "A Message for Gray Days." Paul E. Scherer generally uses subjects that suggest far more than they say, as in his volumes *The Place Where Thou Standest* and *Event in Eternity*.

These examples suggest two contrasting rules, with all sorts of exceptions. On the one hand, when you plan to teach, phrase a topic that every person will understand; but when you wish to comfort or inspire, start with something more poetic. In presenting a doctrine, enforcing a duty, or explaining a passage, you will find the clear topic an asset. In creating an atmosphere, in fostering a spirit, in opening up a vista, rely largely on tone color. Hence you may speak about prayer in terms of "the golden altar," or "a stairway up to God." For a while, however, a young minister does well to specialize on clear subjects, which he will find much easier to prepare.

3. Once more, is the topic *short but not abrupt?* According to experts in the psychology of attention, a line of newspaper publicity should contain no more than four strong words. Through experiments in the laboratory they have found that more than four prominent words tend to distract attention. For an example of a sermon topic with four strong words, take this about the Holy Spirit: "The Power of God in the Lives of Men." Note the strong words: power, God, lives, men. Then see how to weaken it all by watering it down: "The Almighty Power of Our Living Christ in the Everyday Lives of Ordinary People." Such a topic tries to tell too much, scatters where it ought to focus, and suggests nothing for the hearer to see, to feel, to do. Instead of expanding, try cutting the subject down: "The Holy Spirit as Power."

Only an expert can preach well about a single word. A pulpit master has done so with "Procrastination," but in this term he finds more than one idea. He has shown much more skill in naming a book, *The Meaning of Faith*. If he had said *Significance* rather than *Meaning*, he might have cut the book sales in two. Another speaker might hold forth about "The Tremendous Implications of

Unfaltering Trust in the Omnipotent Sovereign of the Cosmic Order," and some of us might look on his pompous verbosity as a proof of scholarship! How much more ability Felix Mendelssohn employed in naming certain compositions, which he first styled *Melodies for the Pianoforte*, but afterwards, *Songs Without Words*.

4. Further, is the topic *rhythmical but not cloying?* When a man's heart moves, his words flow. The beauty of prose rhythm appears in the book titles of John Bunyan, all of which flow: *The Pilgrim's Progress, Grace Abounding to the Chief of Sinners, The Life and Death of Mr. Badman,* and *The Jerusalem Sinner Saved.* On the other hand, a sermon topic might go too far in quest of beauty, as in a succession of messages about "Life's Fitful Fever," "Life's Transient Dream," and "The Sinking Sands of Time." However, the man with taste and self-restraint can keep from seeming sentimental or mushy, even on Mother's Day.

5. More important, is the subject *accurate but not pedantic?* Does it include everything in the sermon and nothing else? Does the tone color accord with the spirit of the message? In short, does the hat fit the head? This test may prove to be the most difficult of all. For examples of accurate topics look at these from Horace Bushnell; note how they keep from scholasticism and yet show the facts: "Every Man's Life a Plan of God," "Living to God in Small Things," and "How to Be a Christian in Trade." Or think about recent topics with varieties of tone color: "The Christ of the Flint Face" (Isa. 50:7), "The Faith That Conquers Fear" (Mark 4:40), and "Thanking God in a Storm at Sea" (Acts 27:35).

6. Last of all, is the topic *religious but not otherworldly?* This question belongs with the one about accuracy, for if a sermon consists of religion in the Christian sense of the term, the name should correspond. A nonreligious label for a Christian sermon might seem like a libel. Even so, many an evangelical message goes out under a name devoid of religion. Take these examples, chosen almost at random: "Conquerors of Mountains," "Strength Measured by Weakness," "When Life Has Meaning," and "Outmatching Defeat." Since each sermon contains a Christian message, it calls for a Christian name.

The point seems important today because of the trend towards secularism. The pastor may insist that he always preaches religion and that he depends on his reputation. When he starts to speak about "Your Unknown Self" or "The Conquest of Fear," [1] the people know that he will stress God more than psychology. But what of the effect on the young preacher who has no prestige? Why not encourage him to put as much religion into his subjects as into his sermons?

The difficulty may come in keeping the balance. When a man speaks about "The Sovereignty of God," the topic suggests an other-worldly discourse, whereas a good subject includes both the divine and the human, often in this order. If the power comes from the divine, the stress falls on the human. For example, J. S. Stewart preaches about "When God's Peace Guards the Door" (Phil. 4:7).[2] Such a topic calls for a message that sings about God as near at hand and strong to save. In naming sermons, therefore, never lose sight of the man in the pew.

The young preacher ought to look on these six tests as practical guides, and not as ironclad restrictions. If anyone keeps them in view for a year or two, he will begin to apply them unconsciously. Fortunately ability to phrase topics keeps growing with use, but still the task may not become easy. Every once in a while even a mature preacher may have to tarry hour after hour before he lays hold of the topic that eludes his grasp. But all this while he can busy himself about other parts of the sermon, and look forward without fear. From past experience he knows that watchful waiting in the spirit of prayer leads to a name that fits the sermon. However, a few suggestions may help the beginner.

THE FORM OF THE SERMON TOPIC

1. Give the preference to *a phrase* rather than a sentence or a single word. A phrase suggests far more than it says, whereas a sentence may tell the whole story. Let the phrase be simple rather than com-

[1] See A. W. Blackwood, *The Protestant Pulpit*, sermons 18, 28.
[2] See *The Strong Name* (New York: Charles Scribner's Sons, 1941), pp. 169-76.

pound. Preach about "The Faith of Our Children" rather than "Faith and Our Children," a topic that suggests lack of unity. Speak about "Being a Christian for Your Boy's Sake," not about "Being a Christian and Loving Your Boy." As in a painting, focus attention on a single point of interest, not on two separate centers. When the divine and the human enter into view, speak about the one with reference to the other, but do not make them move on the same level. Phrase a subject that suggests a sermon full of divine grace for human needs.

A mature preacher may, once in a while, use a sentence as a topic; for example, "Let the Church Be the Church!" The subject raises a thought-provoking question in the mind of the hearer: "What does it mean for the Church to be the Church?" All to the good, if the preacher has won his spurs; otherwise he may seem to be riding roughshod over friends whom he ought to lead gently. For the first few months in the community a young pastor may content himself with appeals to the heart and the head, with never a punch from the shoulder. Gradually he will learn to speak with authority and still not seem pugnacious or pontifical. The fact remains that a certain type of message occasionally calls for a sentence topic, with an imperative verb; for example, "Choose Ye This Day!"

Our working rule calls for another exception: a problem sermon may require a topic in the form of a sentence. The problem may appear as a question; for example, "How Can You Conquer Doubt?" or "How Keep Sunday?" In one case the answer may come through our Lord's dealings with Thomas (John 20:24-29); in the other, from what He taught the disciples (Mark 2:23—3:5). In the message concerning doubt, the preacher brings the hearer face to face with the living Christ. The sermon about Sunday may center round the three sayings: "The sabbath was made for man"; "The Son of man is Lord also of the sabbath"; it is "lawful to do good on the sabbath days."

2. Phrase the subject in *words of your own*. Feel free once in a while to use another man's topic, but as a rule taste the joy of phrasing your own. Form the habit of interpreting the text, and not merely quoting a part. Instead of preaching about "God So Loved the World," speak on "The Golden Text of the Bible," or "The Best

THE PREPARATION OF SERMONS

Thing About God." Instead of taking the subject, "Ye Shall Receive Power," preach on "The Holy Spirit as the Power of God," or "Power from God for the Church Today." Use the topic to throw light on the text; for example, "What Jesus Says About Money," "When a Young Man Finds God," "How the Lord Guides Us Today."

After a man has learned how to phrase topics of his own, he may begin at times to use words from the text. In his published sermons, Brooks uses subjects of his own 67 per cent of the time, but in the remainder of these messages he employs topics from the Bible. Here follow some of his subjects from texts: "The Consolations of God," "Unspotted from the World," "The Candle of the Lord," "The Pillar in God's Temple," "Going Up to Jerusalem," and "The Beautiful Gate of the Temple." If everyone who employs biblical topics would use as much skill and care as Brooks displayed, our laymen would learn much about the beauty of the Bible. But no one ought to follow this method, or any other, all the time.

3. For a while, young man, give the call to *a teaching subject*. Be simple and clear. Choose something within the range of your present powers. Any minister who thinks can label his sermon "The Meaning of God's Providence," "The Peril of an Easy Conscience," or "What Jesus Says About Worry." But if a man confined himself to such clarity month after month, he might fall into a rut. Gradually he should learn how to phrase topics with more beauty and uplift, provided he can wed them with messages full of grace and hope. For example, after Brooks had served an apprenticeship as a craftsman, he could preach on "The Rainbow Round About the Throne" (Rev. 4:3b). In the course of time any minister with imagination can preach on subjects full of grace and charm.

4. Week after week *secure variety*. From Sunday to Sunday let the topics differ both in substance and in form. They will do so if you think for yourself and then look at the sermon as a test of your skill. How can you exercise your intellectual muscles more surely than by fashioning a succession of original topics as different as the sermons themselves? According to Goethe, "Originality does not consist in

saying a new thing, but in saying an old thing in a new way." In other words, be on guard against sameness. If you tend to phrase topics clearly, you may overdo a good thing; if you excel in subjects of the other kind, you may become hazy; if you draw topics from parts of your texts, you may never do anything else. Use imagination! Then you will dare to be yourself, and be different each time.

In a series, however, the topics should follow a pattern fairly uniform. As in the chapters of a book, subjects in parallel form indicate likeness of content. If the general title points to "Beliefs That Matter," or "Beliefs That Build," the topics that follow will show what beliefs stand out today, or which ones tend to build. If the man in charge of "construction" knows how to build with words, he can present similar thoughts in similar forms, and never let them seem wooden. Such a craftsman works like a poet, who can follow a pattern of his own choosing and yet make the truth shine out through words full of beauty and charm.

For many such reasons the novice finds it easier to plan a series of four or five sermons than one of eight or ten. After a few years he may attempt something ambitious, such as a series of ethical sermons, "Bible Teachings about the Family." Without seeming sensational a minister with a happy life at home can work out a series with topics such as these:

> The Primacy of the Christian Home
> The Blessedness of Little Children
> The Meaning of Christian Nurture
> The Building of a Family Altar
> The Importance of Our Young People
> The Christian Ideal of Courtship
> The Bible Teaching About Marriage
> The Lord's Attitude Towards Divorce
> The Beauty of Heaven as Home

A STUDY OF SERMON TOPICS

A study of sermon topics affects all a man does in preparing for the pulpit. In Boston a young pastor became concerned about his preaching, a subject he had treated lightly at the divinity school. Not knowing where else to begin, he started to work on his topics, and to this matter he devoted spare time for weeks. First he studied the topics of master preachers, such as Bushnell and Newman, and then he toiled over his own sermon subjects. In the naming of each message he used all his powers and gifts, and before long he began to find new joy in the work of the study. He noted that the people responded better to his sermons, and that the church attendance began to pick up.

All of this the young pastor reported to the professor whose books had led to the new quest for craftsmanship. After he had listened to the recital, the latter asked: "Do you ascribe all of those improvements to your study of topics?"

"No, sir," the young man replied, "for when I began to fix up the front window, I found that I had to furbish the whole house."

That young man had learned one of the basic lessons about his lifework, for he had begun to look on every sermon as a whole. He did not think of a topic as a thing by itself, but regarded it as a means of strengthening the entire sermon. He also determined never to use a glowing subject with a sloppy discourse. If he had become concerned about some other aspect of preaching, he might have come to the same conclusion. The fact remains that his study of sermon topics led him to a sort of homiletical regeneration.

Does anyone else wish to make a study of sermon topics? If so, begin with a volume or two by your favorite preacher of yesterday or today—Bushnell or Clow, Stewart or Gossip. After you have learned all you can from this preacher's topics, begin to branch out. See if you can find a weak pulpiteer who shows concern about giving every sermon the right sort of name. Then you may conclude: "By the grace of God I shall align myself with the masters and not the dabblers."

No one can hope to become a preacher simply by tinkering with topics, but the man who engages in this kind of discipline week after week has turned his face towards the time when he will present the old gospel with new interest and force.

71279

LINCOLN CHRISTIAN COLLEGE

CHAPTER IX

The Case for Topical Sermons

IN THE HISTORY of preaching, topical sermons have outnumbered all the rest. Among messages that have become famous almost every one has belonged to this order. Especially in the United States during the present century, sermons in print have rarely assumed other forms. At present the trend seems to be toward a larger use of textual and expository methods, but few of us expect preachers to abandon topical sermons. Do these facts mean much or little? Should they cause satisfaction or dismay? All of that must depend on considerations to which we now turn.

THE MEANING OF THE LABEL

A topical sermon means one whose form grows out of the words and ideas in the subject. In a topical sermon the subject dominates everything that follows, just as in a textual sermon the passage governs everything that comes after. Needless to say, these labels fit poorly. Sometimes they overlap and cause confusion. In dealing with a sermon the student may feel at a loss about the identification. In general he may wonder why a topical sermon calls for a text, and why a textual message needs a topic. If he finds the labels perplexing, he should know that the facts themselves seem far from simple. Still we can follow the working description of a topical message as the unfolding of the subject with which it begins.

How should we look on the topical method? As a rule pulpit masters regard it with favor, but certain critics warn the young minister never to preach this way. Many of us who teach have given a place to the topical sermon, but not to the exclusion of other forms. We note, for example, that doctrinal sermons often assume a topical form, as do ethical discourses. Still, we feel that the pulpit of our day would meet human needs more adequately if every young minister learned to

101

preach in other ways at times. Why should anyone rely on a single method of delivering the truth from God?

A critic may ask: "Is it possible to deal with biblical truths topically?" For the answer let us turn again to the history of preaching, here and there. Among evangelical preachers think of Chrysostom, who, at the height of his powers, delivered seven messages about the death of Lazarus. In one of them he dealt with "Excessive Grief at the Death of Friends." He announced as the text I Thess. 4:13, but the sermon itself grew out of the topic. After an introduction that had to do with the text Chrysostom brought out two main ideas, both topical; he showed the folly of excessive grief and the way to ward it off. How would you label such a discourse, if not biblical in substance and topical in form?

As the most eloquent of biblical preachers Chrysostom could have fashioned an entire textual discourse out of what he put into the first few paragraphs. There he dealt with the meaning of death as sleep, and with the Christian limits of grief. Both of these ideas he took straight from the text, and in the same order: "I would not have you to be ignorant, brethren, concerning them which are asleep, that ye sorrow not, even as others which have no hope." But if Chrysostom had followed this trail throughout the sermon, it might not have lived for more than fifteen hundred years. After all, why care about the form of a message that consists of divine truth voiced by a radiant personality in meeting human needs?

For another example turn to Thomas Chalmers and read that famous sermon, "The Expulsive Power of a New Affection." [1] Note how he followed custom by announcing a text, I John 2:15, and how he drew the message out of his topic. In the classroom students insist that he could have used some other text, such as Rom. 12:2, Rom. 12:21, Col. 3:2, or I John 4:18b. After a while they agree on this last text, "Perfect love casteth out fear," but still they admire that sermon, just as it appears, text and all. Why do they stand in awe before that message? Largely because it flows from the topic.

[1] See A. W. Blackwood, The Protestant Pulpit, sermon 6.

Again, we can go to Horace Bushnell, who has become known especially because of two sermons, both topical: "Every Man's Life a Plan of God" and "Unconscious Influence." Each of them warrants our study, but we can think only about the latter. Of course the preacher began with a text, as everyone did in his time: "Then went in also that other disciple" (John 20:8).[2] As in other messages, Bushnell dealt with his text allusively, but he drew the body of the sermon out of the topic. Partly for this reason the message has lived almost one hundred years, and has influenced many a later sermon.

More recently, at Glasgow, William M. Clow often preached textually. Unlike many preachers strongly evangelical, however, he did not eschew topical sermons. In a message about "The Cross and the Memory of Sin"[3] he began with a text, I Tim. 1:13. In the opening paragraphs he fixed attention on the topic, first on "memory," and then on "memory of sin." In the body of the sermon he dealt with three large truths, each of which he derived from the topic, with emphasis on the Cross: "In the first place, *the Cross takes the sting out of the memory of sin*. . . . In the second place, *the Cross makes the memory of sin a means of grace*. . . . In the third place, the Cross shall finally *obliterate the memory of sin*." Then this topical preacher of biblical truth leads up to the final words: "No sin can live under the felt power of the Cross."

In our day, no one has excelled Harry Emerson Fosdick as a master of the topical method. Theologically he often differs from many who admire his homiletics. In a message about "Forgiveness of Sins,"[4] he shows how to deal with a biblical passage indirectly. According to his custom he starts with a topic, or a problem, and he announces no text. But in this sermon he soon begins to deal with the words of our Lord: "Which is easier, to say, Thy sins are forgiven thee; or to say, Arise and walk?" (Luke 5:23). Then the sermon brings out three reasons why our Lord found it hard to forgive sins like those of the man in

[2] *Sermons for the New Life* (London, 1892), pp. 118-32.
[3] See A. W. Blackwood, *The Protestant Pulpit*, sermon 17.
[4] *Ibid.*, sermon 23.

the pew today. Here again, a pulpit master shows how to focus attention on a topic, and how to use it in preaching truth for our time.

THE ADVANTAGES OF THE METHOD

In the hands of a master this kind of pulpit work offers more than a few advantages.

1. It allows the minister to discuss *any subject he thinks needful*. He may feel that the state of the world and of the parish calls for a doctrinal message about "The Meaning of God's Sovereignty," or an ethical discourse about "The Forgiveness of National Foes." In either case he may begin with a biblical passage, and then deal with the subject topically; or else with the topic, and then discuss it more or less biblically.

2. The topical method allows *breadth of treatment*. Within the limits of a broad subject the preacher feels free to roam wherever he can find something for his sheep. At the age of twenty-two, Charles H. Spurgeon preached about "The God of the Aged."[5] He began with a text, Isa. 46:4, and from it brought out a doctrine, the constancy of God's love. Then he dealt with the practical values of this doctrine. Some of the truths Spurgeon got from the text; others, from the topic. All the while he strove to meet the needs of his hearers, old and young, especially those of middle age. Who can object to this way of preaching about the truth wrapped up in a topic?

3. The use of this method *encourages a man to seek unity*. If he phrases a topic with care, he may use it as a test of oneness. For example, take the best-known sermon by John Wesley. In 1758, at the age of fifty-five, at a time when he knew that everyone was thinking about the assizes, he planned to deal with the subject, "The Great Assize." According to custom in an "occasional sermon," he began with the circumstances that suggested the discourse, and then called attention to the text: "We shall all stand before the judgment seat of Christ" (Rom. 14:10c). Soon he launched into a discussion of the subject. Almost a hundred years later, a far different kind of

[5] See *Sermons*, second series (New York: Sheldon & Co., 1865), pp. 361-79.

preacher showed how to use a topic in securing unity. In Boston, William Ellery Channing started with a text—"This is my beloved Son, in whom I am well pleased" (Matt. 17:5)—and delivered a message that has become famous, "The Character of Christ."[6]

Each of these sermons dealt with a single subject, the one with which the speaker began. In his subject the preacher found a sort of polar star, which he followed to the end of the journey. If this matter of unity seems inconsequential, read a number of present-day sermons, and note how some of them suffer from lack of such oneness as goes with any work of art. Do you wonder that laymen find it hard to follow a minister who tries to preach three or four little sermons in less than half an hour? As for a permanent impression, how can they recall the central message of a discourse that lacks a unifying core? If any young minister examines his pulpit work for the past six months, he may discover the need of using a topic in order to secure unity.

4. The wise use of a subject enables a man in the pulpit to *keep moving towards the goal* of the sermon. The topic may serve as a compass to keep the guide on the pathway to his destination. In that message about "The Great Assize," the thought and feeling kept mounting, so that Wesley, moved by the grandeur of his subject, rose to heights of emotion such as he seldom attained. Then he closed with the following words, which have to do with the final appearing of our Lord:

Oh, make proof of His mercy, rather than His justice; of His love, rather than the thunder of His power. He is not far from every one of us; and He is now come, not to condemn, but to save the world. He standeth in the midst! Sinner, doth He not now, even now, knock at the door of thy heart? Oh, that thou mayest know, at least in this thy day, the things that belong unto thy peace! Oh, that ye may now give yourselves to Him who gave Himself for you, in humble faith, in holy, active, patient love. So shall ye rejoice with exceeding joy in His day, when He cometh in the clouds of heaven.[7]

[6] See A. W. Blackwood, *The Protestant Pulpit*, sermon 7.
[7] See *Works*, ed. by John Emory (1856), I, 126-35.

5. This way of preaching, topically, often *brings out a man's literary gifts*. Occasionally, as with Frederick Robertson, a textual and expository preacher has become known for mastery of words, but as a rule topical preachers have won far more favor with lovers of the King's English. For example, turn to the published discourses of Jeremy Taylor and John Tillotson, or the prose works of John Bunyan—three authors whose writings young men study in the department of English at a university. As an object lesson of Bunyan's topical method, study *The Jerusalem Sinner Saved*. See how the name of the treatise includes all that follows, and how the topic leads to the sort of prose that the world shall not willingly let die.

THE OBJECTIONS TO TOPICAL SERMONS

In view of all these facts, why do some evangelical leaders warn young ministers to eschew topical sermons? Perhaps because the method does not work like a machine; in the hands of a bungler a topical sermon may reveal all sorts of flaws. If the most famous sermons in the history of the pulpit have belonged to this type, so have many of the weakest and worst. When anyone warns us against topical sermons, however, let us be sure that we agree about what kind of messages he finds unworthy. Let us also grant that this kind of preaching opens the doorway for certain abuses, which may become serious.

1. The topical method *tends to encourage secularism*. A discourse about a subject rather than a passage may have little or nothing to do with Christianity. The critics rightly protest against turning the pulpit into a forum for the discussion of anything other than "what man is to believe concerning God, and what duty God requires of man." In certain Jewish synagogues, for example, the early parts of public worship come from the Old Testament, but the message sounds like an editorial leader in a political party newspaper. Unfortunately, our Hebrew friends can claim no monopoly on secular preaching. The ministers who visit us from Europe insist that in the United States they hear more than a little pulpit work devoid of religion.

If so, the fault lies with the preacher and his materials, and not

106

with the method. If he discusses world peace, race prejudice, or any other burning issue of the day, he can look on the matter from the standpoint of God and the Bible, or from that of his own opinions and prejudices. From the lips of a gifted man this latter kind of pulpit work may seem as interesting as the other, but what of the fruitage? When has nonreligious "preaching" built up a congregation that flourished after the platform speaker moved away to another field? Since the lay hearers come out of a world where they must listen to the cash register and share in the rush of the market place, why should they not in church hear something other than the lingo of the street? So let us chalk up a black mark against the topical presentation of subjects wholly secular.

2. In other hands the subject sermon may *lack human interest* because it grows out of sweeping surveys and consists in vast abstractions. The preacher may hold forth about the sovereignty of God. Instead of bringing the truth down to earth and tying it up with human needs, he may prate about omniscience, omnipotence, and omnipresence, or else about the supernatural, the objective, and the Altogether-Other. In the study he ought to learn about Rudolf Otto's Numinous and Sören Kierkegaard's mystifications, but in the pulpit today the best of men may deal with a subject beyond his present powers. Would he not be wiser to start with Psalm 139,[8] where the truth about God has to do with one man, like the friend in the pew? This kind of preaching relates to human needs here and now.

3. The wrong sort of topical fare *does not feed the people.* But why condemn a school of domestic science because its methods go awry in the hands of a bungler? Surely the food values in a sermon depend far less on the arrangement of the ingredients than on the presence of proteins and vitamins. Topical preaching has no monopoly of such faults; regardless of method a mechanical preacher must prepare mechanical sermons. But why labor the point? We have already looked at examples of topical sermons that have fed the souls of human beings with abundance of manna from heaven.

[8] See James Denney, *The Way Everlasting* (London: Hodder & Stoughton, 1911), pp. 1-12.

4. The critics insist that the topical method calls for *little work in the study*, because a preacher can get his materials from the daily newspaper or the latest best-seller. He may neglect the Bible, with other works that require a man to think and pray. So the one called of God to interpret His truth may become a reporter of the passing scene. If he shows ability and resourcefulness, the pulpit reporter may interest the hearers week after week. In certain cases this kind of "preaching" calls for cleverness rather than labor, and the lure of the contemporary scene may draw a man away from thinking about the Eternal.

What shall we conclude? Let us recognize the faults that emerge in topical sermons unworthy of the name, and then search for a remedy in the Bible and in theology. Surely no method can ever become a substitute for a message. On the other hand, whenever a man feels a burning desire to share a vision that has come from God, he should feel free to employ any sermonic form he chooses.

Some pastors resort to the topical method too often or too exclusively. If at times they included textual sermons and expository messages, their pulpit work might prove more interesting and profitable. As for the proportion, no one can lay down laws, but here is a practical suggestion. In order to keep away from the pitfalls of topical preaching, do some other kind of pulpit work once every week. After that, employ the topical method as often as the facts warrant.

If the young clergyman has to prepare only one message a week, the parish may suffer through lack of varied food from the pulpit; but if the minister follows the counsel of James Black, the sheep will never look up without being fed:

> At the beginning of your ministry—do not take "subjects," unless for special purposes. Take your chosen passage or text or incident, and deduce from these premises your conclusion and message. In the long run, it is a richer way.... It saves you from giving your own semi-digested views on a big topic, without reference to the touchstone of Biblical truth. If you are dealing with a subject, find out the appropriate passages where it is unfolded, and work outwards from them.[9]

[9] *The Mystery of Preaching*, p. 153.

CHAPTER X

The Art of the Introduction

I N RECENT TIMES more than a few preachers have mastered the art of introducing sermons. In other days many a pulpit master would start slowly and build up towards power at the end, since he could take for granted that the hearers would listen patiently while he got under way. Now a minister needs to gain attention at the beginning, and hold attention until the close. He should look on the first paragraph or two as decisive, and phrase the first sentence or two with all his care. Indeed, no one can overstate the importance of making a good start.

Why must a sermon have such an approach? According to Cicero, a master of the speaker's art, *reddere auditores attentos, benevolos, dociles*. "Arouse interest, secure favor, and prepare to lead." All of this the preacher strives to do in the first few minutes, perhaps in only one or two. If he succeeds, he fixes the attention of every hearer on the truth or duty in hand. At the same time the speaker makes clear the trail over which he wishes to lead. What an undertaking, especially in view of the time at hand! Yet many a preacher in our time almost never fails to start with interest and secure a hearing with favor, by doing well all that he undertakes.

THE TESTS OF AN INTRODUCTION

How then does a man in the study size up an introduction? What has he a right to expect from his own handiwork?

1. Is this approach *interesting but not exciting?* Later in the sermon he may do something else, but first he must gain admission to the "city of man-soul." Now through this portal, and again through another, enter he must, and that soon or perhaps not at all. So he asks himself as he sits in the study: "How can I cross the drawbridge and get in touch with my hearers?" Then he answers, "By being interesting!" This word "interest" points to what the speaker and the hearer possess

in common. If the man in the pulpit knows how to start preaching, the friend in the pew will listen, if only because of curiosity.

Be interesting, but not exciting. An introduction bubbling over with enthusiasm might arouse expectations that the latter part of the sermon could not meet; so why pave the way for anticlimax? The minister who knows the hearts of people schools himself to begin preaching with interest and yet with deliberation. According to Augustine of Hippo, the exordium of a sermon calls for moderation, both in spirit and in tempo.

On the other hand, he tells us, be not too tame. If an occasional preacher ought to guard against making the first few sentences exciting, many of us go too far in the direction of dullness. If in doubt about how far to go in either direction, err on the side of interest. Remember William Magee's saying about three kinds of preachers: the one to whom you cannot listen, the one to whom you can listen, and the one to whom you must listen. Determine by the grace of God to join the smallest of these groups, the third, "a glorious band, the chosen few, on whom the Spirit came."

2. Is the introduction *short but not abrupt?* The sermon today does not run so long as in Puritan times, and the introduction tends to be shorter for much the same reason that the porch of a bungalow does not bulk so large as that of a Southern mansion. If the minister conforms to modern usage and keeps the approach within limits, the hearer may never think about the matter. But if the opening part of the message seems long, the layman may grumble to himself in a stage whisper: "Why doesn't the preacher play ball?"

An abrupt start, however, might do more harm than good. Especially in addressing strangers a wise man spends time in getting acquainted; he may even have to break some ice. Why should he launch into the message before the hearers seem ready to follow? In this art of preparing the audience for what was to follow, Henry Ward Beecher and William Jennings Bryan used to excel. Either of them would have felt that the present-day preacher begins too abruptly; why start to deliver the message before winning the good will of the hearer? At the home church, however, the pastor need not win the favor of hearers who love him as leader and friend.

3. Is the introduction *appropriate but not commonplace?* Appropriate to what? To the occasion, the speaker, and the message. When a pastor leads in the meditation before administering holy communion, he does not begin as in preaching about the Lord's ideals of marriage. In preparing for either discourse he puts himself into the spirit of the hour, and tries to sense the feelings of the hearers. So he forms the habit of planning the introduction after he has the body of the sermon clearly in view. How else could he judge the appropriateness of the first paragraph or two?

Unless the minister takes care, his appropriate introductions may seem so commonplace that he will become known as "Dr. Obvious." A preacher of this type needs to cultivate what Spurgeon called the "surprise power," which calls for saying the appropriate thing in an unexpected way. Beecher used to insist that when he arose and announced his text, no one present could guess what would come next, and that when the sermon had ended everyone there would know what he had heard. Such a way of planning calls for time and skill, with imagination.

4. Is the path of approach *friendly but not effusive?* The friendly speaker knows how to take the people into his confidence. He does not apologize for what he has to say, nor assume the air of Sir Oracle. Still less does he resort to argument, for that would put the layman on the defensive, with no opportunity to talk back. In our day the minister can assume that the hearer has come to church because he wants to become a better man. and that he welcomes a friendly approach:

Take the sermon as essentially a conversation with your hearers, and converse with them, instead of bellowing at them or wailing to them. Above all, be good-natured in manner and in tone. There is a *"curate contra mundum"* way of preaching which gives the impression of a young man standing up alone on behalf of eternal truth, and at the risk of his life defying every member of the congregation to his or her face, even when he is uttering sentiments which it is inconceivable that any sensible person

THE PREPARATION OF SERMONS

would dispute. It is wiser and more effective to . . . take your congregation into your confidence, and speak to them as to people with whom you are on friendly terms.[1]

5. Is the introduction *clear but not anticipatory?* If a man wishes his friends to go with him into some realm of truth or duty, he ought to let them catch a glimpse of the destination. He may do so by announcing the text and stating the topic. After that he can say whatever will lead the hearer most surely and most quickly into the main part of the sermon. According to Charles E. Jefferson, master preacher in New York City, "Unless a man can make the purpose of his sermon stand out broad as a barn door, he ought to go into some work for which the Lord has fitted him." [2] Or perhaps he should learn how to prepare an approach to a sermon!

Be clear, but not too clear! Unless a man uses care and skill, he may tell too much at the start, for only an expert can hold attention after he has explained all that he plans to do in the sermon. In other days Spurgeon or Maclaren would start with a paragraph or two leading up to a statement, part by part, about the plan of the message to follow. In a teaching sermon this kind of opening may seem necessary, but ordinarily a man does better to create a feeling of suspense. Somehow or other he can make clear the goal without letting anyone see the route. He does not let the desire for clarity interfere with the element of interest, and if either must prevail, he lets interest take the lead.

For example, a visiting minister came to preach in the chapel of a university. He arrived there as a stranger, and with a weak voice. Since he had heard about the way the boys treated an unwelcome guest, he knew that he must gain attention at once. Note how he solved that problem. When he stood up to preach, he kept silent until he had caught the attention of everyone in the house. Then he spoke the words of his text, deliberately: "Is thy servant a dog, that he should do this great thing?" (II Kings 8:13). Again he paused, while

---

[1] John Kelman, *The War and Preaching* (New Haven: Yale University Press, 1919), p. 122.

[2] *The Building of the Church* (New York: The Macmillan Co., 1910), p. 87.

everyone wondered about that text, which sounded new and strange. At length the preacher spoke, deliberately: "Dog or no dog, he did it!" After less than twenty words he had won a hearing, for he had made everyone want to learn how some man of old acted like a cur, and why his misdeeds concerned everyone present. In lieu of such a man-to-man approach, many a sermonizer would have started with a disquisition about dogs!

6. Last of all, do the introductions *vary from week to week*, or do they seem as much alike as Model-A Fords? From sermon to sermon, variety has much to do with interest. If a minister speaks to some of the same persons Sunday after Sunday, how can he keep from starting in much the same fashion? By checking up on his past sermons, by searching out new pathways, and by studying introductions from other men. Let him take up a volume by his favorite preacher of today, such as Paul E. Scherer or Ralph W. Sockman, Walter A. Maier or Clarence E. Macartney! How does one of them gain attention and focus it on the truth in hand?

Each of those men starts in a fashion all his own, and differently from week to week. As a builder of sermons no one of them specializes in prefabricated houses, with porches all alike. If one of their volumes contains twenty-five sermons, the reader may find twelve different kinds of introduction. After the parish minister goes through a few books of contemporary sermons, he may say with a sigh, "Other preachers have found twelve different gateways, where I have been using only one!"

THE LIST OF SERMON GATES

Let us glance at twelve gates, some of which may appear much alike. We shall begin with a few of the older ones, and use familiar names.

1. *The textual approach.* This old-fashioned way of starting a sermon has been coming back into favor, for ministers everywhere have found that people like to hear sermons from the Bible. Among laymen of the Methodist Church, a public opinion poll has shown a preference for this kind of pulpit work, if the minister knows how to show

113

the bearing on life today.[3] In a sermon occasionally why not start with the text, and let the first paragraph or two focus attention on that text?

Someone may protest: "A minister ought to begin with the hearers where they are!" Very well, but where are they, mentally, when you rise to preach? For the past twenty-five minutes they have been following the leader up into the mountaintop, where they have stood in the presence of the King, and have beheld His glory. Just before the sermon they have poured out their hearts in a song of supplication, such as "Dear Lord and Father of Mankind, Forgive Our Foolish Ways," or "Spirit of God, Descend upon My Heart." As they settle down in the pews, they should listen for a word from the King.

Then the preacher may announce the text without any preamble: "Come to me, all who labor and are heavy-laden, and I will give you rest" (Matt. 11:28 R.S.V.). After that the next few words may deal with the passage: why does it speak first about rest and then about a yoke, which stands for work? How could the minister start with more human interest than by showing that the "Master Workman of our race" offers "rest unto your souls," but not your bodies? In the pulpit, as in a university debate, why not follow the principle of the man who has coached many a winning team: "Put the discussion at once on the high level, and then keep it there"? But before you plan to start this way, be sure that the people will be with you on that level!

2. *The contextual approach.* Another old-fashioned way of beginning a sermon has been regaining some of its former vogue. If the interpreter wishes to make a text clear and luminous he may start with the background. Early in June, for instance, he may preach about "Christ at a Wedding Feast" (John 2:1-11). After quoting the text he may speak for a little about the wedding at Cana of Galilee, and make everything center round the Lord Jesus. The sermon may lead everyone to see Him now as a lover of home, believer in marriage, and giver of joy. This kind of introduction accords with the tone color of text and sermon.

A different sort of example comes from Robertson in a sermon

[3] See M. H. Leiffer, *The Layman Looks at the Minister* (New York and Nashville: Abingdon-Cokesbury Press, 1947).

about "Obedience, the Organ of Spiritual Knowledge." After the text (John 7:17) the discourse begins with the sentence: "The first thing we have to do is to put ourselves in possession of the history of these words." [4] Sunday after Sunday a man like Robertson or Brooks could begin to preach this way, securing variety by adapting the treatment to the spirit of the text. However, neither of them used the contextual approach all the time.

3. *The dramatic description.* At a vesper service John Bonnell once began the sermon by quoting his text: "Why are ye so fearful? how is it that ye have no faith?" (Mark 4:40). His topic had to do with the faith that triumphs over fear today. He led up to the message by describing a storm he had witnessed on the Sea of Galilee, near where our Lord uttered the words of the text. This kind of introduction lends itself to a sermon where the minister addresses many strangers, but he must know how to make the facts stand out as in a drama. An undramatic account of a moving scene would misrepresent the facts. For many reasons the downtown preacher must excel in the art of making the hearer see the truth at the very beginning of the sermon.

4. *The topical approach.* This kind of introduction assumes different forms, most of them popular today. The majority of preachers would agree with James S. Stewart that the introduction of a sermon ought to concern the interests of the listeners here and now.[5] He would permit exceptions, but still he advises the young minister to use a contemporary approach in presenting a biblical truth. This way of starting calls for emphasis on the topic. For instance, when Harry Emerson Fosdick preached a Christmas sermon about "The Decisive Babies of the World," he began with a reference to a volume that used to be well known, *Fifteen Decisive Battles of the World,* by Sir Edward S. Creasy. Soon the thought in the sermon veered to the central truth: how much more decisive a baby can be than a battle.[6]

This introduction would repay more study than we can give it here. It shows how to start with people who have been thinking much about

[4] See *Sermons Preached at Brighton,* pp. 300-307.
[5] See James S. Stewart, *Heralds of God,* pp. 124-30.
[6] See H. E. Fosdick, *Living Under Tension* (New York: Harper & Bros., 1941), pp. 222-32.

battles and make them think more about babies, especially the Babe of Bethlehem. According to the inductive method, the sermonic trail here leads up to the point where an oldtime preacher would have started. Homiletically, this work shows the appeal of a topical approach in one of its varied forms. Here, as elsewhere, Fosdick shows that he has mastered the art of introduction.

5. *The problem approach.* This way of starting has become associated with the name of Fosdick. In *Harper's Magazine* for July, 1928, he published an article, "What's the Matter with Preaching?" There he insists that much of our pulpit work lacks human interest; it does not seem to matter because it deals with something far away and long ago. He declares: "Every sermon should have for its main business the solving of some human problem, a vital, important problem, puzzling minds, burdening consciences, distracting lives." Obviously, such a way of preaching calls for a problem approach, which constitutes a sort of topical introduction. For examples of the problem approach turn to any volume of sermons by Fosdick.

Such a way of beginning to preach affords all sorts of advantages, especially in the way of human interest. Now and again a pastor may employ the method so exclusively that he causes people to become problem conscious, but many another preacher would bring more zest into his sermons if he dared to wrestle with the problems that beset his hearers today, especially if he devoted an entire sermon to one large problem. As for making people feel problem conscious, anyone can avoid doing that by stressing the use of the Bible, where he will find more about the solution than about the difficulty. For example, in the sixth chapter of Judges he can find "God's cure for an inferiority complex." With such a topic the sermon will call for a problem approach.

6. *A direct statement of purpose.* Here too the man in the pulpit needs to rely on candor, not on camouflage. He stands in no "coward's castle," for he represents the King as the giver of courage. The direct statement of purpose affords another variant of the problem approach, so that once again Fosdick makes himself at home. In a message about "The Return to Discipline" he starts with the words: "Our world

today faces us with at least one elemental necessity—the need of discipline." [7] Then he shows how the major movements of our time all bring to light the need of discipline, which must come from within and not from without. This way of beginning a sermon offers large possibilities, though not to the exclusion of other approaches. Think of the saving in time when the first few words sound the motif of the sermon!

7. *A striking quotation.* Once in a while the minister can vary his approach by quoting words from a man to whom the hearers look up with awe. In a Methodist parish suppose that the minister wishes to speak about the forgiveness of enemies. After quoting a text from our Lord he may pause for a moment and then say: " 'I never forget a friend or forgive a foe.' So spoke a sea captain to John Wesley. Then Wesley replied, 'It is to be hoped, sir, that you never have sinned against God!' " Now that the gateway stands open, the pastor can lead the hearer into the truth as it appears in the text. The words from John Wesley throw light on the saying of our Lord.

In a church with a Scottish background the minister wishes to preach about certain aspects of the Cross. After quoting a text from Paul (II Cor. 5:15), the preacher uses these words from James Denney, of Glasgow: "Christ died for the difference between right and wrong." In this case too the sentence provides the keynote for the sermon. Theoretically, a man could use this kind of approach too often; practically, any minister can start a sermon this way once or even twice a month. However, he must single out quotations that deserve to live, and not begin with platitudes about the "times that try men's souls," and "the challenge of the present crisis." When these phrases first came from the mint, they must have seemed striking, but through constant use they have lost their luster.

8. *The illustration.* This way of starting appeals to many a young clergyman; it serves him well in addressing persons whom he does not know, especially when they show little concern for him and his message. In a downtown church at night, when half of those present may never have visited the place before, an illustration helps the

[7] *Ibid.*, pp. 203-12.

experienced preacher capture attention at once; [8] but not many young ministers face that sort of opportunity. Whenever a man preaches at his own church, with a stable constituency, he can start with something of prime importance, such as the text and the topic. Even at best an illustration serves a secondary purpose, for it throws light upon something more important than itself. Why not put the first thing first? At any rate, many young ministers would secure variety if they did not start so many sermons with illustrations.

9. *The news item or cartoon.* Here again something secondary may help the downtown preacher catch the attention of people with "motion-picture minds." On a Sunday evening before New Year's Day the pastor of such a church in New York City started with a reference to a cartoon many of the hearers had seen in the *Herald-Tribune* a few days before, but that minister would not advise younger brethren to employ such introductions frequently. According to Phillips Brooks, an allusion to current events often "brings in its own associations and prejudices. It is too alive"; it may prove as disappointing as building a porch out of green timbers that sprout. Ordinarily a man does well to start with something of prime importance, but in the hour of need he may resort to this other way of catching attention.

10. *The occasional introduction.* On a special occasion the minister plans to begin the sermon with something about the occasion. If its importance warrants a special message, why not focus attention at once on the reason for the message? Think, for example, about the anniversary sermon, or the home-coming message, the dedication of a church, or the celebration of Easter. Any such message usually proves hard to prepare, but the introduction need cause little concern, except about phrasing. If the speaker begins with something about the occasion, something interesting and important, he catches attention at once. If the calendar for the year includes eight or ten special sermons, he can make each of those introductions differ from all the rest by singling out a distinctive feature of the occasion. But he must guard against playing politics, like a false prophet.

[8] See W. K. Anderson, *Making the Gospel Effective* (Nashville: Commission on Ministerial Training of The Methodist Church, 1945), chap. XVII.

11. *The psychological approach.* This kind of introduction assumes various forms, many of them worthy. For instance, when Nathan stood before King David to rebuke him for adultery and murder, the seer began with a parable about a poor shepherd who had one ewe lamb. How else could the prophet have reached the heart of the Shepherd King? When the apostle Paul spoke on Mars' hill, he began with a reference to the inscription on a statue near by: "To the Unknown God." How else could he have caught the attention of those sophisticated curiosity-seekers? In like manner today, when the minister faces an unusual situation, he may resort to a psychological approach; that is, if he knows how. Only an experienced preacher ought to begin this way; in terms of football, a young man must learn to block and tackle before he attempts a quarterback sneak.

12. *The life situation.* This path of approach, also, may seem too difficult for a young minister during his first years as a pastor. In one of its many forms the life situation sermon begins with a remark the minister has overheard on the street or in an elevator. Again, the preacher may quote part of a letter, or an interview, though never without permission. Usually the life situation approach leads to the discussion of a problem sure to interest the hearers. In a village or rural church, however, this interesting way of beginning may not promote the harmony of Zion. If any young pastor in such a community wishes to start an upheaval, let him gain the reputation of preaching about cases in the neighborhood. However smoothly the plan may work on Broadway, the life situation approach elsewhere calls for caution and tact like that of a family physician, who knows how to deal with each case discreetly.

In the hands of an expert the life situation approach lends itself to many uses, nearly all of them good. Otherwise this way of starting to preach would not have endured from age to age; the labels may have changed, but the thing itself lasts on. Did not our Lord in the days of His flesh deal constantly with life situations? In a book that every minister ought to own and study, T. R. Glover shows that the parables must have come largely from the experiences of our Lord in the home at Nazareth, and from life elsewhere as He mingled with

119

people.[9] From that day to this more than a few pulpit masters have employed the life situation approach, though not under this name. For a series of examples turn to the sermonic essays of F. W. Boreham.[10] Why not learn to start a sermon this way, if only for the sake of variety?

13. *The general statement.* Keep this gateway closed and locked. No matter what the subject in hand, a certain parson starts with three or four paragraphs about things in general; for instance, he may prate about world chaos and atomic energy. Such stuff may cost him nothing and do no one any good. So if anyone feels the urge to start a discourse with a string of conventional generalizations, let him write them out, word for word, and throw them all in the wastebasket. Then he can prepare an approach, specific and pointed, the first few sentences of which will sound the motif of all that follows. These strictures do not concern a ten-talent man with the outlook of a Christian philosopher, or a statesman in the kingdom of God.[11] But even the ablest of men could not preach in the "grand style" two or three times a week, unless he went from place to place and repeated the same sermons.

14. *The double approach.* Keep one of these two gateways closed and locked—whichever one you do not need. Why have two introductions for a sermon? Sometimes the first one precedes the text and the other follows. With two approaches only a man of parts can secure unity, and even he may squander precious minutes. A sermon may have any one of a dozen beginnings, but it needs only one, with no homiletical polygamy! If the warning seems needless, look back over your sermon manuscripts and note how often in the past six months you have confused the issue by starting with two introductions, or with one too many.

We have looked at fourteen approaches, twelve of them worthy and two of them poor. How does a minister determine which of the twelve gateways to use in entering a certain area? Except in a rare

---

[9] See *The Jesus of History* (New York: Geo. H. Doran Co., 1917), pp. 26, 129-32.
[10] A. W. Blackwood, *The Protestant Pulpit*, sermon 19.
[11] See H. H. Farmer, *God and Men* (New York and Nashville: Abingdon-Cokesbury Press, 1948).

case he may not feel sure until he has surveyed the field as a whole. During the preparation of a sermon he may keep thinking at times about how he will start, but he should not make the final decision before he has largely completed the plan. In the actual writing, however, as in the delivery, a man starts with the opening sentence and then goes straight through to the end.

In view of all these choices, the young pastor may appreciate a practical suggestion: plan to build the porch out of materials different from those in the main body of the house. If the sermon proper consists of exposition, begin with something else, but if the main body grows out of something else, start with the text. All the while remember that current practice favors beginning with something here and now rather than something far away and long ago. If you start with something about the text, bring it up to date; talk about it here and now. But do not feel obliged to follow any of these rules save one. That one holds true always and everywhere: start every sermon with human interest. If you do that every Lord's Day, you will secure variety from week to week.

THE USE OF A PROPOSITION

Now that many pastors have begun to engage in a teaching ministry, we ought also to think about the use of a proposition. In other days this matter loomed large in teaching homiletics,[12] but in recent times the proposition has largely disappeared, both from guidebooks and from sermons. Many gifted preachers, however, have formed the habit of writing out a proposition for almost every sermon. John Henry Jowett, for example, used to attract throngs that overflowed the Fifth Avenue Presbyterian Church in New York City twice every Sunday. In speaking to ministerial students he told a part of the reason for his effectiveness: "No sermon is ready for preaching, not ready for writing out, until we can express its theme in a short, pregnant sentence as clear as a crystal. I find the getting of that sentence

[12] See Austin Phelps, *The Theory of Preaching*, revised by F. D. Whitesell (Grand Rapids: Eerdmans, 1947). The proposition takes up almost a seventh of the volume, as in the original work (1881).

the hardest, the most exacting, and the most fruitful labor in my study." [13]

The "proposition" refers to a declarative sentence that contains the substance of the discourse. "Theme" or "key sentence" would mean much the same: "The theme is the sermon condensed; the sermon is the theme expanded." As the terms appear in this book, a theme or proposition differs from a topic or a title. A theme sets forth the gist of the sermon in a single sentence; a topic embodies the same truth in a phrase; a title refers to the name of a book or the heading of a series.

Sometimes the proposition appears as the opening sentence. As we have already seen, Fosdick often begins a sermon this way. In most other hands the theme appears at the end of the introduction, just before the main body. For examples of this usage turn to the three volumes of sermons by Horace Bushnell, notably *The New Life.* Among the twenty-two discourses in that book eleven embody formal propositions. Even Bushnell did not always preach this way, but when he wished to make an idea stand out boldly in a teaching sermon, he embodied that idea in a proposition. When he prepared a volume of sermons for the press, he called for italics in only two parts of the discourse: the text and the proposition. Evidently he wished these two parts to stand out above all the rest of any teaching sermon.

In preaching about "The Hunger of the Soul" (Luke 15:17) Bushnell led up to his theme: "A life separated from God is a life of bitter hunger, and even of spiritual starvation." In dealing with the subject "Duty Not Measured by Our Own Ability" (Luke 9:13), he stressed the proposition: "Men are often, and properly, put under obligation to do that for which they have, in themselves, no present ability." [14] In these two key sentences he dealt partly with negations, but as a rule he preached positively. Whenever he used a proposition, he followed it like a lodestar. Hence he appealed to lawyers, law-makers, and others who loved God with both mind and heart.

Phillips Brooks did not employ the proposition so often or so

[13] *The Preacher, His Life and Work* (New York: Geo. H. Doran Co., 1912), p. 133.
[14] For these two examples see *The New Life* (London, 1892), pp. 32-43, 253-66; for another see *The Protestant Pulpit,* sermon 8.

carefully, but the Boston minister could preach this way whenever he so desired. In a message that he called "Going Up to Jerusalem" (Luke 18:31), the preacher set up this ideal: "Every true life has its Jerusalem, to which it is always going up." With this sentence he opened the first and second paragraphs, and with the same idea he closed the discourse. Towards the end of the sermon he uttered words that will live for decades to come:

O, do not pray for easy lives. Pray to be stronger men. Do not pray for tasks equal to your powers. Pray for powers equal to your tasks. . . . If your Jerusalem really is your sacred city, there is certainly a cross in it. . . . It is dreadful to suffer except in doing duty. To suffer there is glorious.[15]

These examples from two pulpit masters throw light on the meaning of the proposition. Ideally it consists of a complete sentence—simple, not complex; declarative, not interrogative; straightforward, not figurative; positive, not negative. Practically, however, the key sentence may not conform to such an inflexible pattern. Whatever the shape of the theme, or key sentence, it rings out here and there in the sermon. Even when the motif does not sound forth directly, it recurs in the form of an echo. Through such repetition at intervals the dominant note impresses itself on the mind and heart of almost every hearer. Such a device proves doubly helpful in a teaching message.

The use of a proposition aids the minister in preparing and in delivering the sermon. So does this kind of "specific" preaching help the hearer in understanding and recalling the message. Such a way of presenting a truth or duty tends to safeguard the hearers against what James Black terms a "young man's large way of preaching." According to a master teacher of yesterday, "The major problems of sermon development are solved in the framing of a proposition."[16] This mentor would agree with Horace Bushnell in an essay that every minister should "read, mark, learn, and inwardly digest":

[15] See *Visions and Tasks* (New York: E. P. Dutton & Co., 1910), pp. 316-32.
[16] Ozora S. Davis, *The Principles of Preaching* (Chicago: University of Chicago Press, 1924), p. 209.

Now and then a man has capital enough for wholesale preaching, but the particular manner of a retail delivery, both in preaching and in trade, is far more apt to succeed. Hence also it is that a great many young men die out in their generalities and huge, overgrown subjects, and a great many others who appear to be meagre and want calibre, going to work in this hopeful way of economy, will even preach better possibly, and more effectively, than if they were more profusely endowed. They will at least be saved from the folly of trying to do something so great in the general as to do nothing at all in particular.[17]

We have gone far enough to make clear the importance of the introduction. If any young minister wishes to become an interesting and effective preacher, let him learn how to begin every sermon according to its purpose and tone color. For examples of interesting and effective approaches he can turn to almost any volume of sermons today, especially if they have gone out over the radio. But in the long run he should introduce sermons in ways largely his own.

Suggested Readings

Augustine. *De Doctrina Christiana,* Liber IV. Ed. by Thérèse Sullivan. Patristic Studies, Vol. XXIII. Washington: Catholic University, 1930.
Smyth, J. Paterson. *The Preacher and His Sermon.* New York: Geo. H. Doran Co., 1922. Chaps. III, IV.

[17] See *Building Eras in Religion,* chap. VI, pp. 197-98; also chaps. VII and VIII.

CHAPTER XI

The Concern About Structure

CONCERN ABOUT STRUCTURE tends to ebb and flow. Whenever the teaching function of the ministry looms large, structure seems important, because the man who teaches must follow a plan of his own making. But whenever inspiration or something else puts teaching in a secondary place, structure seems less essential, because a person who knows how to enthuse can do so without following much of a plan. In some parts of the Church we have passed through a stage of that sort, but now the trend appears to favor more of a popular teaching ministry. That calls for concern about structure, though not in the way of ugliness. The wise preacher thinks of the sermon as full of life and warmth, and not as the skeleton of a dead man.

The word "structure" here means the bony framework of a sermon that lives and moves so as to reach a certain goal. To the observer nothing of the sort may appear, because good construction calls little attention to itself. Why look at the bones in a horse when you can admire the horse on the bones? Whatever the figure, every message that teaches a truth about God, or a duty for men, ought to embody a bony framework, covered with beauty and charm.

THE IMPORTANCE OF STRUCTURE

The importance of structure appears everywhere in the Bible. The sermons from prophets and apostles, which come to us in the form of reports, show that almost every one of those preachers followed a plan, which may never have appeared on paper. In the Book of the Acts, for instance, the messages tend to follow a certain pattern, and afford a university professor models for use in showing young folk how to prepare a speech.[1]

[1] See Chas. S. Baldwin, *The English Bible as a Guide to Writing* (New York: The Macmillan Co., 1917). This author does not stress the spiritual message of the sermons, but he shows that their popular effectiveness depends largely on structure.

THE PREPARATION OF SERMONS

The same emphasis appears throughout the history of preaching. Almost every sermon that has lived, after the conditions that produced it passed away, has embodied a bony framework. Not all pulpit masters have dealt with structure in the same fashion. Some of them have caused the framework to stand out boldly, while others have not. Among the former, think of F. W. Robertson and Alexander Maclaren. Whenever either of them went into the pulpit to teach, he made it easy for the hearer to see the plan of the sermon.

On the contrary, ministers equally effective and popular seem to have shown little concern about structure. At the first reading, or even the second, one of A. J. Gossip's sermons may appear to be void of a plan. For instance, take that message "But When Life Tumbles In, What Then?" Why has it become better known than almost any other sermon in the present century? Partly because of the occasion, the diction, and the structure, but chiefly because of the message from God to every one who suffers. Since Gossip was preaching for the first time after the death of his wife, he spoke about the testing of a man's soul in a day of disaster.[2]

After a moving introduction, the preacher did two things in the sermon proper, and only two: he showed how everyone must meet a time of testing, and how the Christian can meet such a test triumphantly. This account does slight justice to a message that lives and moves because the man in the pulpit has a sense of human need and a grasp of divine truth. Study the sermon from various points of view, including this: look for symmetry like that of a giant copper beech.

The importance of structure appears in all the other fine arts, notably architecture. In the history of the pulpit almost every master has shown a love of architectural design, a fact that has led more than one master to write about "building" sermons. When Phillips Brooks helped to formulate the plans for Trinity Church, as it now stands in Boston, and when Woodrow Wilson helped to plan the house that anyone can see at Princeton, each of them used imagination much as he often employed it in preparing a public address. For want

[2] See A. W. Blackwood, *The Protestant Pulpit*, sermon 24; also Appendix "How to Study a Sermon."

of better names we term such a use of imagination "constructive," and in its loftier reaches, "creative."

The same holds true of painting. Before an artist mixes his colors and applies them to the canvas, he should know what he wishes to portray, and how. When Raphael painted "The Transfiguration," he followed a plan of his own creation, or he could not have brought unity out of two contrasting scenes, the one at the top of the mountain and the other at the foot. Why does the anguish of the lad down in the valley not detract from the glory of the Lord up near the sky? Because the artist planned that the eyes of the lad, and many of the other lines in the lower part of the picture, should turn towards the transfigured Christ. Hence the picture leads the beholder to feel sure that the Lord of glory will descend into the valley and heal that heart of pain.

In composing a piece of music, also, the artist follows a plan of his own designing. Whether he wishes to compose a hymn tune or a symphony, he must have a pattern, which may exist only in his mind or heart. According to the head of the music department at Princeton University, a composer does not

throw his work at us pell-mell. The Tannhäuser Overture, for example, is plainly enough planned carefully. The first part of it, "The Pilgrim's Chorus," keeps recurring, and each time it recurs we find in it something new to interest us. . . . The plan Wagner had in mind was an important part of his work. It made his Overture more interesting, more dramatic, than it would otherwise have been. Wagner knew what he wanted to do, and how it was to be done.[3]

Still nearer to the spirit of preaching comes poetry. Here, too, except in some forms of free verse, everything from a sonnet to an epic poem conforms to a pattern of its own. Even within the confines of a sonnet Milton or Wordsworth could find freedom and joy. Over in England a professor of theology, John Oman, insisted that young ministers fell short most of all in their knowledge of English

[3] Roy D. Welch, *The Appreciation of Music* (New York: Harper & Bros., 1924), p. 27.

THE PREPARATION OF SERMONS

literature,[4] with its beauty of words drawn from "a well of English undefiled." The professor knew that a love for sonnets and epics would lead to a sense of structure, because a poem never merely happens.[5] Neither does a sermon worthy of the name.

Nowhere else in literature does structure loom so large as in the drama, whether classic or modern. Once when a world-be playwright asked Henrik Ibsen to read the manuscript of a new play, the older man inquired about the scenario. The young man replied that he needed nothing of the sort, because he followed inspiration wherever it led him. In anger Ibsen showed him to the door, and told him that a person who dispensed with a scenario did not know the meaning of a drama and could not write a play worthy to appear on the stage. These facts about Ibsen come from the foremost American teacher of playwrights. a professor who always emphasized the importance of structure:

> The very people who shrink from forcing themselves to work out all the details required by a good scenario are merely dodging the inevitable. They avoid something irksome as a preliminary merely to do this work before the completed play is ready.... Undeniably, a scenario is the most effective way of forcing oneself to know the characters and the story of a play before one begins to write the play in detail.[6]

Testimony of the same kind reaches us from a playwright who taught himself at home. In his autobiography,[7] Channing Pollock tells how he learned to write plays, including two that have brought him fame and fortune—*The Fool* and *The House Beautiful*. Pollock started by making a study of two hundred dramas from the masters. After he had analyzed one of those plays, he would allow himself time to forget the plot, and then he would draw up a plot of his own with the same motif. Because of those studies he put away in his files seven thousand pages of notes about dramas by other men.

[4] See *Concerning the Ministry* (New York: Harper & Bros., 1937).
[5] For an apparent exception in the history of poetry see J. L. Lowes, *The Road to Xanadu* (Boston: Houghton Mifflin, 1927).
[6] Geo. P. Baker, *Dramatic Technique* (Boston: Houghton Mifflin, 1919), p. 463.
[7] See *Harvest of My Years* (Indianapolis: Bobbs-Merrill, 1943), pp. 67, 163, 287.

Meanwhile the student of the drama kept accumulating ideas for plays of his own. During a walk out in the open, or while reading indoors, he would jot down seed-thoughts that might some day grow into dramas. After a number of years he had in his "garden" three thousand seedlings, most of which never developed into plays, for he found he had to thin out the seedlings and then nurture the most promising. This man learned to write plays by discovering how other men had written plays. What he says about that work applies also to preaching:

Becoming an author is like becoming a mother. There must be a period of conception, a period of gestation, labor, and labor pains, with eventual delivery. . . . The vitality of a work may depend on how long it was carried in the conscious or the subconscious mind. In the case of *The Fool*, that was little less than two years.

The importance of structure appears also in fiction, such as Ellen Glasgow's novels about life in old Virginia. Forty-six years after she sent out her first novel, Miss Glasgow wrote a literary autobiography, which includes this advice about technique:

Just as a child must learn to walk and talk naturally, so even the instinctive writer must acquire the simple first principles of his craft. . . . The assembling of materials, the arrangement of masses, may have a greater effect than the materials themselves. . . . As a beginning author what troubled me most was the lack of an adequate method.
. . . .
Technique is valueless . . . so long as one regards it as technique alone. Only after one has acquired it, and forgotten the acquisition, does a formula lend itself to adaptation and become an incalculable help to a novelist. Nevertheless, it is well for every aspiring writer to serve either a voluntary or involuntary apprenticeship.
. . . .
Learn the technique of writing, and having learned it thoroughly, try to forget it. Study the principles of construction, the value of continuity, . . . the revealing episode, the careful handling of detail. . . . Actual writing [is] the hardest work in the world.[8]

[8] *A Certain Measure* (New York: Harcourt, Brace & Co., 1943) pp. 8, 51, 53, 191-93.

THE MARKS OF GOOD STRUCTURE

Think about the other fine arts for many reasons, not least because of what they show about structure. In a formal study of preaching, also, single out qualities of structure, as distinct from literary style. At times you may oversimplify the matter and consider separately things that belong together, but the same holds true in the study of any fine art. In the history of preaching note that strong sermons tend to follow certain laws about structure, the same four laws that govern products of imagination in all of its upper reaches.

1. Most important among the four stands *unity;* so it comes first. In a sermon unity means that the clergyman delivers only one message at a time. According to Newman, "Nothing is so fatal to the effect of a sermon as the habit of preaching on three or four subjects at once." For an example of unity turn to any first-class sermon, such as one by J. B. Mozley, "The Reversal of Human Judgments." In this long discourse note how every part has to do with the topic, which grows out of the text: "Many that are first shall be last; and the last shall be first" (Matt. 19:30). Test the unity throughout by seeing whether or not the text and the topic include everything within the sermon, and nothing else. As for the topic, note how it arches over all the earth and then reaches out into the beyond, where we all shall enter into "the day of reversal, the day of the Lord." [9]

By way of contrast, wholly ridiculous, read a schoolboy's essay about corn. Note how he keeps to the subject, even while he scatters attention where he ought to focus. This example might also illustrate other weaknesses, such as lack of order, but at present the effort shows the unwisdom of starting to write on a subject without first making a plan:

Corn is a very useful vegetable. If it were not for corn there would be no corn cakes with butter and molasses. Corn grows in large fields, and you can plow it with a horse. There was a man who had a cornfield, and he had no horse, but he had a large and faithful wife, who took care of it,

[9] See *Sermons Preached Before the University of Oxford*, 4th ed. (London, 1879).

accompanied by a trusty dog, while he wrote poetry for the papers. We ought to be thankful if we have a good wife, which is much better than hanging round saloons and wasting your time in idleness. Corn is also used to feed hogs with, and it can be made into corn cob pipes, which will make you sick if you are not accustomed to it. Let us firmly resolve that we will reform and lead a better life.[10]

First of all, therefore, in the way of structure, seek for unity. After the plan lies before you on paper, look at the whole and test it for oneness. Remember that preaching calls for the omission of many things not needful at the moment, so as to stress the one truth in hand:

> You will generally do best by taking one important thought and hammering it out on every side, and determining to get that one thought into the minds of the people. . . . Let every sermon be on one subject, one thought, so that you could write it out in one sentence—"This is the thought that I want to impress on the people; this is my clear aim; this is exactly what I wish them to feel; or, this is exactly what I wish them to do." . . .
> Ask yourself in every sermon, "Could the man in the pew tell his wife —or rather in these days,—could the woman in the pew tell her husband in two sentences the central thought of your sermon? If not, why not?" [11]

2. The second law relates to *order*. Unity refers to the body as a whole; order concerns the various parts in relation to the whole and to each other. The impression of unity comes after a bird's-eye view of the entire sermon, whereas the feeling of order follows a study of the message in its parts, one after another. Not only do the main divisions keep moving onward, like the regiments of an army brigade on the march; within each main division the minor parts also keep moving forward, like companies in a regiment. All the while regiments and companies do the will of the officer in command, who has made a plan to secure both unity and order.[12]

For an example showing lack of order, study any of your own

---

[10] Lewis H. Chrisman, *The English of the Pulpit* (New York: Geo. H. Doran Co., 1926), p. 70. Used by permission of Harper & Bros.

[11] J. Paterson Smyth, *The Preacher and His Sermon* (New York: Geo. H. Doran Co., 1922), pp. 67, 108.

[12] "Structure" concerns strategy; "literary style," tactics.

sermons that led to a lapse of memory in the pulpit. Wherever you stumbled, faltered, or omitted a section, you will probably find something out of place. In a sermon ready for delivery each paragraph follows all that has gone before, much as a car on a railroad track keeps its place in the train. If a minister planned to read his sermon word for word, or else use notes at every turn, he could get through despite lack of order. But if he wishes to stand up and speak out, heart to heart and eye to eye, he must have in view a train of thought.

3. The third law has to do with *symmetry*. Since this quality seems less important than the others, it should come neither first nor last. Still the matter of symmetry calls for attention, because the proportion among the various parts has much to do with the beauty of the message as a whole and with the effect upon the hearer. Not all of the main divisions need to run exactly the same length, though Phillips Brooks worked according to some such rule. The law before us now simply requires that every part receive as much time and stress as its importance demands, and no more. In planning a sermon be sure to keep everything in its place, and then all the parts will balance.

Often the novice ignores this law by devoting so much time and attention to the first main part that he feels obliged to skimp the rest of the preparation. He may not even figure out what to say at the end of the sermon. The man who leaves any part of a message to the impulse of the moment needs to be a genius. Otherwise he may pave the way for an anticlimax. In time the beginner learns to plan each successive division of the sermon as carefully as though that division were to stand out alone. In the first main part, if necessary, he practices the art of omission, and in all that follows he plans with equal care and skill. So he may hope for a sermon as symmetrical as a maple tree.

4. The fourth of these laws we may term *progress*, movement, or climax. Here we use the term "progress" to include both movement and climax. This fourth law means that a sermon ought to keep moving forward to its destination, much as a stream flows towards the ocean. At times the course may lead through a level country, and again the waters may dash over rapids. Everywhere a sermon calls for

onward motion, with never a break. If the sweep of the work resembled a merry-go-round, the sermon as a whole would lead to no sense of arrival. At length you would stop and alight, just where you started. Such entertainment may seem harmless, but why call it a sermon? Think of that in terms of progress!

For object lessons of this quality, go to the sermons of Robertson. With the heart of a soldier he planned every message so that the various parts would move forward towards the goal. In his message about "The Three Crosses of Calvary," [13] he dealt with those three crosses, but in what order? Robertson put first the central cross, "The Dying Hour of Devotedness," and in the light of that central truth he looked at the other two. Again, in what order, and why? Second he placed "The Dying Hour of Impenitence," and last of all, "The Dying Hour of Penitence." The speaker must have put this thief last because he repented, just as the preacher wished every sinful hearer to accept the Saviour.

Another preacher would follow a different order for the sake of climax. He would deal first with one of those other crosses, perhaps that of the impenitent thief, and last of all the sermon would come to a climax at the central cross. But how could he make clear why either of those dying thieves should repent? For instance, the most spectacular pulpiteer of his day held forth on this subject, "The Three Crosses," and from Robertson's text, Luke 23:33. As a lover of climax, T. De-Witt Talmage pointed first to "The Cross on the Right—Scoffery"; then to "The Cross on the Left—Repentant Believing"; and last of all, to "The Cross in the Center—Vicarious Suffering." When shall we ministers dare to put the most important thing first, and not second or third?

Must the preacher always arrange his ideas in such an order—one, two, three? No, as we shall see later, a minister needs a variety of sermon plans. As a rule he should keep away from the old three-point outline. But when the facts in view call for that arrangement of the parts, he will dare to follow the facts in the case. Some day the pastor

[13] See *The Human Race and Other Sermons* (London, 1890), pp. 152-62.

will feel an urge to speak about Matthew 6:10, "Thy kingdom come. Thy will be done in earth, as it is in heaven." If so, he may call attention to three ideas in the text, with the most important truth first, where it belongs, as the foundation of all that comes after. He may secure climax through an increasing impact on the will of the hearer. As the sermon draws toward the end, the speaker moves the hearer to act:

1. The kingdom of God starts with the divine.
2. The kingdom of God includes the human.
3. The kingdom of God leads to the practical.

We have been thinking about four laws that concern structure: unity, order, symmetry, and progress. Ideally we ought to look at them all together, for we can appreciate no one of them apart from the others. If anyone feels annoyed because of such emphasis on the mechanics of preparing a sermon, let him remember that all of these laws come from the study of sermons by the masters. If any person had asked one of them in mature years why he did this or that, he would have replied, "I do not know." But in earlier days, while learning his craft, he must have thought about all these things. In the fullness of his powers every pulpit master has followed habit systems that he built up during early years of apprenticeship, so that facility in preparing to preach may become "the easy act of a laborious habit."

Whenever a young man in the workshop grows weary of the drudgery in making plans for sermons, let him remember that others who write and speak have gone through the same kind of discipline. The autobiography of John Erskine tells how in early years he learned to write under George R. Carpenter. The account may cause some readers to regret not having studied under such a professor as Carpenter:

He asked us to bring in a skeleton of the essay, paragraph by paragraph, each paragraph being represented by a single sentence. By the time we had shaped this outline to his satisfaction and our own, nothing remained but to fill out the paragraphs and smooth away the angularities of the frame.

To this day I use no other method in preparing any piece of writing, whether short or long. . . . I do not care to begin a novel or an article before I have worked it out completely in outline. It is easy to write the first sentence when you know what the last sentence will be. I cannot estimate the amount of time I should have wasted, had I not taken that course with George Rice Carpenter.[14]

[14] *The Memory of Certain Persons*, p. 98.

CHAPTER XII

The Variety of Sermon Plans

THE DIFFERENCE between an artist and an artisan appears in their handiwork. The one adapts his design to the end in view; the other works according to a pattern he may have borrowed. In the seminary, or else from a book, the maker of sermons can learn how to "build" structures as much alike as huts in a mill village, where the company employs no architect and the contractor works by rule of thumb. How then can the interpreter of God's truth secure variety of sermon plans from week to week?

For the first few months the young preacher may follow conventional patterns, though not slavishly. Gradually he should dare to try plans of his own, or at least modify any pattern he adopts. In fact, he may discover that sermon plans do not accord with the descriptions for much the same reason that a family physician almost never finds a "textbook case." Even so, the physician has learned the facts about textbook cases, and the minister ought to know about accepted patterns for sermons. Largely for convenience we shall list some of them by numbers, but we must not think of the resulting sermons as machine-made.

THE VARIETY OF NUMBERS

1. *The one-idea sermon.* In a sense every message from the pulpit ought to contain a single idea, large and luminous, and only one. For instance, a college president started with "Life as an Adventure in Faith," drawing the truth from the record about Abraham, who went out by faith, not knowing whither (Heb. 11:8). The speaker dealt with three aspects of that pilgrimage, which called for courage, perseverance, and hope. But such a pulpit master as Thomas Chalmers would have dispensed with these divisions. He would have kept repeating his main idea, first one way and then another, with ever-increasing intensity. So he would have led the hearer to start on that

136

THE VARIETY OF SERMON PLANS

pilgrimage of faith. Needless to say, only a man with talent near to genius could prepare a full-length sermon with only a single idea standing out. But every minister should learn how to speak this way when he has time for only a brief discourse, as in a meditation before the Lord's Supper.

2. *The two contrasting truths.* This kind of preaching has become associated with Robertson. In preparing a morning sermon he would single out a text with two balancing truths. From week to week he secured variety through the choice of texts with all sorts of contrasts. During the hundred years since he began that ministry at Brighton, many of his sermons have found their way into other pulpits, and they may have lost some of their novelty. Still they repay careful study, if only because they show how to secure strength of framework without ugliness. For instance, take his message about "The Irreparable Past" (Mark 14:41-42), a theme suitable for New Year's. In the first main part he dealt with "the irreparable past," and in the second part with "the available future."

This way of planning deserves a wider use, partly because it lends itself to the present-day vogue of brevity and conciseness. Also, this way of preaching helps to prevent a man from dwelling unduly on the negative. At times Robertson dipped his brush into the darkest colors on his palette, and he would never have dreamed of painting a scene without shadows. But he strove to carry out his own injunction: "Preach positively, not negatively." This kind of pulpit work may not seem so interesting as the recent practice of telling why the modern man does not believe in God, and what the preacher does not mean by sin. But in the long run what good comes from negations, save as they throw into contrast the light of God's eternal truth? [1]

3. *The conventional pattern.* Here a man resorts to a threefold division, of the sort in which Alexander Maclaren often took delight, for he "fed the sheep with a three-pronged fork." Once at the City Temple, Joseph Parker spoke to a friend about the published sermons

[1] See James R. Blackwood, *The Soul of Frederick W. Robertson*, chap. IX.

137

of Maclaren: "Good, but all alike!" As a pulpit orator second to none Parker felt that sermons from week to week ought to show variety of structure and style, but he would have granted that certain texts and subjects lend themselves to a conventional threefold division. For instance, a message about the Trinity naturally falls into three parts (II Cor. 13:14). According to a friendly observer of the American pulpit, many of our older ministers use this method too often and some of the sons employ it too seldom. Why should not the two groups secure variety through an exchange of methods?

4. *The fourfold plan.* Many a subject lends itself to a four-square arrangement. Even Maclaren could preach this way. In his volume *The Secret of Power*, thirteen of the twenty sermons belong to this type, and only seven follow the three-point arrangement. In the message from which the book gets its title, Maclaren begins with a text that seems negative, but he throws the stress on positive truth and duty. "Why could not we cast him out? And Jesus said unto them, Because of your unbelief" (Matt. 17:19-20). The resulting sermon grows out of four propositions, three of them positive. Note how the preacher builds up by putting first the most important truth theologically, and last the most practical concern psychologically:

1. We have an unvarying power.
2. The condition of exercising this power is faith.
3. Our faith is ever threatened by subtle unbelief.
4. Faith can be maintained only by constant devotion and rigid self-denial.[2]

In our own country, C. E. Macartney often preaches a "four-square" sermon, and over in Scotland, J. S. Stewart uses the arrangement, though less frequently. Like many another who wishes to make certain truths stand out, Stewart sometimes employs parallelism, repetition, and alliteration. As for parallelism, it appears everywhere in the Scriptures, especially in the poetic passages that young folk were supposed to learn by heart. As for repetition, in skillful hands it increases the effect. As for alliteration, a touch of it may act

[2] See *The Secret of Power* (London: Macmillan & Co., 1882), pp. 1-25.

like pepper, for "just enough adds piquancy, but too much may be worse than none." In a message about "Why Be a Christian?" Stewart uses just enough alliteration, but of course he does not often preach this way. At first glance the order of the four parts makes a reader wonder:

1. The Christian life is happier than any other.
2. The Christian life is harder than any other.
3. The Christian life is holier than any other.
4. The Christian life is more hopeful than any other.[3]

5. *The five-part sermon.* Robert E. Speer often preached this way, especially when the occasion allowed him time to deal with a large subject from various points of view. This kind of pulpit work calls for ability like that in planning a drama with five acts. In the following example William M. Clow deals with the words of our Lord to Saul on the road to Damascus (Acts 26:18). Speaking on the subject "Christ's Last Gospel Message," the Glasgow preacher shows "the rise and progress of religion in the Christian soul. Every one of us is facing one of these five steps in the Christian life." The resulting sermon would have seemed more nearly ideal if the minister had used headings to interpret the text, whereas he merely quoted the five parts:

1. Jesus begins—"To open their eyes"
2. "To turn them from darkness to light"
3. "From the power of Satan unto God"
4. "That they may receive forgiveness of sins"
5. "And inheritance among them which are sanctified" [4]

6. *The six-point sermon.* So we might go on up the scale. Among the old Puritans we could find numbers almost astronomical, but we must stop with six. For an example of a six-point sermon not biblical in substance, turn to H. E. Fosdick. He plans to discuss "Six Ways to Tell Right from Wrong" by setting up "six homely guideposts to the good life." With all of the six headings the minister leaves the impression of unity, because he never loses a sense of

---

[3] See *The Gates of New Life* (New York: Charles Scribner's Sons, 1940), pp. 21-31
[4] See *The Cross in Christian Experience*, pp. 256-67.

direction. Homiletically, the six headings will repay careful study; for they show the value of parallelism and of repetition for emphasis. Each of the six headings follows the same pattern of words up to the end, where the last word or phrase points out the test in view. By repeating this key sentence six times, with only a single change, the speaker stamps it on the hearer's soul:

1. In the first place, if a man is sincerely perplexed about a question of right and wrong, he might well submit to the test of common sense.
2. In the second place, . . . sportsmanship.
3. In the third place, . . . his best self.
4. In the fourth place, . . . publicity.
5. In the fifth place, . . . his most admired personality.
6. In the sixth place, . . . foresight.[5]

Does Fosdick often preach this way? No; neither should anyone else employ such methods often enough to make the layman conscious of sermon mechanics. As for the content, another preacher might begin with Susanna Wesley's counsel to her son John. Then the sermon might consist of five divisions: "Would you judge of the lawfulness or unlawfulness of a pleasure, take this rule—Whatever impairs in tenderness your conscience, weakens your reason, obscures your sense of God, or takes off the relish of spiritual things; whatever increases the authority of your body over your mind— that thing to you is sin."

THE PULPIT USE OF NUMBERS

These examples involving numbers lead to an inquiry about pulpit procedure: how deal with numbers? Should a preacher make them stand out boldly, or let them seem like pillars covered with ivy? The answer may depend on his purpose. If he plans to teach, he makes the numbers stand out, as Fosdick does both in the topic and in the main headings of that discourse about "Six Ways to Tell Right from Wrong." So does Clow in a different kind of message,

[5] See H. E. Fosdick, *The Hope of the World* (New York: Harper & Bros., 1933) pp. 126-35.

"Love in Four Dimensions." Both in the topic and in the headings he calls attention to the four parts of the sermon, which have to do with the breadth, the length, the depth, and the height of God's love, as it shines out through John 3:16.

But when a pastor wishes to inspire or comfort, he need not employ numbers. If he has a plan in mind, he may keep it there. The man who never uses a numerical device could teach better at times if he employed numbers, whereas the one who always does something of the sort may defeat his purpose by overdoing a good thing. Within any sermon a wise man uses numbers sparingly; if he ties them up with the main headings, he omits them elsewhere. Otherwise he might make them as confusing as too many traffic signs along the same highway; e.g., "State Road No. 6" and "National Highway No. 1." Why display numbers at all unless they help to make the trail clear and easy to follow? In the history of preaching men have dealt with the matter of numbers in four different ways.

1. They have used *numbers before and after* and all along the route. In olden times, when Spurgeon or Maclaren felt free to preach forty or fifty minutes, at the end of the introduction he would give a numerical statement about what he proposed to say. When he came to each new division he would stress it again by the use of its number. Towards the end of the discourse he would present a summary, using numbers. In the hands of a master with abundance of time this method often seemed to justify itself, but few pastors employ it today, partly because it consumes time and also because it lessens suspense. Wise men prefer to live in the Book of Acts rather than the Book of Numbers!

2. *Numbers one at a time.* This way of preaching has become far more common. When a man wishes to impress a truth or a duty, he numbers the main headings and somehow makes the numbers stand out boldly. But he deals with only one heading at a time, and only one number. Near the end, of course, he may summarize, but elsewhere he does not bunch the numbers all together. This way of proceeding calls for more ability and work than the older fashion

141

of numbering before and after, but the results often repay the minister for his care in planning to make the trail clear and luminous. This newer method encourages economy of time, permits the use of suspense, and makes the large truths stand out boldly.

3. *Numbers in the practical part.* This third way of preaching affords a variant of the second plan. By employing numbers during the latter part of the sermon, and not elsewhere, the minister stresses what he wishes the hearer to remember and do. The preacher may appear to be dwelling long on the introduction, but really he is preparing the first main floor, all in one room. When he comes to the quarters upstairs, where the members of the family live, he begins to use numbers. Fosdick often preaches this way. After a few words about the problem in hand he devotes forty or fifty per cent of his time to the principle in view, and then he starts to use numbers. Such a way of presenting a truth or a duty affords all sorts of opportunities for variety and effectiveness. Number only the practical parts!

4. *No use of numbers.* The practice of dispensing with numbers began to be common in many circles during the past few decades. Because of a recoil from mid-Victorian forthrightness, young ministers devised ways and means of getting along without numbers. When they succeeded, their pulpit work became worthy of note for human interest and power to inspire. But at present many of these men, now mature, have begun to see the necessity of more teaching from the pulpit. Obviously, no one can become a teacher by resorting to numbers, but if a man has something to say, and wishes the hearer to learn, the teaching minister finds the use of numbers here and there an asset and not a liability. As a witness take one of the most interesting writers about homiletics:

When I began preaching I used not to announce the heads or divisions of my sermon. It seemed to me stiff and old-fashioned. And, of course, like all young preachers, I must be original. I have changed my mind about that. I do not formally announce my divisions, but I take great pains to let my hearers know them. A preached sermon is not like a printed one, where the reader can see the divisions and paragraphs, and where he can look back to the beginning of a passage for the connection. If the audience are not helped to guess at the coming line of thought, they get confused very soon, and you lose their attention.

So much do I feel this that I now begin, after announcing my text, by saying, "The subject of my sermon today will be, etc." Then, when I come to each separate division of my thought, I indicate it clearly by a deliberate pause, or by summing up into a sentence the previous thought. I somehow try to put the audience into the position of a man who has the printed sermon before him.[6]

NEWER WAYS OF PLANNING

1. *The inductive method.* In recent times ministers have been experimenting with the inductive plan, especially in preaching at colleges and universities. For a statement of ideals and methods, see a book by Joseph Fort Newton, *The New Preaching,* where he shows that older preachers relied mainly on deduction. With the Bible or the Church as the fountainhead of wisdom, the man in the pulpit would deduce his findings, much as an attorney before the Supreme Court used to base his plea squarely on the Constitution. In recent times, however, a university preacher may reverse the order. Working inductively he may begin with human experience here and now. If you ask why, he answers, "I must start with the hearers where they are."

This kind of pulpit work stresses human interest. For example, the ministerial guest may wish to tell the college man about "The Duty of Being Yourself." If the message grew out of a text, the words might come from I Sam. 17:39, where young David insists on fighting in his own way, and not with the armor of King Saul. But according to the inductive plan the discourse begins with facts of experience here and now. In the first few sentences the minister raises the problem: How can a young fellow today feel sure of becoming himself, and not a copy of somebody else? The sermon may follow him through home and school, training in a military camp or an athletic team, life in a business or profession, and perhaps other realms of life today. Gradually the trail may lead up to a glimpse

[6] J. Paterson Smyth, *The Preacher and His Sermon,* pp. 115-16.

of Christ and the Cross, where the Son of Man dared to be Himself.

If the man in the pulpit knows his business he can lead the hearer through hills and valleys of human experience, with now and then a glimpse of the God who makes Himself known in such winding trails. In the hands of a master, such as Charles W. Gilkey, of the chapel at the University of Chicago, the inductive method opens the way for all sorts of vistas that should make the hearer sense the nearness of God. In a university chapel some such method may seem wise part of the time, but many of us question the wisdom of such pulpit fare anywhere as a regular diet. Still more strongly do we feel that the young parish minister should not choose as his model a specialist in preaching to university students.

Even university men will respond to deductive preaching, but they want it to come in thought-forms of our own time. At Princeton University and elsewhere many students look on Reinhold Niebuhr as their favorite preacher in chapel. From him they have heard all sorts of sermons about God in Christ, for he follows no homiletical laws except those of his own making. As a rule he begins by quoting words from the Bible, it may be from Paul. The text may come from the Apostle's words about the battle within a man's soul (Rom. 7:23). If so, the sermon deals with God from beginning to end, but never apart from His concern for men, one by one—men like those in the chapel. So it appears that even in university circles the objection to deductive preaching does not come from the man in the pew.

Wherein lies the difficulty of preaching inductively? Perhaps unconsciously the preacher may not correctly present the facts about religion and life. In a sermon from the Old Testament God ought to appear as the chief actor; and from the New Testament, Christ, or the Holy Spirit. But in many a college or university sermon God, Christ, or the Spirit comes to view only near the end of the one-act play. In former times Phillips Brooks and Horace Bushnell knew how to bring God into the forefront of a message. At Harvard or Yale one of those worthies would make the university man feel that he stood in the presence of the God who cared about the student as a human being. Who would ever think of keeping Hamlet off the stage until near the end of a play about Hamlet? So, my young reader, wait for a while before you begin to preach inductively, and then try to give God a square deal.

2. *The life situation sermon.* This way of preaching deserves much more attention than we can give.[7] The method calls for different kinds of sermons, according to the personality of the minister and the character of the life situations. For example, you overhear a businessman telling a friend, "John, the way you and I are living is not worth what it costs." Since you do not know either man, and since you have heard the conversation on a bus, you feel free to start with these words. Then you discuss the subject "Is Life Worth What It Costs?" Or else, more directly, "Is Your Life Worth the Cost?"

After a life-situation approach a message of this kind may assume almost any form. In the hands of a machinist the product might seem mechanical, and a succession of such sermons might make the hearer problem-conscious. But in skillful hands the life situation sermon draws people to the sanctuary; when they come, the message does them good, because it helps them to understand life today through light that comes from God here and now. Hence a young minister should learn to preach this way, but he must be careful not to reveal from the pulpit what he has learned in the pastor's hour, or in any kind of "Protestant confessional."

If a man knows his Bible he can use the life situation approach with a golden text. How else did Robertson preach at Brighton a hundred years ago? If he wished to deal with the problem of despondency, he employed a text about Elijah under the juniper tree. If the life situation had to do with doubt, the light came through a record about Thomas. In either case the sermon had to do with God or Christ rather than Elijah or Thomas. As for that question about whether or not a man's life costs more than it seems worth, why not

[7] See H. E. Luccock, *In the Minister's Workshop* (New York and Nashville: Abingdon-Cokesbury Press, 1944), pp. 50-92; R. W. Sockman, *The Highway of God* (New York: The Macmillan Co., 1942), pp. 118-26; A. W. Blackwood, *Planning a Year's Pulpit Work*, pp. 187-202; and H. W. Roupp in *The Pulpit*, May, June, 1941.

find the answer at the end of the Resurrection chapter? Instead of appealing to a man on the basis of his impulses, lead him to become steadfast in belief, immovable in character, always abounding in the work of the Lord. In view of Christ's Resurrection, a believer's way of living becomes worth far more than it can ever cost him (I Cor. 15:58).

3. *The case method.* This plan too works in various ways. In our seminary courses on pastoral theology, as in the study of medicine or law, young men employ the case method. With such a background the minister of today finds that the plan works also in the pulpit. Sometimes he wishes to discuss "The Gospel in Terms of Health." For case materials he turns to the man whom the Good Physician set free from paralysis. In the record, Mark 2:1-12, the preacher notes the stress on the power of Christ to forgive sins. In the light of this truth the sermon brings out the meaning of sin as the disease of the soul, and of forgiveness as the healing of this disease.

Phillips Brooks employed this method in a different fashion. While he did not use cases in every sermon, he resorted to them so often that he showed the value of hypothetical cases. In a sermon of this kind he would establish a principle, which he drew from the Scriptures; then he would show how the principle worked in the lives of Boston people, one after another, perhaps five or six in all. He did not merely turn to such examples as illustrations; he employed personal facts as building blocks in making the sermon. This way of preaching deserves a wide use, because it enables the pastor to interpret the life of the hearer in light that streams from the Book. The effectiveness, of course, depends much on ability to single out and set forth hypothetical cases true to life in our day and in this parish.

For example, a minister wishes to deal with "Work as a Means of Grace." He may start with familiar words: "Work out your own salvation, . . . for it is God which worketh in you" (Phil. 2:12-13). Like Horace Bushnell, the preacher may formulate a proposition or key sentence: "Under God every man has much to do with determining his destiny." Then the minister can show how the principle works in the lives of men and women, one by one, like those who sit in the pews: the college man with his study, the army man with his drill, the businessman with his money, and the housewife with her routine. If the man in the pulpit uses imagination, he can make this kind of sermon glow; but if he knocks it together with hammer and nails, he will find the effect wooden.

4. *The thematic message.* W. L. Stidger would call this way of preaching "symphonic," a method that he uses with a line or two from a well-known poem or song. At the New Year season a minister can start with the words of Tennyson, "Ring out the old, ring in the new," a motif that calls for the topic "The Music of the New Year Gospel." Then the words from Tennyson ring out in all the rest of the sermon. Again, the pastor begins with words from a hymn by Thomas Moore: "Earth has no sorrows that heaven cannot heal," a refrain that has to do with the healing of a soul here and now. The hymn itself, "Come, Ye Disconsolate," brings God's healing balm to the friend who sits beneath the juniper tree and wishes to die.

Recently William Sherman Skinner of Pittsburgh spoke on the saying: "When God erases, He is making ready to write." The message went back to the words of Paul about believers as epistles of Christ (II Cor. 3:3). The discussion concerned the ways of God in times of world chaos, with a call for reconstruction. After the hearers reached home, and for months to come, they kept saying one to another: "When God erases, He is making ready to write." They found that the thematic sermon suggested far more than it said. Partly because of repetition, the words kept ringing in their ears, and caused many a layman to preach himself a sermon about what God wishes to write today.

5. *The dramatic message.* This way of preaching assumes countless forms, all difficult to classify or describe. In general such a sermon resembles a one-act play. As every observer of the "little theater" knows, the one-act play appears in divers forms.[8] The facts come

---

[8] A minister need not approve of the present-day theater, or attend it, in order to learn why it draws.

out in a book by Percival Wilde, who is said to have written more one-act plays than anyone else in America. In a treatise, *The Craftsmanship of the One-Act Play*,[9] he insists that a person who seems good may become bad, and that one who deserves to be called bad may become good—all within the confines of a play that lasts only an hour. This sounds like the beginning of a message about the greed of Judas in selling his Lord, or about the conversion of Saul on the road to Damascus. When has a one-act play ever included more in the way of dramatic action?

In this kind of sermon you begin with a person or a group of persons. Then you bring out the action, so that the friend in the pew can see someone to admire, someone to dread, someone to be like. The action leads to struggle, the struggle causes conflict, and the conflict involves suspense. After a while comes the dénouement. Why not show the drama of redemption as it appears in the Holy Scriptures? If you learn to preach sermons as dramatic as the scenes they represent, you will never lack a hearing. Especially in a downtown church at night a man must know how to use imagination like that of a playwright.

6. *The Hegelian method.* As a pantheistic philosopher, Hegel would not recognize one of these sermons as anything like his offspring, but his way of thinking has suggested the title. The label goes with a message that consists of three parts with three different emphases: thesis, antithesis, and synthesis. Thus the main parts of the sermon move like the successive portions in a sonata by Mozart. In the sermon first comes the thesis, setting up a truth or an ideal; then follows the antithesis, bringing out the facts of life as they appear today, perhaps in the mud of "Main Street"; last of all, except for the brief conclusion, comes the synthesis or resolution, showing how the truth of God transforms the sordidness of life here below. Needless to say, this kind of pulpit work appears in varied forms, some of which tax all of a man's powers.

In the pulpit wise men almost never employ technical terms such

[9] Boston: Little, Brown & Co., 1923. Also see Fred Eastman, *Christ in the Drama* (New York: The Macmillan Co., 1947).

as thesis, antithesis, and synthesis. But in the study a young minister can use such terms in checking up on his thinking about religion and life. Why not school yourself, again and again, to look at the ideal as it stands out in the truths that come from God? Then take account of the facts as they appear in the home community, and everywhere else today. Best of all, see how God wishes to transform the things of earth. Share this working philosophy with the friends who come to church bewildered and distracted because they have lost their bearings. Whenever you address men and women who spend their working hours amid muck and slime, bid them look up and behold the God who made the beauty of the stars. Better still, lead them to set their affections on things above, where Christ dwelleth. What else does it mean to be Christians today?

The Hegelian method ought to come into more common use. For instance, such a sermon might grow out of the truth that Charles Wesley voiced in the hymn "Christ, Whose Glory Fills the Skies." In the pulpit the first few sentences may concern Charles Wesley as the writer of more than six thousand hymns, many of them about Christ, but the message itself should deal with the truths in the three stanzas of the hymn. First the thesis, "The Wonder of Our Lord as Light"; second the antithesis, "The Sadness of a World Without Christ"; third the synthesis, "The Radiance of a Soul in the Redeemer." Such a message about "The Christian Secret of Radiance" ought to fill many a heart with a desire to sing and pray.[10]

7. *The adverbial plan.* This way of preparing to preach comes up now because it belongs nowhere else. Among evangelical ministers the adverbial method has become too common. Whenever a man has not time enough to think of a method largely his own, he may resort to the old fashion of asking questions, such as "Who," "When," and "Why?" In the hands of a master like Spurgeon this way of preaching may justify itself, at least occasionally; but as a steady diet it becomes as unwelcome as boardinghouse hash. In preaching, as in preparing food, variety comes through use of imagination. Anyone can ask four

[10] For an example of a Hegelian sermon see "The Cloister and the Crowd" by W. M. Clow, in *The Secret of the Lord* (New York: Geo. H. Doran Co., n.d.), pp. 216-28.

or five questions about a subject without opening a book or using his brains. When a man has gone through college and seminary, why should he do the sort of thing he could have done in high school? There he may have run across these lines from Rudyard Kipling. Note especially the closing words, "Give them all a rest."

> I keep six honest serving-men
> (They taught me all I knew);
> Their names are What and Why and When
> And How and Where and Who.
> I send them over land and sea,
> I send them east and west;
> But after they have worked for me,
> I give them all a rest.[11]

We have now looked at seven methods, six of them good. We might go on to see that sermons by the masters differ like stars in the sky. Without pressing the figure too far, we may ask why we do not learn from the stars the appeal of variety. Why not taste the joys of discovering a star that no one else has ever seen? Whenever a man finds a new way of presenting an old truth or duty, he may sing with young Keats:

> Then felt I like some watcher of the skies
> When a new planet swims into his ken.

Before the poet could write such words, he had to master his craft. That he did largely in two ways: by careful study of poems from other men, and by composing ones of his own. So must every young minister learn how to prepare sermons. In this kind of self-discipline he may take to heart words of counsel from the chief exponent of the one-act play—with special emphasis on what he says about imagination. Imagination here means the synthesizing power. Without the use of imagination no one can hope to bring forth week after week a wholesome variety of sermon plans.

[11] From "The Elephant's Child," from *Just So Stories.* Copyright 1902, 1907 by Rudyard Kipling. Reprinted by permission of Mrs. George Bambridge and Doubleday & Co., Inc.

The writing of drama demands the harmonious working of three great faculties: observation, thought, and craftsmanship. The material is gathered by the first; developed by the second; cast into form by the third. A good play is the result of all three. . . .

I have said nothing about imagination. There is little that need be said about imagination. A man either possesses it or lacks it. If he lacks it, it is sheer madness for him to embark upon the writing of either poetry, drama, or fiction. If he possesses it, . . . he will not be able to refrain from transferring some of his ideas to paper. He will find stimulus everywhere.[12]

[12] Percival Wilde, *The Craftsmanship of the One-Act Play* (Boston: Little, Brown & Co., 1923), pp. 25, 16. By permission of the author.

CHAPTER XIII

The Use of Illustrations

OPINIONS differ sharply about the number of illustrations to use in a sermon or in a year's pulpit work. An elderly pastor may insist, "Have none at all, or few at most. Why waste time?" A younger minister replies, "Preachers to common people, from the days of our Lord until now, have relied largely on illustrations." Which side ought to win the argument? Neither! The older man probably employs too few, and the younger one too many. Laymen feel that the elderly minister's abode needs more open windows; the younger one's, more solid walls. Why then employ illustrations?

THE REASONS FOR USING ILLUSTRATIONS

1. For the sake of *human interest*. When a speaker discusses a truth or a duty that seems not to concern the hearers, he can tie it up with something they like. Why did our Lord talk about Providence in terms of birds and of lilies, things to eat and to wear? The Master Teacher spoke about God in relation to persons or things, and about persons or things with reference to God. When our Lord talked about farm or fireside, He wished to interest people in the Kingdom that they could never see with the eyes of flesh. In addressing common folk He never employed abstractions or aimless illustrations. He used facts to throw light on truth or duty and to make the things of heaven attractive to people on earth.

Since an illustration throws light on something beyond itself, the example must fill a secondary place. It must serve as a means to an end, and not as an end in itself. In preparing to preach the mind often follows this rule: "State your truth and define your terms; then discuss the matter and, if need be, illustrate." Another rule often works: "Have something in hand or in sight before you illustrate; then you will find that paragraph after paragraph glows with its own inner light." In our day a vast office building may require few windows, because the light comes largely from within.

Occasionally, however, an illustration may come at the beginning of a sermon. In St. Paul's Church, London, H. P. Liddon once preached about what lies beyond the moment of death.[1] He began by quoting a text that raised a question: "Then shall I know even as also I am known" (I Cor. 13:12b). After the text came an account of an army officer, seventy years of age, who had returned home from the wars of India. Seated amid a group of friends the warrior related all sorts of "hair-breadth escapes," and then he paused. After a little he said: "I expect to see something much more remarkable than anything I have been describing." Knowing that the hearers did not understand, he continued in a low tone, and intensely: "The first five minutes after death!" What a subject, if a man can deliver the goods! And what an illustration! No one but Liddon would have dared to start that way in St. Paul's, and no one else could have gone on to the end of that sermon without anticlimax. Who can wonder that this message has lived ever since 1879? Once in a while, then, you may use an illustration at the beginning to catch attention and rivet it on the truth in hand.

2. *Clearness.* Some other part of the sermon may call for an illustration to make a truth or a duty clear. The truth may come from Rom. 8:28a: "We know that in everything God works for good with those who love him" (R.S.V.). Here a scholastic sermonizer might hold forth about pre-established harmony between the human and the divine, but a lover of common people prefers to tell about God as the Divine Artist. Under His watchful eye the pattern of a good man's life begins to appear: the warp comes from above; the woof issues from earth. In the text "everything" includes strong, somber threads, with which we human beings have little to do save to accept and use them as they come from God, and other threads with their varied hues, which we contribute to the weaving of God's pattern.

[1] See H. P. Liddon, *Forty-Two Sermons* (London, 1886), pp. 25-32.

If the minister tried to argue or prove his point, he might get the ideas tangled. So he may use Joseph or Paul as an object lesson. Since the text comes from the Apostle, take him as a living example of what the words mean, and how the truth works. God had a shaping hand in Paul's career as a whole, day after day. Hence the Apostle could write to the Romans, "We know." He had verified the truth in his own experience, and he had seen it work in the lives of others. Herein lies that "eloquence of Christian experience." Again Joseph's elder brothers planned to kill him, but they compromised by selling him into slavery. There he toiled for thirteen years, and all that time he seemed a victim of fate. In after years he could see that God had overruled those wrongs, wrongs like "the sins that crucified Jesus." "God meant it for good, to bring to pass, as it is this day, to save much people alive" (Gen. 50:20 A.S.V.). No wonder Phillips Brooks insisted that the best illustrations of New Testament truth come from the Old. His own pulpit work shows how to make every such example clear.[2]

3. *Beauty.* The facts about God call for both clarity and beauty, whereas our sermons often make Him seem commonplace and unattractive, even like an "oblong blur." How can anyone tell about the beauty of holiness without misrepresenting the God of all grace? Partly by the use of examples that serve as windows to relieve the monotony of a wall. In a sanctuary the stained-glass windows minister to beauty far more than to illumination. In a sermon by Charles W. Gilkey about "Coincidences," the crowning illustration comes from the experience of George Matheson. Early in manhood, through no fault of his own, he became blind, and because of blindness he attained a new sense of beauty and grace. After more than twenty years of victory over that handicap he could sing:

> O Love that wilt not let me go,
> I rest my weary soul in Thee;
> I give Thee back the life I owe,
> That in Thine ocean depths its flow
> May richer, fuller be.

[2] See A. W. Blackwood, *The Protestant Pulpit,* sermon 13.

This example concerns what the hearer knows and loves; some other time the use of a less familiar illustration may impart a touch of splendor. For instance, turn to the fortieth chapter of Isaiah, or the fifteenth of First Corinthians. Note how the prophet searches heaven and earth for figures to body forth the glory of God, and how the apostle does the same with the wonders of the Resurrection.

For a more recent example go to the last two paragraphs in that sermon "The Expulsive Power of a New Affection" by Thomas Chalmers.[3] First he bids you "conceive a man to be standing on the margin of this green world," with all its promise and glory spread out before him. To that world he would cling, but if "some happy island of the blest had floated by; and there had burst upon his senses the light of its surpassing glories," he would "die unto this present world, and live to the lovelier world that stands in the distance." Such splendor of illustration can come only through the use of imagination in its upper flights.

4. *Completeness.* In preparing a sermon, especially toward the close, the friend in the study feels the need of something more. So he determines to illustrate, not for the sake of interest, clarity, or beauty, but to round out the message and make it live. In a discourse about "The True Simplicity" James S. Stewart has led us to see and desire "the simplicity that is in Christ" (II Cor. 11:3). Near the end he must have felt the need of an example, for he shows how the "Commander-in-chief" can strengthen hearts full of fear.

At the close of a variety entertainment given in London for men going out to the Front, a young officer rose, at his Colonel's request, to express the men's thanks. He did so in genial words of charm and humor. Then suddenly, as if in afterthought, . . . he added: "We are soon crossing to France and to the trenches, and very possibly, of course, to death. Will any of our friends here tell us how to die?" There was a long, strained silence. No one knew what to say. But then the answer came. One of the singers made her way quietly forward to the front of the stage, and began to sing the great aria from the *Elijah*, "O Rest in the Lord." There were few dry eyes when the song was done.[4]

[3] *Ibid.*, sermon 6.
[4] *The Gates of New Life* (New York: Charles Scribner's Sons, 1940), p. 219.

After that illustration the minister spoke only forty-six words, but throughout the discourse he had been leading up to those last few words. If anyone had asked why he used that example, he might have felt nonplussed, but he could have explained that he had sensed the need of illumination that comes best through music. Such use of illustrations calls for the seeing eye and the hearing ear of an artist.

THE VARIETY OF SOURCES

When the novice asks, "Where can I find such illustrations?" some pastor of middle age answers, "Everywhere! Use your eyes!" If the young man does that, he may forget about the needs of the hearer. In an issue of the *New York Times* a half-page ad showed an envelope addressed "To Anybody Everywhere." Above the envelope stood the caption: "Can you, as an advertising man, tell what is wrong with this letter?" Beneath the envelope, without a line between, came the answer: "You're right! It isn't addressed to anybody in particular. That makes a difference in the interest with which a letter, or an advertisement, is received and read." In the words of that copy, it "makes a whale of a difference" also in the way a hearer receives an illustration. Be specific in your aim and then use facts. In that illustration about the soldiers count the number of fact words and phrases. One student finds thirty-two.

In securing examples, therefore, use brains with imagination. Begin with the Bible, especially the portion surrounding the text. Learn to see what you need. At Princeton University most of the newer buildings consist of stones from a quarry near at hand, but the older structures consist of stones imported from another state. If a visitor asked why these newer buildings look better than some of the older ones, a student might answer: "When somebody began to use brains, he found here at home better stones than the builders had been bringing from a distance."

But no example can tell the whole story. If the visitor looked at the oldest of those buildings, he found there all the simplicity and charm of Georgian Colonial architecture at its best. What then shall we conclude? That no person can limit the number and the variety of the fields from which the preacher should draw examples, and that the best examples often come from fields near home. Instead of glancing at those fields once again, turn to the chapter about "The Call for Other Materials." There the discussion concerned the variety of materials that go into the making of sermons. Here we are thinking about the same sources, but from a different point of view. Materials resemble bricks or stones that enter into the walls of a structure; illustrations serve as windows in the walls of the edifice.

Unfortunately the preparation of sermons proves far less simple than this account makes the work seem. Examples from architecture can never set forth the truth about messages that live and move. However, if we keep thinking about the need of materials and illustrations, we shall remember a truth that often escapes notice: a sermon for our day consists largely of facts, facts, facts. Whatever else a message contains, it should embody facts. A study of present-day sermons will show that many a pulpit master relies largely on facts from near and far, but not always as illustrations. In full view of these permutations, let us look at a few working rules.

1. *Limit the number* of illustrations. Concentrate on quality, not quantity, but use examples freely and fully when the audience includes boys and girls. Remember that an illustration occupies a secondary place; so keep a sense of proportion. You will find, however, that certain parts of the structure call for windows, and you will learn to prepare for an example before you put it in place. Phrase every illustration with as much care as any other part of the message. You may wonder why you should devote time and attention to things of secondary concern, but you will learn, perhaps by sad experience, that when an illustration backfires, it may do more harm than good.

For examples of care in the use of illustrations go to the sermons of Spurgeon. In one of his early messages he referred to an old seaman's difficulties in laying hold of God's promises.[5] The seaman had struggled to get his boat up close to the dock. He wished to throw a cable round a post and so keep the boat from drifting out to sea. But before

[5] A. W. Blackwood, *The Protestant Pulpit*, sermon 12.

the old seaman appeared in the sermon, the preacher had been stressing the need for getting close to God and laying hold of His promises. By stating his idea more than once, and then using the example, Spurgeon impressed the truth in hand and not merely the illustration. "I know they are good strong promises [said the seaman], but I cannot get close enough to shore to throw my cable around them." Then the man in the pulpit told him how, but the next paragraph had to do with the promises of God, and not with the old seaman.

2. Within the sermon plan for *a variety of illustrations*. From week to week, also, keep away from sameness. For instance, Clow preached about "The Cloister and the Crowd," by which he meant worship on the mountaintop and service in the valley (Mark 9:5). In the first main part, "The Blessing of the Cloister Hour," he developed a thesis by taking materials from the Bible, chiefly from his context. In the central part, "The Curse of the Cloister Life," he made clear the antithesis by using facts from church history. In the third main part, "The Keeping of the Spirit of the Cloister in the Crowd," he brought out the synthesis by using facts from his own day. Throughout this sermon he kept moving forward in time. A week later he would follow some different plan, go to other sources of materials, and thus insure variety of appeal.

3. In a sermon occasionally, as we have seen, a preacher may *start with an illustration*, and then let it dominate all that follows. In such a case he need not look about for other illustrations. Once Joseph R. Sizoo preached about Christian contentment: "I have learned, in whatsoever state I am, therewith to be content" (Phil. 4:11). The sermon began with an experience on board an ocean liner, where two passengers had been finding fault with everything and everybody except themselves. Their carpings led a bystander to tell a friend: "I hope I shall always be able to take the luck o' the road!"

This phrase, "the luck o' the road," provided the subject for a life situation sermon. In fact, the life situation sermon normally starts with an illustration. When a man chooses a text like this one from Philippians, he can draw from the life of the Apostle other facts. From two sources, the experience of Paul and the scene on the deck, the preacher can take all the local color the message requires. Sizoo used still other illustrations, but he made everything center round the idea of the Christian's life as taking "the luck o' the road." This means accepting life as you find it, seeing it in terms of higher values, and viewing it all in light from God.

THE OTHER SIDE OF THE MATTER

We have been thinking about illustrations in the hands of master preachers, but we should also consider misuses and abuses by other men, who must not appear by name. Sometimes windows in a building weaken the walls and mar the design. When laymen object to the "anecdotal preacher," they ask why someone at the divinity school did not teach the young man how to do this part of his work. Alas, who can impart good taste and a sense for the fitness of things? Nowhere does student preaching fall short more often than in the illustrations. The students have not had enough experience of life, or else they have not learned to use their eyes. A few negative counsels may help them. Since these rules seem obvious, they call for little comment.

1. *Avoid "canned goods."* On the shelves of the study leave no room for books of illustrations, even though they come from Spurgeon or some more recent pulpit master. No such man ever clothed his sermons with secondhand garments. Be yourself!

2. *Never use the preacher's cliché:* "A story is told." If the candidate for admission to the sermon proves worthy, let it in. Tell the facts without any preface. Why waste words? Why prejudice the example by leading up to it with a cliché?

3. *Refrain from relating anecdotes,* especially ones that sound improbable if not impossible. Give the preference to facts from biography and fiction, also to facts from life at every turn of the road. Keep away from anything that savors of unreality, mawkishness, or sentimentality.

4. *Be careful about allusions to persons.* The best examples come from the lives of well-known people, but so do the worst illustrations come from the experiences of persons too well known. Only a pulpit master, and he but seldom, can preach much about his sainted mother,

THE PREPARATION OF SERMONS

his charming wife, and his first-born baby. Away with such domestic illustrations! Be more objective.

5. *Avoid references to yourself*, your prowess, and your exploits. If a young man wishes to say "I," let him say "I," but let him not pose as the hero of any scene. From Robertson or Brooks he can learn how to preach both personally and impersonally at the same time. Each of them kept drawing from his own experiences, but neither of them referred to himself. Be modest!

6. *Do not relate a number of examples* in a row, but plan for one at a time. Occasionally a positive and a negative in succession will show contrasting truths, but when a single example will shed all the light a paragraph needs, why waste the second illustration? Be as thrifty as a Scotsman!

7. *Quote poetry sparingly.* Here and there a pastor can quote verse without calling attention to the disparity between the beauty of the poem and the lack of beauty in the sermon. Such an interpreter can make words from Browning glow, but as a rule the pastor thinks more highly of his quotations than the layman thinks. In poems, as in anecdotes, many a hearer

> . . . wants but little here below,
> Nor wants that little long.

Be not a parrot!

8. Do not employ *a negative illustration* with a positive truth. Here again an exception once in a while may justify itself, but give the preference to light, and not to darkness; make the gospel sound like good news. If this counsel seems needless, pick up a book of illustrations and note how often the examples consist of negations. So do some of our books about preaching!

Enough of negations here! No number of rules can lead to mastery in this field. So let us return to the question with which we started: "How many illustrations does a sermon require?" Who can reply in terms of mathematics? A teacher of our art insists that no minister has ever employed too many good illustrations.[7] Amen, provided

[7] See H. S. Coffin, *What to Preach*, p. 184.

"good" here means helpful in making the sermon effective! In terms of athletics no quarterback ever called for too many good forward passes. If he knows his business, he calls for a play that will be sure to advance the ball!

Still the impression lingers that many young ministers employ illustrations too freely, and that some older men use them too sparingly. In all these matters why not seek and follow the guidance of the Holy Spirit? In any standard church hymnal almost half of the songs about the Spirit refer to Him as Light. When He guides and restrains in the planning of a sermon, He shows the preacher how to use lights and shadows. Then every illustration brings glory to the Author of Light, and blessing to souls in need.

Suggested Readings

Bryan, Dawson C. *The Art of Illustrating Sermons*. New York and Nashville: Abingdon-Cokesbury Press, 1938.
Jeffs, H. *The Art of Sermon Illustration*. London, n.d.
Sangster, W. E. *The Art of Sermon Illustration*. London, 1947.
Spurgeon, Charles H. *The Art of Illustration*. London, 1894.

CHAPTER XIV

The Force of the Conclusion

LET US THINK about the conclusion as the most important part of a sermon, except for the text. In any piece of writing or speaking nothing else bulks so large as the beginning and the end. By the conclusion we mean the last part of a sermon, the part that embodies the purpose. This part differs from the beginning, where a man catches attention and focuses it on the truth in hand so as to prepare for what follows. At the end the preacher guides the hearer in doing the will of the Lord. Ideally a man starts with interest and ends with force, which means effectiveness. Force points to strength of impact, and not to loudness of speech. Strange as the fact may seem, a forceful conclusion calls for a quiet delivery.

In a pastor's workshop the closing part of a sermon may receive less attention than it deserves. In recent years ministers have studied the art of introduction. To the beginning of every sermon a wise man in the study devotes time and care, so that Sunday after Sunday he can start with an appeal to human interest. Especially over the radio preachers today show a mastery of the introduction, but comparatively few seem to appreciate the importance of the conclusion. The same holds true of many published discourses. In preaching a sermon, as in making an airplane flight, the chief test comes at the end.

If these contrasts between yesterday and today seem unfair, single out a dozen sermons by masters in our time, or listen to that many experts over the radio. In almost every message note the skill of the approach, and then see if the discourse leads up to action by the hearer. You may conclude that ministers today know more about human interest than divine power, and more about psychology than God. Fortunately, however, the trend at present gives reason to hope for stronger endings in tomorrow's sermons.

On the other hand, take a dozen messages from the time of Bushnell, Brooks, and Spurgeon. Did those men excel in arousing interest at the start? No; in that day a man in the pulpit could take interest for granted. Sometimes he began with small evidence of skill, but before he got through, he would bring the hearer face to face with God. After such a survey why not resolve to learn from contemporay preachers how to begin, and from earlier masters how to end?

How then should a sermon close? That depends on various factors, most of all on the purpose. Before a man starts out on a journey by land or air, he must decide about the destination. When a minister prepares a sermon for the coming Lord's Day, he ought to have in mind the goal, so that he can lead every hearer to a certain spot. When the guide and his friends reach that destination, the journey should end. Would that the drafting of every conclusion might prove as simple as such an account makes the facts appear! Unfortunately, however, no two sermons ought to end in the same fashion. For that reason we should now consider various ways of closing.

THE VARIETY OF ENDINGS

1. *The direct appeal.* This old-fashioned way of ending a message still deserves a place in the pulpit. The speaker addresses the hearers as a group or one by one. When Spurgeon preached to 3,000 persons, or even 23,000, he could make everyone present feel that God was speaking to him personally. No one would employ Spurgeon's archaic diction, but every preacher can learn from the London man not to fear people. Near the close of many a message Spurgeon dared to speak as man to man. In like fashion L. D. Weatherhead makes a direct appeal in many of his sermons. Here follows the closing paragraph of his message, "Youth Looks at Christ":

Youth, you cannot help loving him, and if you only will look at him, you will find that you cannot thereafter be happy for long without him. ... You will have seen too much. Let me call you back to him now. If you have sinned, he will forgive you. If you are even now intending to sin, he will save you. ... Turn to him now; receive him now. Begin again with him. Keep on looking at him and listening to him. Christianity is Christ. If only I can bring you into living touch with him, he will do the rest.

Where he touches, there is healing. Where he beckons, there the light shines. Where he companions, there is peace.[1]

2. *The practical application.*[2] Such a conclusion resembles the one above, but still the two methods differ somewhat. In making a direct appeal the minister addresses the hearers, often one by one, but in this other way of closing, the preacher may apply his truth without speaking to any hearer directly. In either case the latter part of a sermon ought to answer the unspoken question of the hearer: "In the light of this message what does the Lord wish me to do?" Unlike an essay or a lecture a sermon should lead to action, which may occur solely in the heart.

Take an example of a practical application. In a sermon "The Best Thing about the Church" (Eph. 5:25), the minister has pointed to Christ as Lover of the Church, Believer in the Church, and Transformer of the Church. All of this may sound objective, but the conclusion becomes subjective since it concerns the friend in the pew. For a person to live as a Christian means to resemble Christ in loyalty to His Church. The man or the woman, the boy or the girl, who loves and follows Christ will honor and serve the Church for which He once died and in which He now lives. All of this a preacher can bring home to conscience and will, yet not speak to the hearer directly. For a far better example of the practical application turn to what our Lord says about the man who built his house on a rock (Matt. 7:24-27).

3. *The final summary.* Another old-time way of ending a sermon calls for a recapitulation. When a man does not know how else to round out a message, he may close with a summary. This kind of ending has become common, at least in some circles, perhaps because it costs little in the way of thought. But then it accomplishes little in the way of action. A teaching message lends itself to this way of stopping near the end and looking back over the trail, stage by stage; but

---

[1] *The Significance of Silence* (New York and Nashville: Abingdon-Cokesbury Press, 1946), pp. 29-40.

[2] I say practical rather than personal because I use this latter term with reference to a conclusion that addresses the person or somehow stresses the person. The practical stresses the truth, not the person or persons.

how can you lead the hearer forward while you are looking back? A conclusion ought to differ from a summary, because a summary speaks to the mind, whereas a conclusion appeals to the will, which means the whole personality in action. So if any sermon calls for a recapitulaton, obey that call, and then follow with something that will lead the hearer to act. Never end with a summary looking back.

4. *The contrasting truth.* If the main part of the sermon has led the hearer through the shadows, the conclusion may bring him out into the sunshine. If the pastor has been speaking about "The Dark Line in God's Face," he may lead up to a glimpse of the Cross and its redeeming love. "Had there been no dark line in God's face, there would have been no Cross." If the message has brought out the tragedy of Cain and his way of looking at life—largely in terms of today—the closing part may show the contrast between the spirit of Cain and the Cross of Christ.

Sometimes the contrast runs in the opposite direction. In the first psalm the writer shows the fruitfulness of a tree over against the worthlessness of the chaff. In like manner our Lord shows us a house on the rock and then a house on the sand. In the Scriptures, as a rule, the positive comes before the negative. In preaching from such a passage the interpreter may follow the same order and still close with something positive. According to Schleiermacher, the ablest of German preachers since Martin Luther, no message from the pulpit ought ever to end on a judicial note or with an air of severity. But Spurgeon and Robertson would have dissented, for each of them felt free at times to close with words of warning. Such a way of ending occasionally helps to insure variety.[3]

5. *The appeal to imagination.* This way of completing a sermon calls for making the truth "glorious to the imagination." For an example turn to the conclusion of that message from Chalmers, "The Expulsive Power of a New Affection." For a level not so high, go through a sermon by Brooks, "The Candle of the Lord." In the next to the last paragraph he tells how men of other days prepared candles for the

[3] For a negative ending see "Songs in the Night" by Spurgeon, in *The Protestant Pulpit.*

worship of the Most High, and then he closes with words that cause the heart to glow:

Above all the pictures of life,—of what it means, of what may be made out of it,—there stands out this picture of a human spirit burning with the light of the God whom it obeys, and showing Him to other men. O, my young friends, the old men will tell you that the lower pictures of life and its purposes turn out to be cheats and mistakes. But this picture can never cheat the soul that tries to realize it. The man whose life is a struggle after such obedience, when at last his earthly task is over, may look forward from the borders of this life into the other, and humbly say, as his history of the life that is ended, and his prayer for the life that is to come, the words that Jesus said—"I have glorified Thee on the earth; now, O Father, glorify Me with Thyself forever." [4]

Such a conclusion may leave little to be desired, but only a man with the soul of a poet can mount up as on eagle wings and capture the secrets of the stars. With many another minister the closing portion of a sermon must move on a level more prosaic. Very well, but still the conclusion need not seem commonplace. In quest of a beauty not his own the man in the study sometimes turns to the written work of another; it may be in the form of verse.

6. *The closing poem.* In a book of sermons by Fosdick, three out of twenty-five end with poetry; in a volume by Weatherhead, six of twenty-two; in the book by J. S. Stewart, nine of twenty-four. If every minister quoted poetry as worth while, and used it as well, the laymen would not object. If the man in the pulpit has the spirit of a poet, he can lead up to a few closing words from Emily Dickinson or Edwin Arlington Robinson, Tennyson or Browning. In such a case the wise man keeps the excerpt short, and he closes the majority of sermons in other ways. At the end of a message from God nothing about the sermon must call attention to itself and away from Him.

7. *The closing illustration.* This way of ending has become common, especially among young ministers. If the sermon calls for an illustration at the close, the preacher should obey the call, but as a rule he

The Candle of the Lord (New York: E. P. Dutton & Co., 1881), p. 19.

should close in some other way. Once in a while an illustration at the end may come with all the more force because of the novelty. But unless a man uses care and skill, as in quoting a poem, the illustration may call attention to itself or to him. If so, how can he persuade the hearer to start moving Godward? In short, a minister can employ any form of conclusion that will lead the hearer to act aright.

8. *The missing conclusion.* Sometimes the preacher stops without a formal conclusion. Reinhold Niebuhr does so at times, and this may account for a part of his appeal to university students and professors. Evidently he takes for granted that they can draw their own conclusions after they have listened eagerly to the sermon proper. Many another preacher would bring zest into a sermon occasionally if he closed without the last paragraph or two. But this kind of semiabrupt ending calls for skill in preparation, lest the close seem like a forced landing in an airplane. So for the first few years a young minister does well to conclude his sermons in ways more conventional.

9. *The final sentence.* Whatever the content and the form of the last paragraph or two, the sermon as a whole must lead up to a final sentence, which ought to stand out more boldly and strongly than any other sentence after the text. While Alexander Maclaren committed to memory only a few sentences out of a sermon, he always included one or two at the end. The final one he worded with as much care as a farmer exercises in rounding out a stack of hay. Often a preacher closes with his text, word for word. By doing so he ends on the note with which he began, and he may cause it to seem sublime.

Take an example of closing with the text. Edgar D. Jones has been preaching about "The Light on the Lord's Face." Near the end he has quoted a stanza from each of two hymns: one from William Cowper's "Sometimes a Light Surprises"; another from George Matheson's "O Love That Wilt Not Let Me Go." Then the preacher turns to his text: "For God, who commanded the light to shine out of darkness, hath shined in our hearts, to give the light of the knowledge of the glory of God in the face of Jesus Christ" (II Cor. 4:6). What a text, both for the beginning and for the end of a sermon! [5]

[5] See A. W. Blackwood, *The Protestant Pulpit*, sermon 26.

When a man does not close with the text, he may do well to use words of his own. How can he better put into speech exactly what he wishes to say? For example Brooks has been preaching about rest: "Come unto me, all ye that labour and are heavy laden, and I will give you rest" (Matt. 11:28). In the two paragraphs before the last one he has been dealing with the forgiveness of sins, as this truth concerns the friend in the pew. Much of the time Brooks has been speaking directly to the hearer: "Wrestle, O sinner, with your sin! . . . O sinner in your sin, O mourner in your sorrow, there is rest for you!" Then the sermon closes:

This is the rest which remaineth for His people! This is the rest into which the brave young hearts and the brave old hearts who have gone forth out of our sight into His eternal world have entered. It is a rest full of vigor and activity, a rest which is the same that Christ's own soul enjoyed. It is His peace. Behold! He offers it to every one of you! Behold! He stands before you, your Friend, your Lord, your Christ, and says to you, "Come unto me, O weary and heavy-laden man, and I will give you rest." May His voice so prevail with you that you shall come to Him.[6]

THE PLAN FOR THE CONCLUSION

1. *Make the conclusion appropriate.* Let the spirit and tone color accord with what has gone before. When a farmer builds a stack, when his wife frosts a cake, when their son designs an office building, the crowning touch calls for the eye and the hand of an artist. The maker has to see the end from the beginning. How much more should the ministerial son foresee the conclusion of his sermon! How else can he utter the last few words so as to enlist every hearer for the service of Christ and the Kingdom?

2. *Be simple.* In any sermon have a single conclusion, and by it reach the end in view. Stop before you begin to weaken the impression. On a rare occasion, however, perhaps once in a lifetime, special circumstances may call for a double conclusion. In London, at Westminster Abbey, Brooks preached on the fourth of July, 1880. Because of the national holiday in the United States he knew that the British auditors

[6] *The Law of Growth* (New York: E. P. Dutton & Co., 1910), pp. 148-49.

would expect him to speak about the birth of our Republic a century before. In his message, "The Candle of the Lord," Brooks did not allude to that holiday or to his homeland. But after he had come to the end of the sermon proper, he added a second conclusion. Simply, without embarrassment or apology, he asked those British friends to pray for his country. What tact and what skill! On ordinary occasions, however, only one conclusion for one sermon!

3. *Be short.* As with the introduction, brevity differs from abruptness. If the closing paragraphs call for more time than usual, the wise man keeps on until he has reached the destination. Often, however, the speaker makes the hearers feel that he has arrived at the landing field, but that he does not know how to alight. So he begins to circle, and they start to squirm. With an old Scottish dame they want to cry out: "The dominie's through, but he winna stop!" In the words of Charles R. Brown, "Keep faith with your people when once you awaken the joyful expectation of the end!" Otherwise the sermon may seem long, for even a minute or two of stolen time in closing may create a feeling of ennui. Why become a bore?

4. As a rule *"accentuate the positive."* The sermon as a whole may deal with something dark and awful, such as the wages of sin or the tragedy of divorce. If so, let the final words ring with Christian hope. Send the hearer from the sanctuary with a feeling of assurance and a sense of power. Remember with John Wesley that many a congregation has heard so much discouraging preaching that it has quit trying. However dark the pathway up to the end, lead the hearer out into the sunlight. Open up a vista of hope, even for the weakest and the worst of men, lest anyone begin to feel about the sanctuary: "Abandon hope, all ye that enter here!"

5. *Make the conclusion personal* but not too personal. A wise minister never indulges in personalities, but neither does he close with impersonalities. Directly or indirectly, now one way and again another, he brings truth and duty home to the conscience and the will of the friend in the pew. Like an attorney at the bar the minister pleads for a verdict. Not every message need qualify as evangelistic, but whatever the guiding purpose, the preacher wishes the hearer to

respond affirmatively. For an example of such a hearer-pointed conclusion turn to the closing paragraph of Robertson's message "The Loneliness of Christ." Among other things notice how he brings the truth home to your heart by the use of short, personal sentences:

> The practical result and inference of all this is a very simple, but a very deep one: the deepest of existence. Let life be a life of faith. Do not go timorously about, inquiring what others think, what others believe, and what others say. It seems the easiest, it is the most difficult thing in life to do this—believe in God. God is near you. Throw yourself fearlessly upon Him. Trembling mortal, there is an unknown might within your soul which will wake when you command it. The day may come when all that is human, man and woman, will fall off from you, as they did from Him. Let His strength be yours. Be independent of them all now. The Father is with you. Look to Him, and He will save you.[7]

6. Sound what John Henry Jowett used to call the *"wooing note."* Be persuasive; plan to end quietly. In the last few words of a message from the pulpit God speaks to the waiting soul, not "through the earthquake, wind, and fire," but through "the voice of gentle stillness." In wooing a maiden a young man does not try to carry a citadel by storm, but with quiet intensity presses his claims, pleading that he loves her and wishes her above all else on earth. So if a pastor wishes to end a sermon on the "wooing note," he must fall in love with the people. How else could he lead any of them to do the will of Him who is Love?

For an example turn to the closing paragraph of a sermon by Clovis G. Chappell. Read the entire message about the rich fool (Luke 12:16-21), or rather, about hell. As the preacher draws towards the end, imagine that he pauses and lowers his voice as he speaks with the "wooing note":

> Forever you are going to live. Forever you are going to be yourself. You are going to keep house with yourself for all eternity. Forever you are going to remember. Forever you are going to enjoy or suffer the destiny that you make for yourself while in this life. . . . Remember, too,

[7] A. W. Blackwood, *The Protestant Pulpit*, p. 106.

that though some men are lost, no man needs to be lost. Every man can be saved if he will. This minute you can be saved if you will only be wise enough and brave enough to make a right choice. "Him that cometh unto me I will in no wise cast out." Will you come? Will you come now? [8]

In this conclusion, as in many another, the pastor speaks directly to his friend in the pew. Such preaching calls for courage and tact, but so does all the public and private work of the ambassador from King Jesus. Listen to a master teacher of theology who tells young men how to preach:

Do not be afraid to use the pronoun "you," which is our common usage for "thou." . . . It would be wearisome to speak thus in the second person right through the sermon, indeed it is impossible if there is any development of a theme; moreover, used too persistently and in the wrong way it might give the impression of "nagging," or "browbeating," and of the preacher setting himself on a pedestal. Yet I am confident that such direct address should never be entirely omitted. . . . If there is no point where you can say "you," then it is strongly to be suspected that your discourse is not a sermon, but an essay or a lecture.[9]

THE THINGS TO AVOID

1. Negatively, *never apologize.* "An apology always stinks," and never more than in a sermon, especially at the end. Some of the older preachers fell into this habit. After Spurgeon had lifted the hearers Godward in that message, "Songs in the Night," he ended by saying: "I can not preach as earnestly as I could wish." In a sermon at a seminary chapel the visiting minister did everything superbly until he came to the end of the discourse; then, forgetting his high calling, he fell into an air pocket. After a brief pause he said in closing: "I do not care what you think of me or of my sermon!" In other words, "Forget all about God, and remember me!" What "egotism turned wrong side out"!

2. *Avoid humor.* At the beginning of a sermon away from home a preacher may sense the need of relieving tension, near the middle of

[8] *The Village Tragedy* (Nashville: Cokesbury Press, 1921), p. 105.
[9] Herbert H. Farmer, *The Servant of the Word* (New York: Charles Scribner's Sons, 1942), pp. 63-64.

a discourse he may find the going hard; so he resorts to humor in both cases. About all of this opinions differ; some of us think it possible to speak about God and His children for twenty-five minutes without the sort of comic interludes that Shakespeare put into a three-hour tragedy such as *Hamlet*. But no one can justify humor at the end of a sermon. Neither in a tragic drama nor in a sermon can anyone give a reason for a frivolous note at the close. There the man in the pulpit must neither divert nor amuse. As Reinhold Niebuhr says in a message called "Humor and Faith," there may be "laughter in the vestibule of the temple, and the echo of laughter in the temple itself, but only faith and prayer, and no laughter, in the holy of holies."[10]

3. *Keep from anything boisterous.* Nowhere throughout the sermon does custom today encourage a preacher to shout and scream and tear his hair. Especially as he draws towards the end he must keep his body under control. But, alas, the man who cares most about his message may begin to let himself out. As he becomes more and more excited, he may let his voice rise until it seems to screech like a siren. A man of a different sort may begin to bellow, as though he were bombarding a distant city. Why does he not enter that city at the beginning of the sermon, and talk things over with the friends whom he wishes to enlist for the service of the King?

4. *Never add anything new* on the impulse of the moment. In the study a man toils over a message hour after hour; there he devotes more time and attention to the conclusion than to anything else save the text. In the pulpit, when he draws near to the end of the sermon, he should focus all the rays of light so that they will cause the soul of the hearer to burn and glow. If the preacher has made ready in the spirit of prayer, he should follow a plan of his own making. Does not the Holy Spirit guide and restrain the minister as he prays and toils in the workshop? Strange as the fact may seem, the Holy Spirit prefers to lead according to a plan. Search the Scriptures and see whether or not these statements ring true.

[10] See *Discerning the Signs of the Times* (New York: Charles Scribner's Sons, 1946), p. 131.

5. In the latter part of the sermon *refrain from doing anything to distract.* Why pick up a hymnal, look down at a watch, or do anything else that calls attention to the passing of time and the nervous tension of the speaker? Take as a motto the words of the Apostle: "This one thing I do." Lead every hearer to fix his eye on the goal. Move every heart to do the will of God. Do not distract. Focus!

6. *Do not use the same kind of conclusion* Sunday after Sunday. The ineffectiveness of a man's closing words may spring from lack of variety. If so, he has fallen into a rut. He has tried a certain way of ending a sermon, and has found it effective. So he has settled down to this one mode. Consequently the conclusions of successive sermons may seem as much alike as pieces of metal molded in the same machine. How then can the pastor keep from such sameness? By making a study of conclusions, noting the various types, and by using his imagination. Let him commit to memory and often repeat these lines from *A Midsummer-Night's Dream:*

> ... As imagination bodies forth
> The forms of things unknown, the poet's pen
> Turns them to shapes and gives to airy nothing
> A local habitation and a name.

CHAPTER XV

The Habit of Writing Sermons

T HE WISE YOUNG MINISTER forms the habit of writing a sermon every week. He looks on the composition and revision of that message as the most important task between Sundays. For the writing he sets apart a definite time—it may be Thursday morning. Soon he finds that he can work best at a fixed place, with the same tools. Like Woodrow Wilson he may learn to compose on the typewriter, but as a rule the minister prefers to use his pen. Whatever the details, he soon turns them over to what William James calls "the effortless custody of automatism." What then does the minister need in order to write out a sermon every week?

THE IMPORTANCE OF METHOD

Let us take for granted that he knows what he wishes to preach and why. No amount of writing can atone for lack of a message or muddiness of thought. Let us assume that he has made a plan for the sermon, and that he has the blueprint close at hand. He should also have within reach everything he will need in the way of sermon materials. At length the time comes to set down in black and white the vision that has taken form in his mind and heart. Before he writes the opening words, he can say without boasting, "All things are now ready." So he can pour out the message from beginning to end, preferably without rising from the chair. After he learns how, this way of writing brings a man joy.

At first the novice may work in a different way, which brings no satisfaction or delight. He has watched his grandmother fashioning what she styles a crazy quilt, first cutting out pieces of cloth in all shapes and hues, and then sewing them together whenever she finds nothing else to do. In the right sort of hands this way of working leads to a thing of beauty, but when the grandson tries to prepare a sermon this way, he turns out a thing of shreds and patches. Such a mistaken technique may account for the fact that some ministers never enjoy writing sermons. For this feeling we who teach homiletics and write about preaching must take part of the blame. We have taught much about the parts of the sermon and little about putting them together.

The wise man looks on the message as a whole, and that full of life. Before he puts pen to paper, he can stand up and talk the sermon through, as to an unseen congregation. During the actual composition he can see the faces that will look up to him next Sunday morning as Mexican lilies turn to the rising sun. He knows that people look to him because he comes with light from God. He will find that this way of viewing the whole sermon as a message full of light tends to impart a sense of life and motion, with a spirit of warmth and color. However slowly the idea of the sermon may have come to its present form, the message now begins to live and move. Before it can live and move in the souls of the hearers, it must burn and glow in the heart of the preacher.

In time all of this may become largely a matter of habit. At Harvard, President Eliot used to say that education at its best leads a man to gain the right sort of methods for his lifework, among them the habit of performing a task at a given time. While a minister waits for the impulse to write, he may feel the urge to do something more pleasant. Here he can learn from other craftsmen, such as W. Somerset Maugham. This novelist sometimes deals with dirt, but as a writer he has mastered his craft. In a literary autobiography he tells how the mind of an author works. With this judgment Thomas Mann would agree, and so would almost every other master of the King's English today. Such authors stress the importance of habit and method. Maugham says:

> No professional writer can afford to write when he feels like it. If he waits till he is in the mood, till he has the inspiration, . . . he waits indefinitely and ends by producing little or nothing. The professional writer creates the mood, . . . but he controls and subdues it to his bidding by setting himself regular hours of work. But in time writing becomes a habit.

... You cannot write well or much (and I venture the opinion that you cannot write well unless you write much) unless you form a habit.[1]

If a man goes to work with all his might, sooner or later his mental faculties will awake. Before they start to move, he may put down words and paragraphs that he will need to discard or perhaps rewrite. Very well; let him remain at the desk and keep on at work. Ere long, except in case of illness or jaded nerves, the heart will begin to move, and then the words will start to flow. The writer will catch them as they fly and put them down before they get away. "Write quickly," said old Quintilian, "or you will never write well. Write well, and you will begin to write quickly."

To write well means to use prose rhythm. Whenever a man's heart begins to move, his words tend to flow. As thoughts and feelings surge through mind and heart, the movement tends to surge and recede. Here the waters flow gently, as in the Afton about which the poet sings; at other times the streams of thought and feeling rush over rapids with speed and force. For all these varieties of rhythmical prose turn to the latter part of Isaiah, or to the parables of our Lord. If anyone protests that such writings come close to poetry, the same holds true of preaching at its best. In either case the writer or speaker sees and feels what he wishes the reader or hearer to see and feel.

The man who would write sermons ought to gain a sense of prose rhythm. Let him read aloud the fortieth chapter of Isaiah, "Comfort ye, comfort ye my people"; and the fifteenth chapter of Luke, especially the parable of the loving father and his two sons. By way of contrast the student can take up a piece of prose that does not flow because it lacks feeling. In an old book he can find his way haltingly through words that suggest nothing to see, to feel, or to do, even when they concern hymns full of life and beauty:

This Hymnal was published in October, 1895, with a Preface setting forth the principles which governed its preparation. The present edition marks no departure from these principles, and no change in the general character of the book. It was prepared with a twofold aim.

[1] *The Summing Up* (New York: The Literary Guild of America, Inc., 1938), pp. 181-82.

Such writing lacks rhythm because it conveys thoughts devoid of feeling. What a way to introduce a book full of songs about God as love and Christ as grace! What a pity, also, to put no heart into the preaching of the gospel! When a man puts feeling into his written sermon, it begins to assume a tone color all its own. As in the *Third Symphony* of Beethoven, or the *Seventh*, the tone color keeps shifting from part to part.

Early in the message thought may overshadow feeling, but after a while, when the heart begins to have its way, the words may become like those of a poet. Without falling into a cadence the sentences may flow with a rhythm all their own. For examples of such varying style, according to what the writer puts down on paper, read aloud two passages from Buttrick. In one case he is lecturing about the craftsmanship of the sermon; in the other he is preaching about the mystery of the Cross. Note the shades of tone color:

> The sermon must be written—not as an essay is written, but as a sermon is written; that is to say, with the eyes of the congregation (wistful, hungry, sad, or gayly indifferent) looking at the writer over his desk. Such writing is not an easy task. There will be days when the pen will not move. Preaching is a great art, akin to the painter's art. Every artist knows times when the spirit is inert and the travail of the mind seems barren. These dead hours, with futile struggle for their only life, can be a pain worse than physical pain. They are the cross by which alone, even in preaching, a man may attain unto the resurrection from the dead.[2]

> In that strange play, *The Green Pastures,* a voice sounds off-stage, as though all reverent humanity were speaking, "It's a terrible burden for one Man to carry!" Everybody's sins! My sins! Healed not in the symptoms; healed at their deep and bitter root, by the pains of God's suffering love! ... The Cross was not made of wood: it was made of sin. And the sin and the doubt swept together in one awful darkness to make an eclipse of God: "Eli, Eli, lama, sabachthani! My God, My God, why hast Thou forsaken me?" "It's a terrible burden for one Man to carry!" ... "In whom we have redemption thro' His blood." [3]

[2] *Jesus Came Preaching* (New York: Charles Scribner's Sons, 1931), pp. 156-57.
[3] From *The Great Themes of the Christian Faith*, arranged by Charles W. Ferguson, copyright 1930 by Harper & Bros. Used by permission. P. 22.

THE PREPARATION OF SERMONS

No one else could have written either of those paragraphs, because "The style is the man." But everyone whom the Lord wishes to preach the gospel can learn to write and speak with a touch of beauty. As with any other sort of goodness, beauty in words comes to the man who seeks after something else. When a minister sits down to write a sermon, he has in mind and heart a message he wishes to share with friends whom he can see only with the eyes of the soul. He thinks of them and of the truth they need; then he puts into words the thoughts and feelings he longs to share. He writes with the sort of rhythm that suits the mood of the passing moment. On the contrary, if he sought after beauty for its own sake, he might descend to "fine writing," which calls attention to itself and away from the Saviour.

Why stress the need of beauty? Because every sermon has to do with God the Father, the Author of beauty; with "Fairest Lord Jesus, Ruler of all nature"; or with the Holy Spirit, Giver of Light. In Holy Scripture, as in the Hymnal, the words that body forth the truth about God keep moving the hearts of men because the writers have put down on paper words full of truth and beauty. Where in the Bible, in the Church Hymnal, or in any sermon from a master hand, can you find such jargon as we often employ in speaking about God? The Bible and the Hymnal tell about the Lord as Light, Life. and Love; as Spirit and Father; whereas some of us prate about "the objectivization of the supernatural," and "the exclusiveness of our inwardness." Such mechanistic polysyllables suggest nothing about God except the sort of ugliness He abhors. Leave all such jargon to the classroom and to books! [4]

Does this discussion seem to call for feeling at the expense of thought? If so, turn to the published sermons of Horace Bushnell, who attracted to the North Church in Hartford thoughtful men from all over that city and far beyond. Note how he clothed his thoughts in words of beauty that sang their way into the souls of men. For example, read aloud his message on "Unconscious Influence," noting the beauty of the words and the way they flow. Throughout

[4] For a treatment of jargon see A. T. Quiller-Couch, *On the Art of Writing* (New York: G. P. Putnam's Sons, 1916), pp. 101-5.

the passage that follows think of the Christian in terms of "light, not lightning":

Behind the mere show, the outward noise and stir of the world, nature always conceals her hand of control, and the laws by which she rules. Who ever saw with the eye, for example, or heard with the ear, the exertion of that tremendous astronomic force, which every moment holds the impact of the physical universe together? The lightning is, in fact, but a mere fire-fly spark in comparison; but, because it glares on the clouds, and thunders so terribly in the ear, and rives the tree or the rock where it falls, many will be ready to think that it is a vastly more potent agent than gravity.[5]

That sermon as a whole impresses the reader today because of its beauty. So does many another sermon from Bushnell, such as one about "The Gentleness of God": "Thy gentleness hath made me great" (Ps. 18:35c).[6] This way of preaching accords with Bushnell's essay "Our Gospel a Gift to the Imagination." [7] By imagination he means ability to see what lies hidden from other eyes, and then to use words that others may see. As a lover of beauty that comes from God, Bushnell protests against fanciful writing, a kind of "ornamental, mind's-millinery faculty that excels in the tricking out of subjects in high-wrought metaphoric draperies. . . . The imagination has nothing to do with ornament. It is that which dawns in beauty like the day because the day is in it."

THE ELEMENT OF FORCE

Any correct theory of preaching also encourages a man to seek after force. Force, otherwise known as energy or effectiveness, refers to the impact of a message upon the one who hears or reads. Whenever a minister puts on paper thoughts charged with feeling, under the guidance of a will that the King controls, these words find their way to the conscience and will of the hearer or reader. Life and

[5] *Sermons for the New Life* (New York: Charles Scribner & Co., 1867), p. 189.
[6] *Christ and His Salvation* (London, 1871), pp. 18-38.
[7] *Building Eras in Religion*, p. 265.

motion, warmth and color, beauty that springs from imagination at work among the truths of God—all work together to make the hearer or reader feel that he has come near to the heart of God, and has received a message from the throne. What an ideal!

The style of a sermon differs from that of an essay. The sermon moves the will of the hearer to action, whereas the essay teaches or entertains, but does not try to transform. When Thomas Carlyle sent forth the essays *Heroes and Hero Worship,* he assumed the role of a preacher, but woe be to the local church where the man in the pulpit becomes an essayist. However beautiful the waters of an inland lake as it basks beneath the splendor of the skies, any such body of water needs an outlet, and so does the most beautiful sermon that ever came from human heart and lips. Let us think of beauty, therefore, not as an end in itself, but as a means to glorify God. Was it not always so in the teaching and preaching of our Lord?

The literary form of a message from the pulpit also differs from that of an oration on the platform. Why does the minister stand behind the Book and keep it lying open? Because the man behind the Book speaks in the name of his God: "Thus saith the Lord!" The interpreter of God's truth stands up to speak with a message and a power not his own. Ideally he calls no attention to himself or his use of words. Actually he wishes every eye to behold the King, and every heart to receive Him now. Once in a while, at a stage about which he cannot know in advance, he may rise as on eagle wings until he soars out among the stars and beholds visions never seen on earth; but the closer he comes to the gates of heaven, the more will his style differ from that of a platform performer.

Wherein the difference lies, who can tell? How can a student of preaching put his finger down on anything so elusive as the personality that makes itself known through words? One fact, however, any person can see: the minister speaks for God once or twice a week, month after month, year after year, whereas the orator can bide his time until an hour of crisis calls for a masterpiece. The most eloquent men in history—"Demosthenes, Cicero, Burke, Chatham, Webster, Calhoun, Sumner—have given possibly a score of orations in a lifetime.

It would be preposterous to expect from a minister two score of orations, or more, in a year." Many a pastor, indeed, attempts to address some of the same people over a hundred times within eleven months.

An appreciation of such a difference in style may help to keep the young minister from trying to prepare what Beecher labeled "show sermons." If the pastor were called to serve God as a political orator, he might strive to prepare a few great addresses, but the foremost pulpit orator in our history warned young ministers not to think in terms of "great sermons." He would have deplored the present tendency to stress greatness in sermons rather than goodness:

> Great sermons, young gentlemen, ninety-nine times in a hundred, are nuisances. They are like steeples without any bells in them; things stuck up high in the air, serving for ornament, attracting observation, but sheltering nobody, warming nobody, helping nobody. . . . Great sermons will come of themselves, when they are worth anything. Don't seek them. . . . I do not believe that any man ever made a great sermon who set out to do that thing.[8]

Instead of speaking about sermons as great, why do we not call them good, in the sense that such a message does people good? It leads to Christ the man who has been seeking after Him, and brings near to the Father anyone who longs to know Him better and love Him more. A good sermon makes men and women eager to do the will of God, and then shows them how. For this conception of content and style turn to Brooks. In his sermons you can find all sorts of messages that embody the ideals of the present chapter. Elsewhere you can read his advice to young ministers:

> Never tolerate any idea of the dignity of a sermon which will keep you from saying anything in it which you ought to say, or which your people ought to hear. . . . The sermons of which nobody speaks, the sermons which come from mind and heart, and go to heart and mind with as little consciousness as possible of tongue and ear, those are the sermons that do the work, that make men better, and really sing into their

---

[8] The *Yale Lectures on Preaching*, first series, pp. 32, 226.

affections. They are like perfect days when . . . every man does his best work and feels most fully what a blessed thing it is to live.[9]

Suggested Readings

Donnelly, F. P. *The Art of Interesting*. New York: J. P. Kenedy and Sons, 1920.

Hoyt, Arthur S. *The Work of Preaching*. New York: The Macmillan Co., 1917.

Mather, Frank J. *Concerning Beauty*. Princeton: Princeton University Press, 1935.

Oman, John. *Concerning the Ministry*. London, 1936.

Saintsbury, George. *A History of English Prose Rhythm*. New York: The Macmillan Co., 1922.

[9] *Lectures on Preaching*, p. 151.

CHAPTER XVI

The Marks of Effective Style

THE WRITING OF SERMONS calls for the skill of an artist in the use of words. At one and the same time he can set forth life and motion, warmth and color, beauty and force. All of that, under God, depends on a man's personality, and personality ever eludes our grasp, like quicksilver. But now we turn to something tangible. Not every young minister knows how to prepare a discourse with all of these excellences, certainly not once or twice a week; but every young preacher can form the habit of testing his handiwork, and striving to make it better week after week. So let him take as a motto the words of Paul to young Timothy: "Do your best to present yourself to God as one approved, a workman who has no need to be ashamed, rightly handling the word of truth" (II Tim. 2:15 R.S.V.).

How then should a minister judge his written work? Let us bring the matter down to earth and out into the open. Here lies a manuscript after the first writing. Let us begin with the simplest and easiest test, that of clarity. Clarity refers to writing and speaking that no reader or hearer can misunderstand. Only a visitor among churches can know how many intelligent laymen fail to follow the pastor's sermons. In recent days such complaints have come to one observer from lay officers in churches far from each other and far from his home. In reporting about a pastor with ability, these laymen complain, "Half the time some of us do not know what he is driving at, and we wonder if he knows!"

In his autobiography Joseph Fort Newton quotes the president of a large university:

That is the first sermon I have heard in a long time that I understood. Men have come here to argue about God, trying to prove something that nobody denies until they try to prove it. As a layman I am not up on theology, but you talked about life.[1]

[1] *River of Years* (Philadelphia: J. B. Lippincott Co., 1947), pp. 244-45.

Perhaps those visiting preachers strove to seem scholarly, but if so, they did not know how, and they merely stirred up waters full of mud. In the same book Newton tells how he first sensed the importance of making everything clear to the average man or woman. He concludes that clarity calls for far more ability and work than its opposite.

Among ordinary churchgoers, a gloomy observer estimates that about 2 per cent of the preaching gets across. Now that psychologists have begun to test the "audience response" in church, some of them would raise the proportion a little, but not far. They would also advise the pastor to sit down in his study and test his written work. How? The answer may come from a recent book by an expert in his field, Rudolf Flesch, whose work has nothing directly to do with religion. This author ignores the beauty of written words, and goes into mathematical calculations that do not concern us here. Otherwise his principles will guide any clergyman in checking up on his preaching style.[2]

If a minister wishes to make everything in a sermon clear, he must feel sure about the goal, and then have a sense of direction. He must school himself to state and explain, describe and discuss. At times he must repeat, and perhaps illustrate. For examples of such clarity turn to Macaulay, in whose prose works clear writing comes from clear thinking. On the other hand, alas, clear thinking does not always lead to clear writing and speaking. Hence a minister needs to revise the first draft of his sermon.

Revision may begin with the paragraph. In modern prose a writer or speaker who knows his business pays attention to the paragraph, giving it much the same treatment that the composer of a hymn accords the stanza. Current practice calls for paragraphs of about a hundred words, perhaps a little more. If the units of thought run much over a hundred words, the work may seem heavy. If the paragraphs stop short of a hundred words, the effect may become choppy. Within the limits of a hundred words, or a little more, a writer or

[2] See Rudolf Flesch, *The Art of Plain Talk* (New York: Harper & Bros., 1946).

speaker can state and develop a single idea. If he wishes to say more, he can frame another paragraph. All of this may sound like machine work, but so would any statement about the length of stanzas in a hymn.

Each paragraph may start with a key sentence, clear and crisp. The rest of the hundred words explain and enforce the idea in the opening sentence. After the final revision, when the preacher goes over the manuscript before the hour of delivery, he can size it up by glancing at the key sentences. If he expects to preach from notes, he can write down the paragraph openings; and if he wishes fuller notes, he can jot down both the beginning and the end of each unit. A good paragraph starts with clarity and ends with force. All that comes between the first sentence and the last one helps to round out the whole. For an example of such a paragraph read aloud Lincoln's address at Gettysburg. Better still, divide it into two parts, each with a few more than a hundred words.

Within the paragraph look at the sentences. Are they clear and easy to follow? Does the same subject carry over from sentence to sentence, or does the thought shift back and forth like a tennis ball in a championship match? Does the same tense prevail, or must the attention turn from past to present and from future to past? How often does the speaker expect the hearer to shift his mental gears? As often as necessary to follow the thought, but a wise speaker learns to avoid shifting within a paragraph. Of course someone might apply these suggestions crudely, as with a hammer. But if a man works carefully, as an artist toils over a painting before he counts it complete, the paragraphs and sentences will come out clear.

In each paragraph the final sentence ought to prepare for what follows. In the next paragraph the opening sentence should tie up with what has gone before. Then the successive parts will constitute a train of thought, with never a break from the beginning to the end of the sermon. Such writing and speaking call for the use of connectives, all sorts of connectives except the conspicuous. As coupling pins these words and phrases show transitions from paragraph to paragraph, and often from sentence to sentence. Coupling pins appear more often in the work of a teaching minister than in that of an inspirational speaker. For instance, you find more careful use of connectives in the sermons of Bushnell than in those of Brooks, in the pulpit work of Fosdick than in the pep talks of "Dr. Sunny Jim."

As for sentences, no young minister would try to carry out all of the following suggestions in one week. But in the course of months a few rules may help a man secure clarity.

1. *Avoid making a detour* within a sentence. Keep on the main highway. Never clutter up a sentence with a parenthesis, like the one that follows, in the sort of sloppy stuff that some of us think profound: "In writing a treatise a scholarly author (knowing that the reader can glance back and see where he got off the road) may—like a playwright in an 'aside'—employ parentheses such as these, but twice as long and much more tortuous."

2. Keep the *subject close to the predicate*. As a minister grows older, he tends to introduce explanatory clauses, and so to become increasingly incoherent. When he comes to the middle of a sentence that rambles over the hills like a rail fence, he forgets where that section of the fence ought to end. If any reader feels that he has learned how to keep from rambling, let him secure a recording machine and have an expert take down the sermon and the prayers next Sunday morning. Only an exceptional leader goes through an hour of public worship without using sentences that wobble or break down in the middle.

3. Keep *most of the sentences short*. In the words of Flaubert, a master of the novel, "Banish the semicolon. Whenever you can shorten the sentence, do. And one always can. The best sentence? The shortest!" In the handiwork of a dunce the habit of using short sentences might lead to nonsense or even bathos, but why should a dunce try to preach? Even if a dunce did preach, he would not write out sermons and then revise them with care. Only a wise man does that. But not every wise man keeps his sentences short. Gossip feels free at times to use ones that run beyond a hundred words, whereas Flesch recommends an average of about seventeen.[3] The best wisdom of our day

[3] *Ibid.*, pp. 31-39.

calls for prose sentences shorter than those of yesterday, but still not choppy.

4. Within the sentence *watch the sequence of ideas* by keeping your eye on the ball. Avoid saying, "When the people assembled for worship, a beautiful Cross was seen." Fix attention on the people, or else on the Cross. Form the habit of using an active verb to show action: "When the people gathered for worship, they beheld a beautiful Cross." This habit of keeping the mind moving in the same direction may help a man to avoid embarrassment. In the copy for next Sunday morning's bulletin he may have to correct an item from the church secretary: "At the Women's Society last Thursday, Miss Minerva Brown spoke on 'Personal Devils'; sixty-five were present."

THE CALL FOR INTEREST

We might go on to think about clarity in the use of words, but we turn to human interest, only to find it more important and more difficult to attain. Needless to say, the two terms overlap, for both clarity and interest have to do with words, sentences, and paragraphs, even with whole sermons. Sometimes, however, the claims of clarity and those of interest seem to conflict. Clarity may call for short sentences, but a succession of them, too much alike, might become as monotonous as ties in a railroad track. When the use of short sentences begins to attract attention to itself, the speaker has employed one too many. In short, keep your balance!

Any child of ten can write short sentences, straight and stiff, like pickets in a fence. But a man who knows his Bible can use sentences that accord with the tone color of what he wishes to say. Often he employs something with a balance that resembles Hebrew parallelism, much as our Lord spoke about treasures on earth and treasures in heaven. Robertson preached this way, if only for variety. As an example of a balanced sentence take this one about Great Britain: "The king has glory without much power; the prime minister has power without much glory."

Robertson framed many of his sentences this way because his mind

THE PREPARATION OF SERMONS

and heart dwelt much on truths that balanced. For a more recent example of a balanced style turn to part of a message by Henry Van Dyke. At a university chapel he spoke on "The Meaning of Manhood," from the text: "How much then is a man better than a sheep?" (Matt. 12:12).

"How much is that man worth?" asks the curious observer. "That man," says the walking business directory, "is worth a million dollars: and the man sitting next to him is not worth a penny." . . .

What can this man make; how much has that man made; how much can I make out of this man's labor; how much will that man pay for my services? . . .

Those little children that play in the streets—they are nothing to me or to the world; they are worthless. Those long-fleeced, high-bred sheep that feed upon my pastures—they are among my most costly possessions; they will bring an enormous price; they are immensely valuable. "How much, then, is a man better than a sheep?" What a foolish question! Sometimes the man is better; sometimes the sheep is better. It all depends on the supply and demand.[4]

The use of balance in sentences and elsewhere in writing calls for ability and practice. The mastery of the periodic sentence affords a still more conclusive proof of a man's education and culture. In our day, however, through no fault of his own, many a college graduate seems never to have heard of the periodic sentence. When a seminary student asks what the term means, the professor may quote an example: "Though I speak with the tongues of men and of angels, and have not love, I am become as sounding brass" (I Cor. 13:1). If the Apostle had stopped there, he would have used periodic structure, but the sentence goes on with another phrase that adds to the charm: "or a tinkling cymbal." In the verse as a whole note the alliteration and the assonance, the rhythm and the repetition for emphasis.

In reading or speaking a periodic sentence the minister needs to sustain his voice, with a sort of suspense, and not let it fall until he comes to the word that completes his thought the first time; in this

[4] W. H. Sallmon, ed., *The Culture of Christian Manhood* (New York: F. H. Revell Co., 1897).

case, "brass." In that message from Van Dyke the use of balanced sentences gives way at times to the periodic; for example, "If wealth is really the measure of value, if the end of life is the production or acquisition of riches, then humanity must take its place in the sliding scale of commodities." More tersely, a concert artist tells a beginner: "When you stand up to sing, if you feel nervous, slowly inhale three full breaths." In like manner, young minister, if you would add to the variety and appeal of your spoken words, learn to use a periodic sentence occasionally, if only for the sake of variety and suspense.[5]

In that sermon from Van Dyke the closing paragraph illustrates another "rule of the road": a few successive sentences alike in form often prove more effective than an equal number of statements all diverse. In the appeal that follows note the use of parallelism, the quietness of rhythm, the repetition for emphasis, and the willingness to stop before repetition tires. Also see how Van Dyke as a pulpit master spoke to the heart of the university student:

> Come then to Christ, who alone can save you from the sin that defiles and destroys your manhood. Come then to Christ, who alone can make you good men and true, living in the power of an endless life. Come then to Christ, that you may have fellowship with Him, and realize all it means to be a man.

"All it means to be a man!" What an ending for a message about "The Meaning of Manhood"! The ability to speak with clarity and interest depends almost as much on mastery of words as of sentences. "No material with which human beings work has so much potential energy as words." Through everyday use of the dictionary, and through the companionship of books, the minister can discipline himself to speak correctly and precisely without seeming pedantic. He knows that "few" relates to number and "less" to quantity, that a farmer "sows" wheat and "plants" corn, but never feeds "fodder" to sheep. In the church bulletin and elsewhere the pastor avoids referring to "Reverend Jones" in lieu of "The Reverend John Henry

[5] For a discussion of sentences see Reed Smith, *Learning to Write in College* (Boston: Little, Brown & Co., 1939), pp. 69-87, 188-235.

THE PREPARATION OF SERMONS

Jones," "The Rev. Dr. Jones," or occasionally, "Rev. John H. Jones."
Much more important than such precision is human interest. If a
preacher wishes to use words that appeal to ordinary people, let him
widen the range of his vocabulary. Where a novice would employ the
colorless word "great" to describe everything from a sonnet to a
cyclone, Bushnell or Gossip would give the call to live words, fact
words, action words, words with "hands and feet." By using live words
the speaker can show the hearer a succession of motion pictures. For
examples of live words go to the teachings of our Lörd, especially to
that parable about the two builders: "I will liken him unto a wise man,
which built his house upon a rock; and the rain descended, and the
floods came, and the winds blew, and beat upon that house; and it fell
not: for it was founded upon a rock" (Matt. 7:24-25).

In these forty-three words note the number of appeals to see, to
feel, to do. Of such live words a student has found fifteen, or one
out of every three. Whatever the number, it exceeds that on many a
page of sermonic prose. Once again, note how the Master Teacher
heightens the effect by going on to repeat His words, this time
negatively, about the house on the sand. In each half of the word
picture he points to one builder, not to eight or ten, and to one in
action, not in repose. The Teacher also throws His stress on nouns and
verbs, especially verbs of action. Except for "wise man" and "foolish
man," each of which points to a single builder, He employs no
descriptive adjective or adverb. By such artistry in the use of words
He attains a beauty like that of a rainbow after a storm in June.

> God wove a web of loveliness,
> Of clouds and storms and birds,
> But made not anything at all
> So beautiful as words.[6]

By way of contrast, see how not to use words. In 1768 a New
Testament "scholar," Edward Harwood, issued what he styled an
"elegant rendering" of the parable we all know best and love most.

[6] Anna Hempstead Branch, *The Shoes That Danced* (Boston: Houghton Mifflin,
1905), p. 156.

In this excerpt note the scarcity of live words, and then look at the "duds." See how the use of modifiers weakens the effect in detail and mars the picture as a whole:

A gentleman of a splendid family and opulent fortune had two sons. One day the younger approached his father, and begged him in the most importunate and soothing terms to make a partition of his effects betwixt himself and his elder brother. The indulgent father, overcome by his blandishments, immediately divided all his fortune between them.

Today no one but a pedant would resort to such pomposity. However, with a jargon all our own we of today can make the prodigal son and his elder brother seem commonplace or unreal. Even when we refer to the father who forgave his younger son, we may talk in terms of "reaction," "characterization," "realization," and "implications." We may overwork "particularly"—a word especially difficult to articulate. In other connections we may refer to "this war-torn world," "the far-flung battle line," and "needing no introduction to this audience." Why should an educated man ever resort to a cliché? A wise minister, though a Protestant, can set up an *Index Expurgatorius;* at least he can follow the injunction of Alexander Pope:

> In words as fashions the same rule will hold,
> Alike fantastic if too new or old:
> Be not the first by whom the new are tried,
> Nor yet the last to lay the old aside.

Fortunately no one minister needs all of these counsels. If in college and seminary a young man has formed the right sort of habits, most of these matters take care of themselves. In lieu of such discipline in the past a young preacher may need to check up on his ways of using words, sentences, and paragraphs. The man whose pulpit speech tends to be clear and dull needs to discover ways of securing interest, whereas the one who knows how to grip the hearer, only to leave him confused, needs to strive after clarity. In the pulpit human interest far outweighs clearness, but still many an interesting preacher ought to study the words of our Lord: "He that received seed into the good

THE PREPARATION OF SERMONS

ground is he that heareth the word, and understandeth it" (Matt.
13:23).

Does any pastor wish to enjoy writing a sermon every week? If so, let him determine to prepare every message as well as his abilities permit. In the service of our King, whatever a man does well he begins to enjoy, and whatever he enjoys he tends to do well. "Learning to write may be a serious business, but it need not be a solemn one." As for ability to write with ease, and at times with a touch of distinction, all of that comes to the man who lives with good books, especially poetry, and then writes something every day—it may be a prayer. "Write much, if you would write well."

What an ideal! To transform drudgery into delight! Even if this ideal eludes a man's grasp, the pursuit will bring him satisfaction of heart. As the biographies of countless artists make clear, every man who would become a master of words must toil at his task. For instance, when still a young man John Masefield, afterwards poet laureate, looked out at a sailing vessel and then sang about the effect on his mastery of words:

> When I saw
> Her masts across the river rising queenly,
> Built out of so much chaos brought to law,
> I learned the power of knowing how to draw,
> Of beating thought into the perfect line;
> I vowed to make that power of beauty mine.[7]

Suggested Readings

[7] From the original version of *Dauber*. Used by permission of the author.

CHAPTER XVII

The Preparation for Speaking

THE POPULAR effectiveness of a man's pulpit work depends largely on his ability to speak. The spiritual value, under God, comes mainly from the purpose of the speaker and the content of the sermon, but in the eyes of many laymen neither purpose nor content bulks so large as ability to speak effectively. In other times the same feeling prevailed; for example, according to a Methodist editor of ability who had studied public speaking through the ages, George Whitefield as a preacher became popular rather than powerful; John Wesley, powerful rather than popular.[1] Whitefield excelled in the delivery of sermons, and John Wesley in most other aspects of preaching. How else could Whitefield have moved throngs of people to tears with a spoken message that now in print seems commonplace?

Those two men illustrate the description of preaching as truth through personality: in Wesley truth stood out, and in Whitefield, personality. In the pulpit today truth still voices itself in two ways, and in only two, known technically as homiletics and public speaking. Of the two, as Whitefield and others have shown, speaking has more to do with popular effectiveness. If most laymen now had to choose between a minister who speaks well but does not shine homiletically and one who excels as a maker of sermons but not as a speaker, they would prefer the former. For this fact a young minister should give thanks, because he will find it easier to excel as a speaker than to master the art of preparing sermons. Ideally, of course, the two sorts of work belong together as closely as husband and wife, whom no man can put asunder.

So let us watch a young pastor in the study on Friday or Saturday morning, and see how he prepares to deliver a message at the coming

---

[1] See J. M. Buckley, *Extemporaneous Oratory* (New York: Methodist Book Concern, n.d.), p. 363. Also see Ezek. 33:30-33.

service. As a wise man he apportions his study time, because it belongs to God and to the people. At least for the first few years, while learning his craft, a young preacher may devote to sermon preparation fifteen or twenty hours a week. Fosdick reports that through the years he has spent in preparation an hour for every minute of delivery; and elsewhere he refers to a sermon—not over the radio—as calling for thirty-five minutes. Not every young preacher can give that much time to the preparation of a sermon, but the example suggests a working ideal: in the study devote enough time to make ready for every message.

How should a man distribute these hours between homiletics and public speaking? Many who teach the former plead for more time and attention to making ready for delivery. We dare not lay down laws like those of the Medes and Persians, but we wish that every young pastor would start with the habit of devoting all his God-given powers to preparation for the delivery of every sermon. Early in the seminary course, the earlier the better, the student ought to decide which of four methods he will adopt.

THE FOUR METHODS OF DELIVERY

1. *Preaching without notes:* This way of speaking appeared among all the prophets and apostles, not to mention our Lord. When did Isaiah or Paul ever read a message from a scroll or repeat it by rote instead of speaking from heart to heart and eye to eye? The same held true of their successors until comparatively modern times, for not until after the Reformation did any considerable number of conscientious preachers begin to adopt other ways of delivery. Although the prophetic and apostolic tradition about speaking does not come to us with the force of law, the fact that the mightiest of God's heralds in olden times preached without notes ought to create a presupposition in favor of this method now. In what other fashion can any minister today speak so naturally?

Preaching without notes assumes various forms. Here we refer to only one, which calls for mastery of the sermon plan and for memorizing only a few sentences. Like Alexander Maclaren, Charles R.

Brown, former dean of Yale, commits to memory only the first and the last four sentences of a sermon. No doubt he also has in mind a few other landmarks which he wishes to point out in delivery. Otherwise he plans to utter words that well up from the heart when he rises to speak for God. In the study he has filled both heart and mind with truth and duty that he wishes to share with his lay friends, and in the pulpit he trusts God to supply the overflow in the form of words. What a natural way to speak from the pulpit, and how difficult a way to prepare in the study!

This kind of delivery calls for skill and courage. The skill appears in the study, not in the pulpit, for a wise man calls no attention to how he speaks. In the study he maps out the route and then pores over the trail, so that he could follow it with ease if his vision began to grow dim when he rose to preach and did not clear up until he had finished, or at an evening service if the lights went out when he began and came on again during the benediction. In either case he might shorten the sermon, but not because he had lost the way "amid the encircling gloom." Even in the best-regulated edifice, the lights do go out at inconvenient times, with no warning. Sometimes even the most circumspect preacher who wears spectacles must rise to speak with no such aid. Then he thanks God that he has prepared to preach without notes.

The courage appears when a man goes to the pulpit without any paper and trusts the Lord to guide him in the delivery of the message he has prepared. In the sanctuary such a minister forgets all about his training in homiletics and public speaking. During the earlier parts of public worship he need not think about his sermon. Indeed, he cannot do so if he joins with the other children of God in corporate worship. When at length he rises to preach, his knees may shake and his pulse beat fast, but he looks on all that as a test of courage. Why should a man of valor shirk what he finds hard?

This way of preaching, after careful preparation, appeals to the majority of churchgoers today. If a man of mature years has something to say, and if he knows how to put a sermon on paper, some of his hearers do not object to his use of notes, or even to his reading a manuscript. However, most laymen feel that the minister has a whole week to prepare, and that he ought to speak like an attorney at the bar, who can plead for an hour with never a manuscript or a note. In the vernacular speech of an old Virginia woodsman, a hunter with a keen eye and a steady hand "shoots without a rest."

In this judgment about the most effective delivery, psychologists agree with common people. In the laboratory scholars who specialize in the psychology of attention have found that public speaking at its best interposes no barrier between speaker and hearer. When tongue and eye should work together to body forth the truth of God, why let a piece of paper intervene? Remember that the mind of the hearer tends to follow the eye of the speaker. Why then look at paper rather than people? According to a master teacher of the art a piece of paper in the hand, or a manuscript on the pulpit, "puts a spot in the eye" rather than a picture in the soul. However, when a man reads a lesson from Holy Writ, he should call attention to what he reads, and not to himself.

2. *Speaking from memory:* What if a young man lacks skill enough to prepare and courage enough to preach without notes? Then he may commit the sermon to memory, word for word, or at least imperfectly. In certain cases this method accords with the workings of a mind which may have powers almost photographic. In such a case the friend in the study can write out his message, revise it with care, and then read it through once or twice, knowing that in the pulpit his memory will enable him to reproduce it all verbatim. If he has schooled himself to speak naturally, and not like a phonograph or a parrot, he may soar to heights that other preachers seldom attain. In France during the seventeenth century a group of pulpit orators in the Roman Church rose to fame largely because of sermons delivered *memoriter*. In the Protestant pulpit, also, such "pulpit oratory" has been more common than many hearers have supposed.

Few ministers, however, can rely on such powers. Beecher, for instance, always insisted that he had a poor verbal memory. In the cathedral at Glasgow, Lauchlan MacLean Watt reports that he cannot trust his memory to reproduce the simplest hymn publicly, no matter how well he knows it in private. If some ecclesiastical court decreed that ministers had to commit sermons to memory word for word, some of the ablest preachers would have to leave that branch of the Church. Every man could rely on his memory more fully if he exercised it more often, but psychologists have found that ability to memorize and recall differs with various persons, according to their make-up. As the Apostle tells us, we ministers "have this treasure in earthen vessels" (II Cor. 4:7), which sometimes means that God blesses the pulpit work of a man without a phenomenal memory for words. In any case, why not dare to speak without notes?

3. *Preaching from a manuscript:* In the history of the pulpit since the Reformation more than a few of the mightiest preachers have read their discourses. Some men read word for word; e.g., Hooker, Taylor, South; Newman, Liddon, Farrar; Jonathan Edwards, Channing, Bushnell, and George A. Gordon; with others who adorn the pulpit today.[2] In fact, the most impressive preaching many of us have ever enjoyed has come from the manuscript. Whenever John Henry Jowett or Henry Van Dyke entered the pulpit, he would read the sermon. Ah, but what reading! At Harvard, the head professor of public speaking used to send his students to chapel to watch Van Dyke as a model in public address. Every once in a while that master of assemblies would glance down at his written sermon, perhaps to note the beginning of a new paragraph, but most of the time he kept looking at the hearers, eye to eye. So he might almost as well have been speaking from notes consisting of paragraph headings.

The ordinary reader of sermons from the pulpit, however, seems to lose himself in the manuscript and forget the hearers. In self-defense he may plead that Chalmers always read his messages, word for word, and that he would set the hearts of the hearers on fire. If Chalmers could return to the pulpit now he might inflame the spirits of men, but his mantle as a prophet of fire seems not to have fallen on his ministerial admirers. Since he came close to being a

[2] For a list of preachers using various methods, see John M. English, *For Pulpit and Platform* (New York: The Macmillan Co., 1919), chap. V, especially pp. 77-78.

THE PREPARATION OF SERMONS

genius, why should he serve as a model for a pastor with two talents, or even for a man with five? Except in the hands of a minister with rare pulpit gifts, the use of a manuscript constitutes a handicap. Such a statement obviously involves no criticism of the manuscript preacher with superior powers, or of any man who reads a sermon once in a while, on a very special occasion.

The minister who adopts this method ought to do so with open eyes. If he plans to carry a manuscript into the pulpit, he should make no concealment or display and offer no apology. But he ought to understand that he appears to be tacitly making three claims. He seems to be setting up three hurdles such as few men can clear successfully Sunday after Sunday. (1) "I have here a message so masterly that I must present it exactly in this form." To a disbeliever in the method that sounds like a claim of "verbal inspiration." (2) "I have written with such artistry that I must call attention to my literary prowess." Perhaps so, from a given viewpoint, but who can produce a masterpiece of literature every week? (3) "I can read with such skill that no one will dream I am reading." Interesting, if true, and plausible—all of that plea. But only an exceptional minister can preach this way without calling attention to himself and his powers.

4. *Preaching from notes:* The majority of parish ministers prefer this fourth method. They consider it the easiest for the average minister from week to week and the best for the hearers at an ordinary service, because this way of preaching calls for less preparation in the study, and involves less nervous strain in the pulpit. Ideally notes of the proper kind interpose no mental barrier between speaker and hearers. If he knows how to make sermon notes in the study, and how to use them in the pulpit, he may in preaching glance down once in a while without calling attention to what he is doing. Practically, however, few ministers can keep from calling attention to their use of notes.

> O wad some Pow'r the giftie gie us
> To see oursels as ithers see us!

Pulpit notes of the right sort give a bird's eye view of the manuscript that reposes on the table in the study, so that the bony frame-

198

work of the message stands out boldly on two opposite pages of a loose-leaf notebook about five by seven inches. This notebook contains in order every piece of paper the minister will need during the service. The two pages of sermon notes consist of key words, which the roving eye will catch at a glance and comprehend with ease because the "see-er" has put the markers there. On the way home after the service the "sky pilot" may recall that he did not need to look down once to get his bearings. He had been over the route so often mentally that he knew the way straight to the destination. But still he felt a sense of security because of those beacon lights.

In preparing to speak from notes a pastor may work in various ways, notably in two which differ much. At the morning service he may deliver a message that he has written out quickly, and revised with care, so that the notes give a résumé of the manuscript. At the second service, or more than once on a weekday, he may speak on the basis of a careful and extensive plan, of which the pulpit notes give the high spots. If a minister follows these two ways of preparation in the study week after week, he gains benefits that accrue from both ways of working: those that come from writing in full, with careful revision, and those that come from preparing less formally, with more appeal to the heart. But all the while, the written manuscript, carefully revised and ready for the storehouse, ought to serve as the norm. In the course of years the pastor's files will become full of such treasures, all of his own minting and more precious than gold.

So the young pastor must choose among four methods of preparing to deliver a sermon. He may reply to this suggestion: "I use all four at the same time! After I write out a sermon and revise it as carefully as time permits, I learn it by heart, but not word for word. Then I make an abstract which I carry into the pulpit. In the delivery I aim to speak without notes, but if I falter I find them a present help in time of trouble." Wherein does the young man err? Perhaps not at all! If this way of preparing to speak brings him peace of heart and enables him to meet human needs, let him rejoice. But if he brought seminary students a lecture on how to prepare a sermon, he would not recommend this way of getting ready to speak.

Many of us advocate preaching without notes, but we do not feel that this method fits all ministers alike, or the same man all the time. A certain pastor, for instance, made it a rule to speak without notes every Lord's Day but one—the one when he presented the financial program for the coming year. Since the officers in charge asked him to prepare such a special sermon, he wrote it out in the first draft and then submitted it to these lay friends. In the revised form he embodied all of their suggestions that he found feasible. In the pulpit, before he began to read the "co-operative sermon," he told the people what he had done and why. The fact that he did not read any other sermon all year, or even use notes, made this message the most memorable in the twelve months. What a wise way of safeguarding one's steps, and of making a special sermon appear distinctive!

Now for a word of caution: preaching without notes can never become foolproof. As everyone knows, some of the weakest pulpiteers patter and prate or ramble and roar without notes or anything else except wind and gall. But they need not concern us now, for men of that ilk never read books about preaching, or bother about doing it better. On the other hand, the wise man studies the facts in the case, including his own abilities and limitations. Then he chooses a method of speaking. He chooses deliberately, and for life. Let us hope that he decides to preach without notes, at least most of the time.

The man who approaches middle age may need counsel of another sort. If so, let him read the autobiography of Bishop Edwin H. Hughes, who sent out that work when seventy-six years young. In speaking to a friend who asked about the prevailing sin of ministerial life, the bishop declared:

Extemporaneousness! . . . This temptation comes in the middle years. . . . There is "a destruction that wasteth at noonday." . . . The habit of the pen is not only a taskmaster that commands to industry; it is a guard against carelessness. . . . I have a tremor when I recall how I almost succumbed to extemporaneousness. . . . When we are careless in our preparation we are not good men. . . . Extemporaneousness may spell the loss of character. We are followers of One who said, "I must work." [3]

THE PREPARATION FOR SPEAKING

Outside the pulpit any man with brains enough to preach can learn to talk correctly and pleasingly. If he wishes never to make a grammatical blunder or a rhetorical slip in the pulpit, he should avoid everything of the sort in private conversation, because either good form or bad becomes a matter of habit. The same holds true in the pronunciation of words such as "saith" (seth) and "apostle" (aposle), or "wash" (wŏsh, not warsh). If a pastor wishes to hold the respect of high-school students, he does not split the infinitive and break other rules that they learn from the lady professor of English. Especially should he beware whenever he puts in the bulletin or reads from the pulpit anything he has written, for as one college student said to another: "It sounds strange to hear a college and seminary graduate reading grammatical errors of his own making. Why doesn't the man correct his own copy? Perhaps he doesn't know how!" [4]

In the study a minister needs to deal with such matters much more directly. After he has a sermon in shape, all written out and revised, he should go through it with care to be sure that he can pronounce every word correctly and to decide which parts he ought to emphasize most.[5] On the manuscript he may underline any word or phrase he wishes to stress, and make a vertical mark to indicate a pause, with two such marks to show a longer pause. Even if a minister expects to speak without notes and without having memorized more than four or five sentences, he ought to prepare for the right sort of emphasis. To most of these matters we shall return in the next chapter, but we cannot state them too often or stress them too much.

In the delivery, even more than in the composition, the effect of

---

[3] *I Was Made a Minister* (New York and Nashville: Abingdon-Cokesbury Press, 1943), pp. 311-14.

[4] See L. H. Chrisman, *The English of the Pulpit.*

[5] For a painstaking treatment see R. W. Kirkpatrick, *The Creative Delivery of Sermons* (New York: The Macmillan Co., 1944).

a sermon depends largely on emphasis, and that depends in part on the pause. A skillful speaker forms the habit of stressing in each sentence the thought word or phrase. If he follows the principles of this book so far, he depends on nouns and verbs more than on other parts of speech, stressing nouns because they provide power and verbs because they show power at work.[6] But if anyone writes and speaks in some other way which calls for anemic nouns and inactive verbs, he will need to stress other parts of speech.

As with all man-made rules about work for God, this idea permits exceptions. In a golden chapter from Isaiah, for instance, the order of the Hebrew calls for stress on the pronouns: "He was wounded for *our* transgressions" (53:5a); but after the first appearance of this pronoun, the stress may begin to shift. The same kind of exception appears in the words of our Lord: "Come unto *me*, all ye that labour and are heavy laden" (Matt. 11:28a). On the other hand, why break up the rhythm and misinterpret the meaning by constantly thumping secondary words, as in the following verse: "Seek *ye* first *the* kingdom of God, and *his* righteousness; *and* all these things *shall* be added *unto* you" (Matt. 6:33)? Fortunately the verse contains no modifiers for any minister to maul. An English lover of preaching states the matter succinctly but perhaps too simply:

Always accentuate new matter, and only new matter. A pronoun having an antecedent is never new matter. To this there are only two exceptions. You do not accentuate the negative, even when it is new; and you accentuate the positive, even when it is not.[7]

Most laymen, however, will pardon errors in emphasis if they can hear with ease and satisfaction. Some of them have begun to grow slightly deaf, all unconsciously, and though they sit back near the door, they insist on hearing every word as clearly as the church bell. They find it hard to catch the words of a man who rants and roars, rushing along pell-mell, as if fleeing from a forest fire. Still less can they follow the speaker who swallows words at the end of a

[6] See Rudolf Flesch, *op. cit.*, chap. VIII.
[7] John Oman, *Concerning the Ministry* (London, 1936), p. 111.

sentence and mumbles others in the middle. Unwisely they demand that the pastor speak louder,[8] whereas they ought to pray about his articulation. So be sure to "carve every word before you let it fall."

For an object lesson of a "carrying voice," carrying because of articulation rather than volume, read about Whitefield or Spurgeon, William J. Bryan or George W. Truett. As a growing boy in North Carolina Truett liked to talk things over with a brother who could not hear ordinary conversation. By practically forcing himself to speak deliberately and articulate distinctly, the future minister of the vast First Baptist Church in Dallas unknowingly prepared for his lifework.[9] In later years, when he spoke in the open air, either from the steps of the Capitol at Washington, D.C., or to cattlemen on the plains of West Texas, he could make his voice heard at any distance, without effort by speaker or hearer. So he could preach out under the sky with assurance, like the Master Himself on the shore of Lake Galilee.

Even if the preacher makes himself easily audible, the succession of soothing words may induce sleep, or at least a desire for sleep. In his autobiography Bishop Hughes protests against much pulpit work of today as too tame. He insists that preaching of late has often lacked life and motion, warmth and color. Because of belief in a conversational style—a belief that every intelligent person shares—some preachers have fallen into the habit of monotonous soliloquizing, whereas the spirit of the evangel calls for something of adventure and romance. When delivered as an absorbing conversation with the friends in the pew, such a sermon may resemble a journey through the hills and valleys along the upper Susquehanna River rather than a trip through the Sahara Desert.

The delivery of a sermon calls for earnestness, which comes to be second nature with the preacher who believes what he says and longs for everyone present to believe as well as act. Of his work in the study week after week the pastor should be able to say: "While I was

[8] See E. E. Calkins, *Louder Please!* (Boston: Little, Brown & Co.); also *And Hearing Not* (New York: Charles Scribner's Sons, 1946).

[9] See P. W. James, *George W. Truett*, revised edition (New York: The Macmillan Co., 1945).

musing, the fire burned." Whenever such a prophet of fire goes into the pulpit, his words flow into other hearts and cause them to burn. If a preacher's heart burns with a consuming desire to see men and women transformed by the grace of God and enlisted in the work of the Kingdom, he must speak with enthusiasm, which here means "God in a man of His own choosing." In other days such a spirit of contagious enthusiasm went by the name of "unction," and on the higher levels, "holy passion." [10]

On the other hand, no one today desires a return to "hifalutin" oratory, so called. Why should an apostle of peace and joy ever become so excited that he shouts and screams as he rushes along and makes sensitive hearers squirm? The ambassador of King Jesus ought to manifest self-control: "Be not like a torrent; pause sometimes." Otherwise, impassioned speech may seem like

> . . . a tale
> Told by an idiot, full of sound and fury,
> Signifying nothing.

These words from *Macbeth* suggest others from *Hamlet* equally well known:

> Do not saw the air too much with your hand, thus, but use all gently; for in the very torrent, tempest, and, as I may say, the whirlwind of passion, you must acquire and beget a temperance that may give it smoothness. O, it offends me to the soul to hear a robustious periwig-pated fellow tear a passion to tatters, to very rags, to split the ears of the groundlings, who for the most part are capable of nothing but inexplicable dumb-shows and noise. . . . Suit the action to the word, the word to the action; with this special observance, that you o'erstep not the modesty of nature.

"The modesty of nature" leads a man to keep his balance and call no attention to his ways of speaking. If he has inherited a nervous temperament, like that of Peter or Martin Luther, the preacher should learn to maintain poise and self-control. If he tends to be phlegmatic, he should train himself to stand up and speak out with prophetic

[10] For "conversational delivery" see Luke 24:13-35, especially vs. 32.

boldness. In either case a minister ought to enter the pulpit with a rested body and a fund of physical reserves. So get the brunt of the week's toil out of the way before you draw near to the Lord's Day. Avoid anything strenuous on Friday evening and all the next day, especially on Saturday night. In short, plan to enter the pulpit with all the fullness of your Christian manhood.

For an object lesson of effective delivery look again at Spurgeon. In a day when pulpit work sometimes oozed with gloom, he became known as a "happy" preacher. "As soon as he begins to preach he begins to act, not as if declaiming on the stage, but as if conversing on the street. He seems to shake hands all around, and put everyone at ease."[11] Whenever he spoke for God, he did so with joy, joy that he longed to share with everyone who helped to throng the London Tabernacle.

Now for a study motto to hang on the wall, facing the minister as he prepares to deliver sermon after sermon:

> The Lord God hath given me the tongue of the learned,
> That I should know how to speak (Isa. 50:4).

Suggested Readings

Brown, Charles R. *The Art of Preaching*. New York: The Macmillan Co., 1922.

Jefferson, Charles E. *The Minister as Prophet*. New York: T. Y. Crowell Co., 1905.

Speer, Robert E. *How to Speak Effectively Without Notes*. New York: F. H. Revell Co., 1909.

Storrs, Richard S. *Conditions of Success in Preaching Without Notes*. New York: Dodd, Mead, 1875.

[11] W. Y. Fullerton, *C. H. Spurgeon, A Biography* (London: 1920), p. 97.

CHAPTER XVIII

The Delivery from the Pulpit

L ET US follow a young minister to the pulpit in his first charge, and watch how he does the most important work of his life. We shall assume that he accepts the ideals of this book up to the present stage, and that he stands up to deliver a morning sermon. We cannot even glance at his leadership in other parts of worship. So we ask three questions, all about his speaking and mostly about details. First, ideally, how should the preacher deliver this sermon? Second, practically, what should he avoid in delivery? Third, synthetically, how can he improve this part of his work? What an undertaking in a single chapter! Why not a book, and that by an expert? Alas, most of the books about speaking from the pulpit have come from men who know more about homiletics than about public speaking, or vice versa.

THE WAY TO DELIVER A SERMON

Every man ought to speak from the pulpit in a fashion all his own, and that ought to differ from sermon to sermon. How else could anyone voice the manifold truths of God through his personality? Here lies much of the fascination in the delivery of sermons with all sorts of truths to meet all sorts of needs. In full view of divergencies we may stress the ways in which all preachers and all sermons ideally conform to the same rules about delivery.[1] If the form seems dogmatic, that comes from a desire to set forth the rules compactly.

Before you go into the sanctuary, think about your personal appearance. Conform with parish custom about wearing a robe or a clerical collar, perhaps both. Put on black shoes, polished with care fore and aft; if shirt and collar appear at all, let each look whiter than snow. Let all your garments come to the sanctuary "unspotted

[1] These rules have come largely from experts in the field, notably here at Princeton Seminary.

from the world." With face neatly shaved and hair closely trimmed, show everyone that you love the holiness of beauty.

Early in the morning of the Lord's Day go to the pulpit and make everything ready. Open the Bible, see about the hymnbook, and put everything else in place, the fewer things the better. At other times of the week arrange about ventilation of the room and adjustment of lights if they ought to go on or off. Follow an order of service that will lead everyone to rise and sing just before the sermon. When at last you stand ready to preach, wait for a moment or two silently, in the spirit of prayer, but not with eyes closed. Look at the people, kindly, and when you hear nothing but your own heartbeat, you may begin with the text or with an ascription of praise that calls no attention to yourself; e.g., "In the name of the Father and of the Son and of the Holy Spirit. Amen."

The effect of the sermon will depend in part upon your posture, especially at first. Since you represent the King of kings, stand on both feet and stand erect, with one foot in advance of the other for the sake of comfort. Once in a while, throughout the sermon, shift your posture to rest your muscles or to indicate a transition in thought; but move deliberately, and not while saying anything important. Except when you make a gesture, keep both hands where nature put them, down beside your body, and keep them still without seeming stiff. In the pulpit every motion of the body, and every lack of motion, must mean something, good or bad. Above all, hold your head fairly still and far enough up to permit free use of the throat. So with all of your body; use it for the glory of God. "Do you not know that your body is a temple of the Holy Spirit within you, which you have from God? You are not your own; you were bought with a price. So glorify God in your body" (I Cor. 6:19-20, R.S.V.).

Adopt a friendly attitude towards the people. When you come from the holy of holies with the gospel of redemption, assume that everyone present desires to learn the will of God in order to become a better man or woman. Imagine that you can hear this friend or that whispering Tennyson's plea:

And ah for a man to arise in me,
That the man I am may cease to be!

Then show him how. Throughout the sermon let the expression on your face accord with what you are saying. As a rule be sure to look happy; the people have troubles enough of their own without sharing yours. In short, look and act like a bearer of good news.

Be specially careful about the use of your eyes as a sort of "second voice." School yourself to look hearers in the face, without seeming to stare them down. Keep looking at them throughout the sermon if you wish them to keep looking at you. In the synagogue at Nazareth the eyes of everyone present were fixed upon the speaker. Look at one friend and then at another, but never turn the back of your head towards any part of the congregation. When you speak in a large edifice, broad rather than long, keep looking at those in the central part of the throng, particularly those in the rear. The eyes of the man in the pulpit always speak, either effectively or ineffectively.

Most important of all, so far, be careful about the opening words. Speak them deliberately, distinctly, and with the lowest tones that come to you naturally. From sermon to sermon let the opening words vary according to content and tone color, but always make the first words easily audible and pleasant to hear. Speak with the poise and the assurance of a man with a message from God.

The effect of the opening words, and of the entire sermon, depends much on the use of your voice. Now that almost every home has a radio or two, and almost every public school gives instruction in music, young people and many others have become voice conscious. Whether or not people agreed with what Franklin D. Roosevelt said in his "fireside talks," everybody liked to hear his radio voice. When people come to the sanctuary, they wish to hear a voice clear as a bell, sweet as a harp, strong as an organ, and full of overtones like those in Mendelssohn's *Songs Without Words*. According to students of church history, no minister without an unusual voice has ever attained first rank as a preacher to the common people.

The man with a pleasing voice has learned the secret of breath control. He breathes with the part of his body below the diaphragm, and he does so often enough to keep his tones sustained by a volume of air, so that no tone sounds hollow or weak. In all of this a wise man schools himself to relax and then follow the laws of nature, which bid him breathe deeply, silently, and fairly often. With such an unfailing support in the form of internal resources, a man merely opens his mouth far enough to let words flow out through a throat free from stress and strain.

Throughout the delivery secure variety of pitch. Since the voice tends to keep rising as the sermon proceeds and feeling mounts, start with low tones, as low as you can make pleasant for others and easy for yourself. Whenever you shift the pitch, at the end of a paragraph or a longer section, bring the voice down, though not always to the same level. Emphasis calls for low tones rather than high, and for distinctness rather than volume. As a recording machine makes clear, a skillful speaker runs the gamut of his pleasing tones; when he wishes to make any part of the message stand out, he lowers the pitch, slows the tempo, and adds to the intensity. Fortunately a minister can school himself to do all of this as a matter of second nature. Such discipline calls for work outside the pulpit.

Also regulate the volume of sound. Ability to make yourself heard depends far more on articulation than on volume. A whisper from a man who knows how to speak carries far more clearly than ranting by one who roars. But still a preacher must guard against seeming underkeyed, even anemic. If he starts with volume enough to suggest assurance and strength, without seeming loud, he must maintain volume enough to make the beginning, the middle, and the last part of every sentence audible to an elderly person dull of hearing. Especially in speaking through a microphone the preacher must maintain a fairly even volume, with only enough ebb and flow to accord with the changing moods of thought and feeling. Whenever he shifts to the use of more volume, or of less, he must guard against abruptness, by increasing or decreasing gradually. All of this may in time become largely a matter of habit.

Among the rules so far, no one can compare in importance with the following: be careful about articulation, or enunciation. Technically articulation has to do with the skill of the speaker; enunciation, with the effect on the hearer. Articulation concerns the production of sounds clear and distinct; enunciation enables another to hear with ease and satisfaction. Practically, however, these terms often appear interchangeably, because they refer to exactly the same physical processes. Ability to articulate and enunciate comes to the man who schools himself to make consonants sound clear and precise, and vowels seem instinct with beauty. He may slightly prolong some of his vowels, as in "from glo-ry unto glo-ry"; but not any of his consonants, especially an r, as in that overworked word "gr-r-reat." [2]

In order to articulate and enunciate distinctly a man needs to think clearly. Those who listen to student sermons almost never hear mumbling of phrases or swallowing of words on the part of a man who thinks clearly and feels correctly. But even such a speaker finds it easier to make himself easily audible when he relies mainly on short words and short sentences. On the other hand, a clear thinker and speaker may know almost nothing about beauty. If so, he may need to put feeling into vowels as he puts intelligence into consonants.

An experienced speaker, such as Winston Churchill, makes frequent and effective use of the pause. Where a tyro might strive to emphasize by raising the pitch, increasing the volume, and quickening the pace, the man who knows how to speak does the reverse. Especially does he pause when he wishes to stress a word or phrase. Sometimes he pauses momentarily just before he utters the significant word or phrase; more often he pauses afterwards. At times he may pause both before and after. Thus, paradoxically, the most impressive parts of a sermon may come while the speaker remains silent, waiting for the Spirit to impress on the hearer's mind and heart an idea or a picture. "Be still, and know that I am God" (Ps. 46:10).

Mastery of the pause enables a preacher to interpret the text by repeating it at the beginning of the sermon, and at times thereafter,

---

[2] On paper, unfortunately, as in a cartoon, such distinctions stand out too sharply; sometimes they grate.

for emphasis. In every sermon a pastor may strive to leave on the hearer's soul an illuminated text. Ability to do that depends largely on emphasis, which in turn depends partly on the pause. Naturally every preacher ought to quote a text in his own way, and perhaps a little differently at times, according to his purpose. Here is how one man deals with Matt. 11:28—"Come unto me (pause), all ye that labour (slight pause) and are heavy laden (pause), and I will give you (very slight pause) rest" (stop). Again, take these familiar words: "God is (slight pause) love." "Jesus (slight pause) wept." What a test of a man's artistry and self-restraint!

In dealing with words for the glory of God a minister needs ability to phrase. In public address "phrasing" refers to keeping a group of words together as a unit of thought and feeling. When a man "trips along lightly" over a section of road that affords little to see or feel, he phrases in fairly long units. But when he wishes to make something stand out boldly, he may resort to shorter phrases. In all of this he follows feeling rather than rules. On the one hand, if he never paused until he came to a punctuation mark, he might rush past words and clusters of words that he ought to pause and enjoy. On the other hand, if he made all the phrases short and of the same length, he might sound like a girl in the first grade.

Ability to phrase goes far towards making a passage clear and luminous. Like everything else in this realm, such ability comes partly through listening to speakers like Madame Chiang Kai-shek, and more through a desire to interpret the spirit of every sentence. Hence a working rule may help the inexperienced preacher: the more momentous any part of your utterance, the more careful the phrasing. It simply consists in keeping together all the members of an immediate family, and in letting them live somewhat by themselves but never out of touch with their neighbors. For an object lesson of such phrasing listen to any radio speaker who always has rhythm but never cadence. If you investigate you may find that he has long since fallen in love with Hebrew parallelism and with Anglo-Saxon rhythm. As for cadence, it usually comes at the end of a sentence, and consists in something of a sickly singsong pattern, which quickly cloys.

Closely allied with phrasing comes tempo, or timing. In fact many of these things belong together almost inseparably. Should the man in the pulpit speak slowly, moderately, or rapidly? That depends in part on his temperament, and more on his message. In reply to such a question Francis L. Patton, former president of Princeton University, showed part of his secret as a masterly speaker: "No one but a dunce would proceed at the same rate all through a sermon. Begin at a moderate pace, and later at times trip along lightly. When you come to something you wish the hearer to remember, be sure to say it slowly." In this judgment most students of the art would concur, but with a single caution: Tend to be deliberate rather than hasty. Do not rush!

For examples of such speaking turn to the history of preaching. At Geneva, John Calvin had to speak slowly because of asthma,[3] a thorn in his flesh for which the hearers must have thanked God. According to Spurgeon's stenographer,[4] the London preacher averaged 140 words a minute, but he never spoke at the same rate in two main sections of a sermon. In driving a team of horses on a long journey he would have varied the rate of speed, and from time to time slowed down. Here is salient advice for the preacher of today:

No seasoned radio speaker ever proceeds at a machine gun pace. He knows that each thought he expresses can hit its target only once; so he moves slowly enough to allow his first shot to sink home before he fires a second bullet. The rate of your delivery should be based upon the material you are [preaching] and your particular speaking style. Average [preaching] speed for radio ranges between 120 and 150 words a minute. President Roosevelt, who is generally conceded to have been the most effective speaker in American radio, sometimes spoke as slowly as 110 words a minute and seldom exceeded 135; Lowell Thomas uses 145 words a minute; Edward Murrow, 120.[5]

A matter much less important, that of gestures, may cause perplexity. In Bible days public speakers appear to have used both hands

[3] See T. H. L. Parker, *The Oracles of God* (London, 1947), p. 40.
[4] See *The Autobiography*, four vols., compiled by his wife and his private secretary (New York: F. H. Revell Co., 1898), IV, 76.
[5] Parker and Others, *Religious Radio* (New York: Harper & Bros., 1948), p. 203.

THE DELIVERY FROM THE PULPIT

...

freely. When Raphael painted the apostle Paul speaking at Mars' hill, the artist showed him with both hands extended. In eastern lands today, and in certain sections of our own country, preachers use gestures freely, sometimes profusely. But in certain localities, especially where ministers wear the robe and read sermons, one of them may go for a year without making a gesture in the pulpit. In view of such divergent customs, why not seek for the golden mean? Use gestures at times, but not early in the sermon, and not often at any one stage. When in doubt, don't!

In our day pulpit work calls for "animated conversation," and that opens the way for the use of your hands. Did you ever converse eagerly for twenty-five minutes without making gestures, perhaps with one hand, then with the other, and sometimes with both? Why? Because you wished to make a certain point clear, another one luminous, and a third one emphatic. As the minutes flew by, and you become more enthusiastic, you "talked" more frequently with your hands. Since you were not thinking about yourself or your gestures, you made them seem as natural and as necessary as breathing. Why forfeit any of that spontaneity and enthusiasm when you stand up to preach? But remember, no waste motions!

All of these considerations, including the ones about gestures, have to do with the need of variety. From stage to stage, in a message full of life and motion, the speaker ought to secure variety like that of a journey through the Trossachs. But how can a preacher tell when to vary his mode of address? By letting the various lights and shadows of his thought and feeling guide in the delivery of each successive part. In the right sort of conversational delivery the tone colors keep shifting as much as lights and shadows on a hillside in the afternoon, under a canopy of cirrus clouds. "Tone color" here means the way a speaker puts into voice and action the inner spirit of his thoughts and feelings as they come and go. In all of this we must think ideally, for only an artist can excel in the use of tone color.

From week to week the tone color of a man's sermons ought to vary still more, according to the spirit of the truths that shine out through his personality. During the Lenten season, for example, he may draw sermon materials largely from the mountain country in the Fourth Gospel. From chapter thirteen he may bring a message about "The Meaning of Christian Service"; from chapter fourteen, "The Christian Gospel of Comfort"; from chapter fifteen, "The Deepening Friendship with Christ"; and so on to the end of a brief course about Christ. In order to prepare any such message the friend in the study saturates his soul in the spirit of his passage, and then uses that passage in meeting the needs of the congregation. In each passage he finds a different sort of tone color, and this he embodies in a sermon, so that no two messages seem exactly alike, either in literary form or in delivery.

As for the conclusion, it should overshadow everything else except the text. In a sermon by a pulpit master "the end crowns all." Hence the delivery calls for the spirit of an artist in the use of the voice. Towards the end of his message this kind of preacher relies on "the wooing note," with its "quiet and measured close." While each of his sermon conclusions differs from all the rest, he would agree with J. S. Stewart that every message from God to men calls for a quiet rather than a stormy ending:

> Cultivate the quiet close. Let your last words of appeal have in them something of the hush that falls when Christ Himself draws near. Remember that, even at the best, "we prophesy in part," and that "whether there be tongues, they shall cease." But if, when our poor stammering words have fallen silent, there comes forth . . . the one eternal Word; if men are able in that silence to hear even though only dimly . . . the challenging and healing cadences of the voice of God, the work will have been done, and we shall not have preached in vain.[6]

After the service, as soon as you can, begin to relax. Indeed, the relaxation ought to start a day or so before the delivery of the sermon. Beecher, with all of his rugged physique, "took special care of his body at least twenty-four hours before the time" for a morning sermon. As the Lord's Day drew near, "he made it a rule to eat less and sleep more." His friend and neighbor in Brooklyn, Theodore L. Cuyler,

---

[6] J. S. Stewart, *Heralds of God*, pp. 139-40.

did much the same before every morning service, and after that he began storing up energy for the evening service by spending several hours in bed, asleep.[7] When such a man enters the pulpit, either at the morning or the evening hour, he stands ready to taste the joys of preaching as earth's nearest approach to heaven.

THE WAY NOT TO SPEAK

Now let us look at the other side of the case. All unconsciously a preacher may keep breaking all the rules that govern the delivery of sermons. If so, he may need a method of checking up on his ways of public address. During Spurgeon's first few years in London he received once a week a letter from an unknown critic who listed the young man's faults, such as his way of saying "covechus," and his repeated use of the line: "Nothing in my hand I bring." In later years, after Spurgeon had corrected such faults, he thanked God for those anonymous criticisms, and regretted that he could not thank the self-appointed censor.[8] In lieu of such searching critiques, why not use a check list, such as the one below? The twenty points vary in importance, but you can give them equal value and roughly compute your score, with a passing grade of seventy-five.

1. *Impression on others.* Seems hot and bothered? Lacks poise and self-control? Nervous? Bashful? Cocky? Untidy?

2. *Posture in pulpit.* Slovenly? Stiff? Sometimes slumps? Hands in pockets? Behind back? Folded in front? Arms often akimbo? Head seldom still? Defiant? "Gooseneck stance"? Teetering on toes? Never stands still? Impression of instability? "A wooden Indian"?

3. *Attitude toward hearers.* Supercilious? Patronizing? Belligerent? Effusive? Neutral? Indifferent? Absorbed in self? Lost in sermon?

4. *Facial expression.* Stern? Fixed? Often frowns? Funereal? Facial contortions? Constant grin? "Poker face"?

5. *Use of eyes.* Fixed on space? Often on ceiling? Sometimes on floor? Gazing out of window? Over heads of people? Vacant stare?

[7] J. M. Buckley, *Extemporaneous Oratory*, pp. 265-68.
[8] See *The Autobiography*, II, 227.

6. *Opening words.* High? Loud? Rapid? Indistinct? Insipid? Inconsequential? Irritating?

7. *Use of voice.* Produced from chest alone? Constricted? Throaty? Heady? Nasal (due to obstruction or laziness)? Metallic (lack of breath control)? Little variation? Piercing? Rasping? Subject to "preacher's sore throat"?

8. *Control of breath.* Labored? Inhales too slowly? Exhales too rapidly? Breathes too seldom? Too much speech in one breath? Often seems breathless? Voice sometimes breaks (lack of air support)?

9. *Volume.* Insufficient for room? Too little at first? Too much? Loud at end? Indistinct at end? Inconsistent throughout? Abrupt shifts? Unsuitable for microphone?

10. *Pitch.* Starts too high? Neglects lower tones? Sense of strain? Effect unpleasant? Monotonous? Soporific?

11. *Tempo.* No sense of timing? Too fast at first? Too slow at times? No relation to content? Little variation throughout sermon? Same pattern from week to week?

12. *Rhythm.* Lacking? Excessive? Tendency to cadence? Prettiness? Sonorous sameness? "The grand style"?

13. *Phrasing.* Units too long? Too short? Mechanical? Lack of variety? Pauses at wrong places?

14. *Pronunciation.* Accent correct (e.g., har'-ass, re-sourc'-es)? Syllabification (glō-ry)? Consonants distinct (govern*m*ent)? Vowels euphonious? Pedantry? Foppishness? Provincialism? Carelessness?

15. *Enunciation.* Indistinct? Fading at end of sentence? Mouthing in middle? Carelessness? "Schoolmarm" preciseness?

16. *Emphasis.* Needless stress on prepositions? Pronouns? Conjunctions? Interjections? Adjectives? Adverbs? Little stress on verbs? Nouns? Tendency to thump "thought words"? Stress on too many words? Practically none? Monotony?

17. *Inflection.* Too many rising inflections? Impression of uncertainty? Unreality? Insincerity? Confusion? Mechanical precision?

18. *Gestures.* None? Too many? Too early in sermon? Too much alike? Too low down? Constricted? Jerky? "Pump handle"? Teacher's index finger? Fighter's clenched fist? "Babbling" with hands?

19. *Conversational style.* Monologue? Private meditation? Personal display? Impersonal lecture? Needless animation? Excited utterance? Forced feeling? Tameness? Boredom?

20. *Imagination.* Lack of life? Motion? Warmth? Color? Variety? Harmony with content? With occasion? Tendency to overdo?

Second-rate preachers always overdo. They use too many adjectives, too many gestures, too many ideas, too much force. They pound the pulpit, and this invariably pushes the people further off. You cannot pound an idea into the human mind. An idea is like a flower. You can shake its perfume on the air, but that requires no bluster. . . . [Speaking] style is perfect when it cannot be seen.[9]

THE WAY TO IMPROVE YOUR SPEAKING

When a young man begins to use such a check list he may become discouraged, finding that he knows little about how to deliver a sermon and less about how to correct his faults. If he makes such a discovery, let him thank God and take courage. When he rises to preach, must he remember all these twenty headings, and all these scores of questions with points as barbed as porcupine quills? God forbid! Whenever he goes into the sanctuary on the Lord's Day, let him forget all about technique, and join with the people in their corporate worship. In delivering the sermon let him not think about public speaking, lest he call attention to himself and away from his message. "The best speaking voice never is heard."

But a day or two later, after he has rested, let him take out the check list and read it through once more. Then let him determine to find out the facts about his delivery. A wise man does something of the sort with his body; once every year he goes to a specialist in internal medicine and asks for a complete physical diagnosis. Why not do the same with your speaking, especially your voice? As for the counsel that comes through books—including this one—a teacher of the art declares: "Nobody can put down on paper how a thing ought to sound." Once again, if anyone dissents from this saying, let him

[9] C. E. Jefferson, *The Minister as Prophet*, pp. 139-44.

write for a ministerial gathering a paper on how to lead in repeating the Lord's Prayer.

Few ministers, alas, consult specialists in public speaking. In a metropolitan center the best-known teacher of the art reports that during the past twenty years he has had only one ministerial applicant for coaching, and that this request almost caused the professor to faint. When the good man recovers from such a shock, he may start the check-up by using a recording device. As with an X-ray machine or a fluoroscope in the hands of an expert, a recording device brings out the facts, both good and bad. After a senior in the seminary had heard the recording of his class sermon, he exclaimed: "That sounds like Donald Duck!"

"Yes," said the coach, "so did the sermon!"

Under a coach with skill and tact a mature minister, also, can improve his delivery. If many a pastor devoted to his speaking as much time, attention, and money as he gives to golf, he might begin to reach the men who say that they like him everywhere except in the pulpit. A businessman might as well report about a certain make of blotter: "It can do everything but blot!" So let the preacher become a speaker! In terms of golf, let him learn never to press or let down, but enter into the spirit of the game. Soon he will begin to find in the pulpit new effectiveness and power.

Suggested Readings

Curry, S. S. *Vocal and Literary Interpretation of the Bible.* Boston: Expression Co., 1903.

Fairbanks, Grant. *Voice and Articulation Drillbook.* New York: Harper & Bros., 1940.

Monroe, Allen H. *Principles and Types of Speech.* New York: Scott, Foresman & Co., 1935.

Phelps, Arthur. *Speaking in Public.* New York: Harper & Bros., 1930.

Sarett, L. R., and Foster, W. *Basic Principles of Speech.* Boston: Houghton Mifflin Co., 1946.

Tarbell, Cobert. *Psychology of Persuasive Speech.* New York: Longmans, 1942.

Woolbert, C. H., and Nelson, S. E. *The Art of Interpretive Speech.* New York: F. S. Crofts & Co., 1946.

CHAPTER XIX

The Helpfulness of the Radio

WHETHER or not we rejoice in the fact, radio has come to stay, and with it television. How does all of this affect the work of the preacher? The replies differ widely. One pastor looks on the radio as an asset; he also welcomes the prospect of television. He exults in the opportunity to broadcast a period of worship, with a message for our day, because he has learned to speak through that "interrupter" known as a microphone. The pastor may exaggerate the size of his vast radio audience, but still he can win many unseen friends and influence many unknown people. So he can appeal to a larger parish, and gradually increase attendance at the sanctuary.

But what about the ninety and nine parish ministers who almost never speak over the radio? In any such attempt, occasionally, the novice may flounder because he has not learned how. Some of these men regard the radio, religiously and otherwise, as a liability, if not a menace. They insist that it makes churchgoers captious about the music, critical about the prayers, and censorious about the sermon. They also contend that radio preaching has interfered with church attendance, especially in a time of rain or snow. In some congregations attendance began to decrease when metropolitan preachers started broadcasting sermons. If more people have been coming to church of late, perhaps they have begun to grow weary of the radio.

Many of us sympathize with these parish ministers who have no outlet over the radio. In the seminaries we train young men to rely on other methods. Sometimes our friends wonder why we do not prepare men for preaching over the radio, but we prefer to concentrate on the ninety and nine who most need our help. However, any student or mature preacher can learn much from the radio. No isolated pastor need now complain that he never can hear music, prayers, and sermons to strengthen and uplift his soul. What then should a minister learn from the radio?

THE IMPORTANCE OF PREPARATION

At the national broadcasting stations experts have made a study of the speaker's art. They agree about the importance of preparation before a man speaks over the radio. What they tell us about broadcasting applies to a minister's sermons anywhere. Ideally, the speaker ascertains "what interests the radio audience. He finds out by asking the schoolboy, the soldier, and the businessman; the workman, the cop, and the teacher; the motorman, the nurse, and the housewife." Such an interpreter of life today "reads a lot, listens a lot, and thinks a lot."[1] Notice here the use of facts, and the stress on persons, one by one. If you would be interesting today, use facts about persons!

After the radio speaker has learned what he needs to know about the hearers, he begins to take stock of his own resources. As an interpreter of God's truth today, what has a minister to offer? Let him preach about what he knows best and loves most. At Boston University a professor of Old Testament literature spoke over the radio about the burning bush. Because his own heart burned, he could make other hearts glow, even when he could not see those distant faces. Unfortunately, even television does not enable a man to see the light in the hearers' eyes. If radio preachers could do that, they might speak more often about familiar passages of Scripture, such as the twenty-third psalm, as Sockman once did effectively.

Another radio preacher has dealt with our Lord's parable about being a good neighbor. Instead of talking about the Good Samaritan, the broadcaster pointed to an American traveling man over against two churchmen, one a pastor and the other a deacon, both of old Colonial stock. One after the other they passed by a Jewish victim of hijackers as he lay writhing by the roadside. The traveling man came by in his Chevrolet, rendered first aid, and went far out of the way to start that victim back towards health and strength. By such use of facts as they had to do with persons, one by one, the speaker depicted action and struggle, conflict and suspense, with the right sort of

[1] See *Making Friends with the Microphone* (New York: Columbia Broadcasting Co., 1945).

climax. This kind of preaching calls for the use of brains in the study and of imagination before the microphone.

Must the radio sermon always come from the Bible? Evidently not, according to some experts, but of late the trend has been moving towards a larger use of the Scriptures. However, preaching from the Bible may not set younger brethren a worthy example. On a Lord's Day two weeks before Easter the hymns and other music over a national network had to do with the meaning and glory of the Cross. So had the prayers and the reading from the Scriptures, but the sermon harked back to the forty-sixth psalm. A week later, on Palm Sunday, everyone had a right to expect an evangelical preacher to speak about the triumphal entry or about the Cross, but the Christ-centered worship led up to a message about the 121st psalm. Consequently, each service moved backward in time, and failed to meet the needs of the hour.

Later in the season either of those psalms might have met the needs of many hearts. In the heat of midsummer, when listeners over the radio must battle with diseases of the soul, words from the psalms come with healing on their wings. But at a season when people everywhere are thinking about the deepening shadow of the Cross, and when the other parts of radio worship lead every hearer to expect a message about the Redeemer, why turn to some other part of Holy Writ? Why not preach as a Christian minister, and not like a Jewish rabbi?

These suggestions apply also to pastors who cannot speak over the radio. What interests men and women when it issues from a stranger speaking at a distance would appeal far more if it came from their friend in the pulpit at home. Whatever the source of the message and whatever the form, preaching today calls for the interpretation of life here and now, in light that comes from God. If the man in the pulpit knows how to preach, he need never dread the competition of a broadcaster who must remain unseen and appear impersonal.

THE IMPORTANCE OF LITERARY FORM

Students of the radio also emphasize the form of the sermon. They insist that the preacher begin with something sure to catch and rivet attention. Away with the old-time tedious introduction! In other days the preacher felt free to use a few minutes in getting warmed up, but the speaker over the radio must be ready before he starts. From the first sentence onward he must not let down, but must become more and more appealing. From start to finish the radio sermon calls for human interest, and that depends in part on literary form.

In the opening sentence or two the radio preacher may induce the hearer to ask a question, and then the sermon deals with that question. In the message as a whole the preacher gives the unseen friend something to mull over all the rest of the day, if not all week. Religious broadcasting often consists in teaching, sometimes biblical, interesting because it concerns what the hearer wishes to learn. The art of the speaker consists in making the teaching attractive, and that calls for labor in the study.

The radio preacher uses skill in repetition, because he wishes a few ideas to stand out. Even in a fifteen-minute sermon he finds it better to say one thing in ten different ways than to touch ten different things, each in passing. As a broadcaster Fosdick has owed much of his effectiveness to skill and care in repeating what he wished the hearer to remember. For example, in a message about "Things That Money Cannot Buy" he never let the hearer get away from the central thought. In the printed form, longer than over the radio, almost every one of the twenty-five paragraphs ends with an allusion to "things that money cannot buy."

The experts also insist that a radio preacher write out his sermon, word for word, and then revise the manuscript, sentence after sentence; that he use short words, short sentences, and short paragraphs; that he write about persons, one by one, and never let the hearer lose sight of some person or persons, preferably in action. This kind of preaching calls for facts, facts that live and move and press onward towards the goal. In short, make ready as for a one-act play. On the other hand, keep away from radio jargon, such as "and I quote," or "end of quote." When people come to church, why remind them of the radio at home? Poor psychology!

THE HELPFULNESS OF THE RADIO

THE IMPORTANCE OF DELIVERY

The radio preacher who knows his business prepares to deliver the message as though he were chatting with friends at their fireside. Like Franklin D. Roosevelt, the minister talks with animation, but without excitement. "Every time I hear you broadcast I feel as though I were listening to a friend." What a tribute! Why should not the layman feel so whenever he comes to the home church and listens to a sermon by the pastor? There the man in the pulpit need not use a manuscript, as he would in broadcasting from a booth. In addressing friends at home a minister can speak from heart to heart and from eye to eye. If he does not, why should the layman come out through the rain when he can hear the same kind of impersonal preaching over the radio?

By listening to the right broadcasters the young preacher can learn much about delivery. He can see the wisdom of keeping the voice down where it belongs. As a radio preacher Sockman owes much to skill in using a rich bass voice with all sorts of overtones. If a man normally speaks with a tenor voice, he can keep it down on the lower ranges. Jowett did not broadcast sermons over the radio, but if he had done so, he would have charmed everyone with a tenor voice as clear and moving as a flute in the hands of a master. Not every local pastor can command such an instrument, but everyone can learn not to let his voice rise until it almost screams and shrieks. On the other hand, not one preacher in a hundred needs to guard against undue use of his lower tones.

Listening to the radio also makes a man see the folly of rapid-fire utterance. Many preachers over the air afford worthy examples of deliberate speaking; others do not. The same holds true in the realm of sports. On New Year's Day, when some of us follow the accounts of the football game out in the Rose Bowl, we enjoy the reporter who takes time to make every play stand out distinctly, but we soon grow weary of the "interpreter" who fusses and fumes in an endeavor to make us share his excitement. What do we care about his hysterics? We want to follow the game! After turning away from one broad-

223

caster because he becomes incoherent and dialing in on another who takes time to make everything clear, the ministerial auditor may ask himself: "Which way do I preach? Do I keep rushing, as to a fire which may burn out before I arrive?"

An occasional minister speaks too slowly. He pauses too long after each period, or else he breaks up sentences into fragments that mean nothing when they stand alone. How then can anyone know whether he speaks too rapidly or too slowly? By listening to the radio he can see that the ablest speakers talk more deliberately than the majority of ministers who do not broadcast sermons. For instance, take Madame Chiang Kai-shek, Winston Churchill, and Franklin D. Roosevelt, no one of whom spoke rapidly. When any of them came to a pause, he made it impressive, at times even memorable. Whether or not the hearer agreed with one of those three international speakers during World War II, anyone could learn much from those ablest broadcasters of their time. Out of such experiences let us formulate a working rule: "Speak so that no one will notice how you speak. Be natural. Secure variety. Be on the safe side; tend to be deliberate."

We have been thinking about radio speaking by the masters. The same holds true about radio preaching. But if some of the ablest sermons come over the air, so do many of the worst. Hence the young man who would improve as a preacher must know which broadcasters to select as models. Some would vote for Fulton J. Sheen, and others for Walter Maier, who is said to command the largest radio audience of any religious broadcaster in America. Here again we may venture a working rule: "Study the methods of the radio preacher whom your most thoughtful laymen enjoy, and figure out the secrets of his effectiveness. You will find that he depends mainly on being natural and in earnest." Long before the days of broadcasting Chalmers set countless hearts on fire through "blood earnestness."

All of this applies in part to speaking through an amplifier. Sooner or later every minister will preach in a sanctuary with some kind of broadcasting device, perhaps a loud speaker or a public address system. The preacher ought to stand directly behind the microphone, keeping his face turned all the time in that direction and maintaining an even tone, which need not be loud. If he strolled about over the platform or let his voice abruptly rise and fall in volume, he might annoy the listeners. Worse still, if he caused the Bible or the hymnal to bump against the instrument, he might make it sound like a bull of Bashan. Worst of all, if the preacher worried about the business, he might talk like a phonograph. In view of these facts, why not hunt up a church with such equipment and ask one of the lay officers to give you a lesson or two in speaking through the microphone?

What then shall we conclude? Since radio and other mechanical devices have come to stay, shall we ministers look on them as assets or as liabilities, as friends and helpers of the local church, or as rivals and enemies of the home pulpit? If the pastor learns from radio preachers all that they stand ready to show about appealing to people, he will thank God for such a postgraduate course in preaching the gospel today. As for amplifying systems, he can learn to use them as means of grace. In short, let him claim the blessing of God on the preaching of the Word, with or without the radio and the amplifier.

Suggested Readings

Barnouw, Erik. *Handbook of Radio Writing*. Revised ed. Boston: Little, Brown & Co., 1947.

Cantril, Hadley, and Allport, Gordon W. *The Psychology of Radio*. New York: Peter Smith, 1941.

Crews, Albert. *Professional Radio Writing*. Boston: Houghton Mifflin Co., 1946.

Loveless, Wendell P. *Manual of Gospel Broadcasting*. Chicago: Moody Press, 1946.

Parker, E. C., and Others. *Religious Radio*. New York: Harper & Bros., 1947.

Sayers, Dorothy. *The Man Born to Be a King*. Toronto: Ryerson Press, 1943.

Welch, J. W. *The Church and Religious Broadcasting*, a booklet. London, n.d.

CHAPTER XX

The Problem of Sermon Length

THE QUESTION NOW BEFORE US concerns every preacher and every sermon: how long should a pulpit message require for delivery? Answers differ sharply, sometimes without reason. The history of the pulpit shows no uniformity, though in Bible days prophets and apostles seem not to have spoken long. In an evening service of farewell the apostle Paul held forth until midnight (Acts 20:7), but in view of the consequences he may not have repeated the experiment.

In the Early Church, also, the fathers seem not to have preached long at any one time, for that custom appears to have originated after the Reformation.[1] Over in Germany, Claud Harms used to tell about a discourse that lasted all day—fortunately in winter, when nightfall comes sooner than in summer. Among English Puritans a message that lasted only an hour did not seem long, and in our land some of us remember ministers who excelled as long distance racers, never running out of wind.

THE LENGTH OF SERMONS NOW

All of that has changed; in our time the pendulum has swung to the other extreme. "Not a few of our younger clergymen are eager to see the sermon whittled down, and reduced to the vanishing point altogether, like the cat in *Alice in Wonderland*, with only the smile behind." These younger ministers have watched throngs of men and women, boys and girls, on their way to the Roman parish church, and coming back within half an hour. In those thirty minutes the people have listened to a Latin service, with an English sermonette five minutes short. Why do they attend week after week? Largely because of the service apart from the sermon. On the other hand, could the

---

[1] See *Blackwood's Magazine*, Edinburgh, February, 1868. On this subject not all students agree.

226

Protestant Church survive on the basis of five-minute sermonettes, however skillful?

Over the radio, too, a religious service usually lasts no more than thirty minutes. After the music, the reading, and the prayers, all of them brief and pointed, comes the message, which may last fifteen minutes, but no more. Sometimes the entire service calls for only fifteen minutes, with a message half that long. Such pulpit fare suits many people with "motion picture minds," or lack of minds. The tempo of life has speeded up since the days of the Pilgrim Fathers, but still there remains a question about how far the pulpit should go in yielding to the spirit of the age. More than a few thoughtful people wish for something more substantial than the snacks they sometimes get in the way of radio sermonettes.

Why then do churchgoers object to long sermons? Not because of length, but because of boredom. They protest against monotony and dullness. They cannot enjoy sermons "untroubled by a spark." If the discourse runs forty minutes, they have twice as much of an opportunity to find fault as if it lasted only twenty. Often they feel that the pastor tries to handle more material than he has been able to master and illuminate. When he deals with an episode in the life of Joseph, or of Moses, they wonder why the sermon must survey the hero's whole career. They wish that the pastor would begin with something specific, and then keep his eye on the ball. Alas, they forget that pointed preaching would call for the expenditure of more time and brain power than many a pastor's working schedule allows. Hence he has to ramble, often starting back with Adam.

Such critical hearers object to any sermon that seems tedious; they may grow impatient with the man who talks only fifteen minutes. They begin to squirm if he reads a text so long that he cannot repeat it from memory, if he makes a leisurely approach instead of beginning at once to preach, and especially if he draws out the concluding paragraph with "finally" after "finally." They feel that he calls attention to lack of preparation, that he shows no use of imagination, and that he should learn how to preach. In their plea for shorter sermons these friends may not know that the preacher often finds it harder to prepare a fifteen-minute discourse than if he could speak half an hour. The same holds true in making a cameo over against a statuette.

The desire for short sermons may originate with the minister, rather than the laymen. Because of zeal for the enrichment of the service more than one pastor has begun to give the sermon a secondary place. If so, why not put it back where it belongs, in the heart of public worship to Almighty God? In more than one parish church of late thoughtful people have been complaining because their minister substitutes bright little talks for soul-satisfying sermons. They do not object to the man who speaks twenty-five minutes, provided he has something to say and knows how to say it effectively. The majority of our laymen do not insist on shorter sermons so much as better ones.

Over in England a brilliant scholar and essayist has aroused certain church leaders by a discussion of "The Empty Pews." As a layman who has grown lax in church attendance he insists that the man in the pulpit ought to feed the sheep and not merely "amuse the goats."

What the absentees require, and fail continually to find, is something in their church that will interest and challenge them. Their most frequent disappointment is in the sermons—not, as many parsons too modestly suppose, because they are too long, or because they give offense, but for the opposite reason, that they are too scanty, that they do not strike deep enough, that they are too conciliatory and timid. . . . When the sermon begins, what they wish to hear . . . is the priest who, fearlessly and without compromise, refers his subject, whatever it may be, to the innermost truths of Christianity.[2]

The trend towards brevity in sermons has come during the time when the pulpit has suffered a decline in prestige. Years ago a foremost writer on homiletics warned his brethren against the fashion of curtailing sermons.[3] He predicted that the custom would lead to widespread ignorance of the Bible and to avoidance of Christian doctrine.

[2] See Charles Morgan, *Reflections in a Mirror* (Toronto: The Macmillan Co., 1947), pp. 146-48.
[3] See Austin Phelps, *My Portfolio* (New York: Charles Scribner's Sons, 1882), pp. 117-22.

Since that day many sermons have become shorter than the professor would have thought possible, and during the intervening period many of our laymen have lost their concern about the Scriptures and about Christian doctrine. Whether the short sermons have constituted the cause or the effect, who can tell?

At the beginning of the twentieth century the tendency in view had got under way, so that in Britain a scholar and theologian raised his voice in protest. Now that this man's books have been coming back into print, his words about preaching call for attention. P. T. Forsyth has had more than a little to do with the present-day revival of concern for the Scriptures and for doctrine. If the words that follow sound extreme, remember that they came at a time when messages from the pulpit threatened to grow shorter and shorter. In some quarters clergyman had even begun to call for "a moratorium on preaching." In more recent times, thank God, theologians and parish ministers have begun to think highly of preaching and theology, both of which belong together. Still we all need to ponder this warning:

> The demand for short sermons on the part of Christian people is one of the most fatal influences at work to destroy preaching in the true sense of the word. How can a man preach if he feels that the people have set a watch upon his lips. Brevity may be the soul of wit, but the preacher is not a wit. And those who say that they want little sermon because they are there to worship God and not hear man, have not grasped the rudiments of the first idea of Christian worship. . . . A Christianity of short sermons is a Christianity of short fibre.[4]

Today the trend in many quarters seems to be turning towards more of a popular teaching ministry. If any minister wishes to teach from the pulpit he must allow time to develop a subject. If he stands up to deal with a biblical doctrine or a Christian duty, he must take time enough to make that truth or duty clear, luminous, and practical. If he plans to set forth the truth and light in a paragraph from the Gospels, or in a golden chapter from Isaiah, the interpreter must have time to bring out the salient facts, and then show their value today.

[4] See *Positive Preaching and the Modern Mind* (New York: Hodder & Stoughton, 1907), pp. 109-10.

Only a master of public address could hope to do all of that in less than twenty-five minutes.

THE PATH OF WISDOM TODAY

Wherein lies the path of wisdom today? No one wishes a return to the interminable sermons of yesteryears, for in other times more than a few divines ran to extremes of prolixity and profusion. They set so full a table that they threatened to cause indigestion, but in more recent times some of their ministerial descendants may have gone too far in reducing the pulpit fare. Where then can we find the golden mean? Every pastor must look for the answer in his own parish, where he ought to think about the traditions of the past and the needs of today, especially the latter. However, a few suggestions may help.

1. The length of the sermon ought to *vary according to the character of the service*. At the hour of morning worship boys and girls ought to be present and remain through for the benediction. If so, the man in charge of planning for the worship may think of it all in terms of sixty minutes. He need not call attention to time, or announce that he will stop at the stroke of twelve. But if he knows that the organ prelude will start at ten forty-five and stop exactly at eleven, he can arrange for the service to close at twelve, or shortly thereafter. Within that hour he can deliver a sermon not longer than twenty-five minutes; Buttrick is said to think in terms of twenty-two.

2. The needs of the hour may call for a *longer sermon at a special occasion*. The congregation, for example, wishes to celebrate the one hundredth anniversary of its founding, and the burning of the mortgage on the present edifice. The officers invite a speaker to come from afar and deliver this address. They wish a message like that of John A. Broadus years ago in the Second Baptist Church of St. Louis. At the dedication of the sanctuary he spoke about "Worship,"[5] in a way that must have helped to make that congregation a power ever since. The pulpit master did not have to address people all worn out with other exercises, or feel obliged to stop with the ringing of a dinner bell.

[5] See *Sermons and Addresses* (London: Hodder & Stoughton, 1887), pp. 1-25.

Rightly or wrongly, the guest minister often feels that special services run too long, and that the sermon starts after the hearers have begun to feel jaded, if not surfeited. When the occasion calls for a message longer than usual, why not shorten the other parts of public worship? Such a procedure need involve no disparagement of the music, the readings, and the prayers, all of which deserve places of honor. On the other hand, in case of need, the man in charge ought to plan for a short message, so as to allow time for something else. In any event, never prolong the time of worship beyond the powers of human endurance today, especially on the part of boys and girls.

3. On a special occasion the service may lead up to an *act of corporate worship*. If that part of the service lasts more than a few minutes, the pastor should plan for the climactic feature to start before the people have begun to think about going home. For example, in a Chicago church the Holy Communion comes once a month, alternating between the morning and the evening service. On other Sundays the hour of worship culminates with the sermon, which takes the place once given to the Mass. But on the high day of the Sacrament, the Lord's Supper itself constitutes a sermon in action: "As often as you eat this bread and drink the cup, you proclaim the Lord's death until he comes" (I Cor. 11:26, R.S.V.). This word "proclaim" literally means to "preach."

On this high day the people should come to the Lord's Table as earth's nearest approach to heaven. Especially in a large congregation the spirit of the hour may call for the shortening of the worship that leads up to the Sacrament. Instead of preparing a regular sermon the pastor may use a meditation calling for fifteen minutes, or only twelve. He does not attempt to teach a doctrine or enforce a duty, since he wishes to create an atmosphere like that on the Mount of Transfiguration. In such an "air of greater visibility," the lay friends ought to "see no man, but Jesus only," and then be transformed into His likeness. The preparation of such a message calls for ability and work, all in the spirit of prayer.

4. In order to meet the needs of the parish the officers may plan for *more than one service* on the Lord's Day. If so, the second ought

231

to differ from the first: if the morning hour affords uplift, with a message that inspires, the other service may appeal more directly to people who like to think. Not all who attend in the morning will return at night or at vespers, but if the second service assumes a form of its own, and meets a different kind of need, other people will begin to attend. So in time the church ought to reach persons of various types. In the later service, at least occasionally, the sermon may last for thirty-five minutes, but even then the entire period of worship need not run beyond an hour. However, if the people wish for a song service beforehand, they will not object to an hour and a quarter.

In Washington, D. C., the program of a downtown church calls for three services every Lord's Day, and the leaders think of adding a fourth. In a downtown church elsewhere the fourth service comes at the noon hour on Thursday. During Lent, in this nonliturgical body, the noon meetings come every day of the week except Saturday. Each period of worship lasts only thirty minutes, and the message calls for ten. Whatever the details in the local parish, the program ought to meet the needs of that field today. After the minister becomes acquainted with the facts, he should welcome the counsel of Beecher:

The length of sermons . . . never should be determined by the clock, but upon broader considerations,—short sermons for small subjects, and long sermons for large subjects. It [practical wisdom] does not require that sermons be of any uniform length. Let one be short, and the next long, and the next intermediate. . . . The true way to shorten a sermon is to make it interesting. The object of preaching is not to let men out of church at a given time. . . . You cannot discuss great themes in a short compass, nor can you by driblets—by sermons of ten or twenty minutes—train an audience to a broad consideration of high themes.[6]

5. *A mature clergyman may need* to prepare *shorter sermons*. He may protest that he used to hear Charles E. Jefferson of New York City in a series of doctrinal messages, each one lasting sixty minutes, before a throng that filled Broadway Tabernacle. But that master preacher did not always hold forth for an hour; in fact, he never did

[6] *Yale Lectures on Preaching*, p. 234.

so unless he had a message that called for sixty minutes, and if he were living now he would probably stop within forty-five. As for men without his talents, they do well to think of twenty-five or thirty as the upper limit. Unfortunately, as a minister gets older he begins to feel that he ought to be heard for his much speaking.

6. *The young preacher*, on the other hand, may need to consider the wisdom of *preaching longer* than twelve or fifteen minutes. If he listens only to the people who prattle about his sermons, he may not decide the case on its merits; but if he studies the history of preaching, he will find that the ablest ministers, as a rule, have taken time to develop the subject in a sermon. Fosdick, as we have seen, refers to a normal message in the pulpit as lasting thirty-five minutes. Some of us think in terms of twenty-five, with a little leeway in either direction. In other words, we recommend a golden mean.

Regardless of age, deal with the matter prayerfully. In every sermon do what will bring glory to God and a blessing to the people. If you preach well, the hearers will think little about the passing of time, but if you ever run out of anything to say after the first quarter of an hour, stop while the people wish you to go on. Determine by the grace of God to make every sermon long enough to present the subject adequately and short enough to be interesting. If at any time you feel uncertain about whether to prepare a long sermon or a short one, err on the side of brevity. When at last you retire from the pulpit, however, you will feel grateful most of all not for your shortest sermons but for the ones that have done most good.

Suggested Readings

Brown, Charles R. *The Art of Preaching*. New York: The Macmillan Co., 1922. Chap. IV.

Burton, Nathaniel J. *In Pulpit and Parish*. New York: The Macmillan Co., 1925. Chap. VI.

James, William. *The Principles of Psychology*. New York: Holt, 1908, I, 402-58, "Attention."

CHAPTER XXI

The Message for Boys and Girls

THE LEADERS of every congregation ought to think much about reaching boys and girls, how to enlist them for public worship and prepare them for church membership. In all sorts of parishes the absence of boys and girls from morning worship causes much concern. Unless they form the habit of regular attendance before they reach the age of ten or twelve, likely they will never become regular churchgoers. In many parishes the decline in regular attendance by adults started about ten years after boys and girls quit coming to church. Herein lies either the most serious problem of Protestants or else the most attractive opportunity.

THE PLANS IN USE TODAY

In order to attract boys and girls to the church on Sunday morning the leaders have devised three methods, which we describe as good, better, and best. Any method serves better than that of ignoring the issue and waiting to see what will happen when the present churchgoers die off. Under God, the welfare and progress of the congregation depend chiefly on men and women, old and young, who come to church whenever they can. Many of them attend regularly because they formed the habit before the age of ten or twelve; so let us consider three methods of recruiting young churchgoers for years to come.

We shall be thinking chiefly about the man in the pulpit, and we shall find no fault with any minister save one who shuts his eyes to the seriousness of the situation. We may count the first plan good, because it works in an exceptional church; the second one better, since it operates more widely; the third one best of all, because it will work anywhere. If someone has found still another way of enlisting boys and girls for public worship let him rejoice. However, he will probably discover that it resembles one of these three.

1. *The junior church.* This plan calls for personnel and equipment

234

such as only a large congregation can afford. A church with a thousand members or more includes enough boys and girls to form a church within the church. This would consist of lads and lasses old enough to attend the public schools but not yet ready for senior high. As for children below school age, they do not concern us now. They too call for tender care, but not as members and officers in the junior church, which ministers to boys and girls who think of themselves as growing up, and do not relish the name of "children."

This sort of program necessitates a chapel suitable for worship and far enough away from the chief sanctuary so as not to cause competing sounds. More important still, the church staff must include a person able to lead boys and girls in group worship, including the most difficult kind of preaching. As a rule the junior church assembles at the hour of the morning service in the main sanctuary. Under the right sort of leadership the plan commends itself; but still it raises one question, that of transferring boy and girl graduates over into the main stream of congregational life and worship. Unless someone takes care, they will drift away from the church when they cease to attend worship all their own.

2. *The junior sermon.* Sometimes this alternative plan goes under the name of "children's sermon," but boys and girls of the age in view deserve a title that encourages them to look up, not down. The junior sermon assumes many forms, most of them worthy. Over in England a pastor may use with boys and girls a brief message as a prelude to the sermon for adults. This way of planning resembles the course of the Passion play at Oberammergau. While the actors behind the main curtain prepare for the coming scene from the New Testament, some of the other actors portray a similar episode from the Old. If the next scene is to deal with the Lord's Supper, the tableau portrays the giving of the manna. If the later scene is to show how Judas betrayed his Lord, the tableau presents the sons of Jacob selling their brother Joseph.

Such a sermon appears most nearly ideal when the boys and girls sit with their parents in family pews, and remain there until the end of the hour. If any parents do not attend, their sons and daughters can

THE PREPARATION OF SERMONS
THE PREPARATION OF SERMONS

sit with Bible school teachers. Where lads and lasses bunch up in the front pews they become the observed of all observers. If they all troop out while the older people try to sing a hymn, those who leave the sanctuary forfeit much of the value in public worship. However, the advocates of the junior sermon rightly insist that twenty minutes every week with God in His house will do vastly more for boys and girls than any sort of "absent treatment."

3. *The regular service.* The third plan calls for nothing new; it goes back to the old-fashioned idea that the morning hour of worship should enlist boys and girls, with their fathers and mothers. In preparing the hymns and the other music, the readings from the Bible, the prayers and responses, the minister and the other leaders of worship strive to make everything attractive to these younger friends. If the plan succeeds with boys and girls of ten or twelve, the leaders will find small reason for concern about the fathers and mothers, not to mention the grandparents. Such older folk love the church that cares for the men and women of tomorrow.

For light on these matters, turn to a book by Willard L. Sperry,[1] of the divinity school at Harvard, who has made a special study of public worship, past and present. In this little volume he publishes the substance of what he told club women in New York City. He insisted that the morning hour of worship afforded the best opportunity for bringing a boy or girl close to God, and for developing the right sort of habits through later years. In this judgment many of us concur, since it accords with our own experience and with our observation of churches near and far.

A certain professor of preaching spent most of his active ministry in two parishes near state universities. At first he thought much about ways of attracting students and professors, and then he made a discovery that changed his whole outlook. He found that students and professors liked to attend a church where boys and girls felt at home, and that university folk could understand and appreciate everything of interest to boys and girls ready for junior high. He did not keep

---

[1] *What You Owe Your Child* (New York: Harper & Bros., 1935).

all the worship on their level, for he wished them to sense the mystery of the faith, and to keep reaching up for something beyond their grasp. But in each main part of the hour—in the hymns, the readings, the prayers, and the sermon—he strove to include something for his younger friends, whom he regarded as the most important members of the congregation.

Above all, the minister covets the presence of boys and girls during the celebration of the sacraments. At the time they may comprehend little of what they see and hear, but then who of us older folk can enter far into the mystery of the gospel as it shines out through these holy symbols? In years to come, when these boys and girls have become lay officers and ministers, or missionaries beyond the seven seas, they will look back on the times when the Lord God made Himself known to their little hearts as they witnessed the washing with water and the breaking of bread. Anyone who desires to follow this trail farther may begin with a life of Albert Schweitzer or Walter Rauschenbusch. As a boy not yet old enough for membership in the church, wee Albert found God near and wondrous during the celebration of the Holy Communion, and little Walter as he witnessed the ordinance of baptism.

"How early in life should a boy start attending church?" This question came to a professor from a member of the senior class. Being a Scotsman, and thrifty with opinions, the teacher asked the entire group: "How many of you attended morning worship regularly when you were six years old?" Out of ninety men present almost every one raised his hand. If any person had felt disposed to argue about the matter, he might have inquired: "Has either of the alternative plans led many young men and women into the ministry and the mission field? Where in biography can you find such testimonies as those of Schweitzer and Rauschenbusch? At least you grant that the old-fashioned way works? Then why not give it a trial?"

THE HEARTS OF BOYS AND GIRLS

The old way still works—sometimes; why not always, and everywhere? Partly because many of us leaders do not understand the hearts of boys and girls. How should the man in the pulpit appeal to boys and girls of ten or twelve? In order to answer this question a minister needs to know something about psychology. He may not delve into the subject so extensively as Weatherhead, but every pastor needs a working knowledge of human hearts, especially of boys and girls. At least he ought to understand something about the native impulses or tendencies, formerly known as instincts. Regardless of their origin and their number, these traits appear in the young friends whom the pastor wishes to reach for Christ and His Church. The following list comes from Arthur T. Quiller-Couch, of Cambridge University.[2] He says that in addition to food and exercise every normal boy or girl desires:

1. *To talk and to listen.* Especially to talk! These listeners feel happy when they can join in repeating the text, and in other parts of the service. They welcome "co-operative preaching," with a give-and-take that consists in talking things over with their friend in the pulpit. This communicative tendency on the part of boys and girls may cause us to alter some of our ideas about their being "seen but not heard." On the other hand, if the man in the pulpit does not know how to lead them in attending to a sermon as an act of worship, some lad may try to show off. Who but their pastor should lovingly guide them through the spoken word?

2. *To act,* as in a drama. They enjoy taking part in a procession, as in entering the sanctuary fully robed, especially on Palm Sunday. They want to stand up for the responsive reading, and they enjoy taking part in responses after the prayers. Sometimes they would prefer the responses without the prayers, which seems remote from their needs. They relish the sermons of the man who preaches imaginatively, not pontifically, who takes up a case and shows a truth or a duty "with hands and feet." All of this sounds like an up-to-date brand of homiletics and public worship!

3. *To draw, paint, model.* Boys and girls like the preacher who sees what he says, and says what he sees. They enjoy him all the more if

[2] See *On the Art of Reading* (New York: G. P. Putnam's Sons, 1920), p. 56.

his love of beauty reveals the soul of a poet. They want him to use live words, which show them something to feel, to see, and to do. If he talks about David and Goliath, they can see that slingshot and those five stones from the brook. In fact, they would like to use paper and pencil to illustrate the pastor's talk. At least they can make such drawings after they reach home, if they care to remember the sermon that long.

4. *To dance and sing.* Here we need to think only about the singing! Why not start a junior choir, with both girls and boys? At least once a month let the order of worship include a special number by these sons and daughters of the church. Almost every Lord's Day let one of the hymns appear in the bulletin as "a song for boys and girls," or as a "memory hymn." Single out a song that has lived for years because of its beauty; e.g., "Fairest Lord Jesus, Ruler of All Nature." Instead of two long anthems by the senior choir, be content with one, not too heavy, and leave room for three full hymns that the boys and girls know and love. Perhaps, to your amazement, you will find that most of them love real music.

What has all of this to do with getting them to hear sermons? The character of the music in the sanctuary Sunday morning shows whether or not the pastor loves boys and girls. If he arranges for music that will appeal to them, he will find them concerned about the message that comes from their friend. Boys and girls soon figure out that the minister cares for them, and they love to hear whatever he says, at least everything near their range. However, as Quiller-Couch says, he must keep from jargon, the "infirmity of speech" that leads a man to "use circumlocution rather than short, straight speech," and "habitually choose vague, wooly, abstract nouns rather than concrete verbs." [3] What a test of a man's brains, and of his humility!

5. *To know the why of things.* The normal boy wishes to learn; so does his little sister. They like the preacher who appeals to their sense of wonder and awe. According to an expert in this kind of pulpit work, they enjoy two kinds of subjects, and only two: things that

[3] See A. T. Quiller-Couch, *On the Art of Writing*, pp. 101-05.

they know and things that they do not know. Then the expert suggests: "If you talk about what they know, tie it up with something they find new and strange. If you bring out something they find new and strange, show how it relates to something they know and love." All of that sounds like the way Susanna Wesley taught John and Charles and her other children at home. As Sperry has said, in speaking to boys and girls begin and end with wonder; fill up the interstices with admiration. What an art!

6. *To construct.* These young friends want to build. A boy likes to play with blocks; his sister, with dolls. Both of them show concern about homes for human beings, and they like to hear the preacher who talks about religion and life in terms of building. They may not know that Paul and his Master often taught this way, and that each of those preachers must often have paused in the midst of a busy day to watch a carpenter or a mason at work on a new house. Today whenever a ministerial kibitzer goes into the pulpit, he meets with a response from young would-be builders.

What about the use of object lessons in the pulpit? A few at times may justify their presence. A New Testament or a hymnal, a fountain pen or a watch, may not call undue attention to itself. But anything foreign, especially if large, might distract. When boys and girls watch a man in the pulpit blow bubbles from a pipe or fondle a black kitten, they may find it hard to think much about God, especially if the bubble bursts or the kitten miaows. If their pastor and friend comes down from the sacred desk and meets them on their level, they may like him all the more, but are they forming habits of worship for years to come? Often they think of object lessons as entertainment, not worship. The older people, too, enjoy, but do they worship?

So we might go on to other "native impulses," as they appear in the writings of William McDougall and kindred psychologists, and we might discuss "the laws of habit." But we have gone far enough to show the difficulty of preaching to boys and girls. A friendly observer of visiting preachers objects most of all to their junior sermons: "Man after man tries to tell three or four things when he has time for only one, and uses words so long and abstract that they show the young hearers nothing to see or feel. The preacher talks too fast and too long. He should learn to say one thing, and say it twenty times, in twenty different ways. Why doesn't someone at the seminary teach every young preacher to work like an artist at his easel?" For an example of what the critic has in mind, look at this excerpt from a junior sermon by Charles E. Jefferson. Especially note the repetition about the pile driver, which every boy can see with the inner eye:

It takes a great deal of repetition to get a big idea into a small boy's soul. Did you ever see a pile driver driving piles? The pile driver shoots up into the air a great mass of iron, and without a moment's warning lets it drop upon the head of the pile. The pile does not mind the first blow very much, and stands almost as proud and tall as before. But the pile driver keeps right on at its work. It lifts the iron into the air and lets it drop five times, ten times, fifty times, perhaps a hundred times, and by and by the pile is driven down deep into the river bed, and is so firm and sure that men are not afraid to make it part of the foundation of a house.[4]

If any young minister learns how to reach boys and girls by his sermons, and how to lead them in other parts of worship, he may double his usefulness.[5] How can anyone engage in a more practical study of homiletics and liturgics? For many reasons the pastors who have excelled in appealing to boys and girls have also moved the fathers and mothers. The man who speaks to the hearts of these young friends and brings them close to God needs to have "the simplicity and the purity that is toward Christ" (II Cor. 11:3, A.R.V.).

Suggested Readings

Bowie, Walter R. *The Armour of Youth*. New York: F. H. Revell Co., 1923.

Cavert, Walter D. *Story Sermons from Literature and Art*. New York: Harper & Bros., 1939.

Coffin, Henry S. *The Public Worship of God*. Philadelphia: Westminster Press, 1946. Chap. IX.

[4] *My Father's Business* (New York: T. Y. Crowell Co., 1909).
[5] For the other side, see Brooks, *Lectures on Preaching*, p. 96. Also see E. R. Micklem, *Our Approach to God* (London: Hodder & Stoughton, 1934), pp. 197-204.

Hutchison, S. Nye. *The Voice Within Us*. New York: F. H. Revell Co., 1932.

Jeffs, H. *The Art of Addressing Children*. New York: Geo. H. Doran Co., 1904.

Jones, Mary A. *The Faith of Our Children*. New York and Nashville: Abingdon-Cokesbury Press, 1943.

Kerr, Hugh T. *Children's Parable Story-Sermons*. New York: F. H. Revell Co., 1945.

Orr, W. M. *The Fingerprints of God*. Nashville: Cokesbury Press, 1939.

Schofield, Joseph A. *A Year of Children's Sermons*. Nashville: Cokesbury Press, 1938.

Sherrill, Lewis J. *The Opening Doors of Childhood*. New York: The Macmillan Co., 1939.

Stewart, R. W. *The Singing Mountain*. London, 1946.

CHAPTER XXII

The Ethics of Quoting Materials

MUST A MINISTER give credit for everything he quotes?" This problem illustrates the difficulty in discussing practical ethics without going to extremes of severity or laxness. If a minister writes for the press, the whole matter becomes subject to laws he should know and obey, but all of that does not concern us here. Otherwise, the problem relates to what Jeremy Taylor calls "the liberty of prophesying," and to what Josiah Royce terms "the higher prudence." As a man of honor the pastor thinks more about his reputation for integrity than about the laws of the state, and more about the Golden Rule than about the Ten Commandments. He understands the two sayings from the Apostle: "Where the Spirit of the Lord is, there is liberty" (II Cor. 3:17*b*); and "Abstain from all appearance of evil" (I Thess. 5:22).

This whole problem has arisen largely since the Reformation. In olden times, according to a historian of the Church, the practice of appropriating materials wholesale and without credit "was not disapproved when it was done with skill, and when the ideas or words taken from another were used with success. The literary offence lay in the ignorance and incapacity displayed when stolen knowledge was improperly applied."[1] Much the same attitude prevailed throughout the Middle Ages, especially whenever the work of the pulpit drew near to the nadir. Among parish priests the appropriation of sermons abounded; so did books full of sermons ready for use without alteration.

One of those collections went out over Europe under the title *Sermones Dormi Securi,* and became so popular among priests that it passed through twenty-five editions. The reason for the name, *Sleep Well Sermons,* appeared in the preface; otherwise the uncanny priest

[1] See Wm. M. Ramsay, *St. Paul, the Traveller and the Roman Citizen* (New York: G. P. Putnam's Sons, 1901), p. 242.

243

might have supposed that the hearers were supposed to do the sleeping. As for the possibility of the book's falling into the hands of church-goers, few of them could read anything such as this:

> Here happily begin the Sunday Sermons with expositions of the Gospels through the year, quite well known and useful to all priests, pastors, and chaplains, which also are called by the other title of Sleep Well, or Sleep without Care, for this reason, that without much study they may be appropriated and preached to the people.[2]

Those last few words will repay a second reading: "Without much study they may be appropriated and preached to the people!" All of this may seem as harmless as Joseph Addison's essay about Sir Roger de Coverley, the old country gentleman who declared that "Sunday clears away the rust of the whole week." According to *The Spectator*, Sir Roger instructed his curate to read from the sacred desk sermons by the masters. The practice involved no deception, for everyone knew the facts in the case. Not only could the curate busy himself about other things all week, and then "sleep well" on Saturday night; the people too could have slept serenely through the sermon if the dear old autocrat had not decreed that nobody slumber except himself. In those "good old days," however, most parish ministers prepared their own sermons.

In recent times the problem has become more complicated. Laymen now have access to books of sermons, which they sometimes use in checking up on the pastor. They wish to know whether he works in the study or loafs most of the week, whether he does his own thinking or relies on the fruits of other men's toil, whether he feeds the people with food of his own raising, or chiefly from tin cans.

Does all of this seem like armchair soliloquizing? If so, read part of a letter from a layman who wrote on a Sunday afternoon: "Our pastor has now completed a series of eight sermons lifted from Dr. Fosdick's latest book; and according to the bulletin the coming series will follow Dr. Weatherhead's latest volume, both of which books I

[2] See E. C. Dargan, *A History of Preaching* (New York: A. C. Armstrong & Son, 1905), I, 309; see also p. 187.

have read with care." By way of evidence the self-appointed reporter enclosed a copy of the bulletin for the day, checking the announcement of the coming series. That statement consisted of a paragraph, word for word, from the Preface of Weatherhead's book. Then followed, word for word, eight sermon topics lifted from his chapter headings. The sermons, too, followed the source book closely, but neither in the bulletin nor anywhere else did the preacher refer to Weatherhead or, in the other series, to Fosdick. What do you suppose the lay reporter thought of a minister who preached only one sermon a week, and that not his own?

These laymen love their church so much that they feel jealous about its prestige and the good name of the pastor. They would not object if he told them occasionally that he had been reading a volume of sermons by Dr. X, and wished to share some of the insights of that book. But as a rule they wish him to preach messages distinctly his own. Since he has gone through college and seminary, and has six days every week between Sundays, he ought not to appear publicly in used garments, even if they have come from a metropolitan preacher. In view of such feelings, wherein lies the path of wisdom? Must a preacher always refer to his sources?

THE LIMITS OF CHRISTIAN LIBERTY

Whenever a minister preaches a sermon not his own, even in large measure, he should frankly tell what he is doing. Once a visiting pastor delivered the substance of that famous sermon by Brooks, "The Fire and the Calf." In its revised form the message pleased and helped the people, especially those who had never read the original. The few that had read the sermon by Brooks wondered why the borrower did not say that he was treading in the footsteps of the Boston preacher. Even though that use involved the direct quotation of not a single sentence, still the speaker should have guarded his reputation by a reference to Brooks and his sermon. Would that the facts about borrowing always proved this simple!

Much the same principle holds when a minister uses another man's outline, especially if it seems striking. Perhaps some other preacher has recently followed the same trail locally, and that without reference to any source outside himself. What then should the layman conclude? This question arises chiefly concerning messages to boys and girls, perhaps because most pastors find such sermons hard to prepare. If a young man gains the reputation of preaching his own sermons of fuller length, he need not hesitate to let his older hearers know that he gets help from abroad on some of his junior sermons. In a year or two he should find such help no longer necessary.

Why call attention to the source of a sermon for boys and girls? What do they care about where their friend gets his ideas if he makes them interesting? But what if a boy has received from his grandfather as a Christmas gift *The Armour of Youth*, by Walter R. Bowie; *Holy Ground*, by S. Nye Hutchison, or one of the story-sermon books by Hugh T. Kerr? What will the lad tell his chums after the pastor preaches the substance of a sermon from such a book? The elder who wrote that letter about the borrowing of sermons by his pastor never revealed the facts to anyone in the parish, but the boy would excel as a broadcaster. Why should the pastor not keep on the safe side?

What if he does not know the source of a sermon plan? Have not some such patterns for sermons become common property, perhaps too common? Take the time-worn way of treating Psalm 119:11—"Thy word have I laid up in my heart, that I might not sin against thee" (A.S.V.). "The Best Book, in the Best Place, for the Best Purpose." Who could improve on this way of impressing the truth on the heart of a boy or girl? If a young pastor wishes to follow this form of sound words, let him say in passing, and without emphasis, something like this: "Years ago a preacher spoke from this text, and showed how it told three things." So the young minister avoids suspicion on the part of anyone who heard much the same thing a few months before. If the man in the pulpit knows the value of repetition for emphasis, he can make the sermon plan linger in a boy's memory for years, if not forever.

A wise pastor does not often resort to this kind of structure, or to any other. But some time he may wish to speak about II Cor. 8:9—"You know the grace of our Lord Jesus Christ, that though he was rich, yet for your sake he became poor, so that by his poverty you might become rich" (R.S.V.) "How Rich He Was, How Poor He Became, How Rich He Made Us." In a message about "The Riches of the Incarnation" where else could anyone find such a glorious text and such a glowing plan? Perhaps unfortunately, no one hereabouts has identified the author. Even so, somehow the preacher today ought to guard his good name by a passing remark: "Did you ever hear about the sermon by a minister of old?"

An extended quotation also requires some sort of acknowledgment, but that need occasion no difficulty. If the excerpt comes from a well-known book, the minister refers to that work by name and to the writer. Such a reference heightens the effect of the quotation. Then, too, such a speaker as Robert E. Speer always read what he quoted. This author of *How to Speak Effectively Without Notes* never read from pulpit or platform anything except the Scripture lesson and the words of a quotation. He quoted often and much, at times perhaps too much, but he quoted well. By reading a passage from someone else he made it stand out in contrast with what he said in his own name.

These precautions do not apply to quotations from the Scriptures and from other classic literature. In either case a man should commit the words to memory and say them from heart to heart, without glancing down. He need call no attention to the fact that "these familiar words may be found in the First Epistle of Paul to the Corinthians, the fifteenth chapter, and the fifty-eighth verse"; or to the fact that "Lord Tennyson, erstwhile poet laureate of Britain and the favorite bard of countless Christians, penned the lines 'Ring out the old, ring in the new.'" Assume that the hearer has sense and you will save his time.

A poem less familiar calls for a different treatment. When a man recites from memory a poem by Sidney Lanier, "A Ballad of Trees and the Master," the name of the poet ought to come out clearly. If that name deserves to become better known locally, it may appear before the quotation and afterwards. In determining how much stress to put on the name of the author the preacher tries to put himself in the place of his friend in the pew. Then the preacher does whatever will most impress on the memory these words of truth and beauty.[3]

In preparing to speak over the radio a minister has to do still more. Here let him listen to experts:

Before incorporating a poem into your radio sermon, check with the station or network management to be sure no copyright infringement is involved. Two poets whose works cannot be used are Henry Van Dyke and Rudyard Kipling. . . . So be sure to furnish the station, well in advance, the title of the poem, the name of the author, name of the publisher, and the name and date of the magazine or book in which you found the poem. . . .

Copyright laws also cover prose quotations of more than fifty words taken from a copyrighted text. This should give the sermon writer little concern. A fifty-word quotation is too long for the radio sermon. In addition to the danger of deflecting from the main line of thought, there is the peril of using something that doesn't quite fit.[4]

THE WAY TO KEEP WITHIN LIMITS

"What about plagiarism?" Every seminary graduate knows that plagiarism means the improper use of another man's materials. Obviously every minister worthy of the calling desires to keep within proper limits, but he feels confused when he tries to figure out the dividing line between right and wrong, or rather between things proper and things inexpedient. Literally the word plagiarism comes from a Latin word connected with kidnaping, and the Latin springs from a Greek root meaning "oblique, crooked, tortuous, treacherous." But why employ such a harsh term to describe most cases? Frequently they involve some sort of "white lie," or false pretense, rather than theft or larceny.

We ministers may employ euphemisms to gloze over what we term our faults, foibles, and frailties, but why should we rationalize what other men condemn? For example, a young man from Harvard went to a seminary where some of the students sneered at his university as "godless." In that school he had learned to think of plagiarism as a

[3] See Luccock and Brentano, *The Questing Spirit*.
[4] Parker and Others, *Religious Radio*, pp. 115-16.

248

serious offense that usually led to expulsion with no redress. But within the first six weeks in the seminary he heard two of those "pious" students deliver sermons they had taken from books, word for word, with the omission of enough paragraphs to fit the limits of time. One of those men took his message from Henry Drummond and the other from Spurgeon. If the students had known that their classmate reported the facts to the professor in charge, they would have branded the "tattletale" as a traitor. When the professor took up the matter with each delinquent in private, neither of them could see that he had done anything out of the way other than "pull a boner by being caught with the goods."

We who listen to countless sermons by students almost never run across such a flagrant case, but sometimes we meet one near the border line. For example, a certain congregation sends out a monthly folder, skillfully edited and attractively printed. The current issue contains a "lead" by the pastor under the heading "How to Know Right from Wrong," an excerpt from a recent sermon. The preacher sets up four standards, or tests:

> The first of these is the test of publicity. If you are confused about a moral issue ask yourself this question: "If all the world were to know, would I still go on with this action?" Ask yourself: "Would I go ahead with this if my mother and father knew about it, if my best friend was aware of what I was doing? What about my business associates?" In other words, submit your problem to the test of publicity.

Let us apply this test to the sermon itself. Fortunately we need not think harshly about the pastor involved, for he must not have sensed the need of applying the test to himself. He did not commit plagiarism, for the message as reported contains not a word of the sort. However, it bears some resemblance to that sermon by Fosdick, "Six Ways to Tell Right from Wrong," a resemblance like that between an automobile with four cylinders and one with six, each embodying the same design. Since the excerpt bears directly on the problem before us, let us look at part of Fosdick's handiwork, as it came from his workshop fourteen years before the later model:

In the fourth place, if a man is sincerely perplexed over a matter of right and wrong he may well submit the question to the test of publicity. What if everybody knew what we are proposing to do? Strip it of secrecy and furtiveness. Carry it out into the open air, this conduct we are unsure about. Suppose our family and friends knew about it. Imagine it publicly talked of whenever our name is mentioned. Picture it written in the story of our life for our children afterwards to read. Submit it to the test of publicity.[5]

Now for the practical application. If you were the pastor of that congregation, would you be willing to print in the monthly news letter the two paragraphs that appear above in small type? If not, why not? So let every minister resolve anew to safeguard his reputation. He may read printed sermons, but not with a view to reproducing any of them without credit. At St. Paul's in London, H. P. Liddon used to read a sermon every day of the week, but in the pulpit he voiced the gospel according to Liddon, and not according to John Donne, Jeremy Taylor, or John Tillotson. Through constant reading and study Liddon aimed to keep the reservoir so full that whenever he wished to prepare a sermon he could count on the overflow.

Such a minister thinks for himself. He keeps away from homiletical helps, most of which prove to be hindrances. Why waste time on secondhand stuff? Give no shelf room to books of sermon outlines or canned illustrations, even if they come from Spurgeon or some recent master. Do the same with homiletical commentaries, which deprive the preacher of lasting joy in using his intellectual muscles. In exegetical commentaries you can find the meaning of any passage in its own background, and then use imagination in determining how to make the truth live. As for the possibility of quoting the words of exegetical commentaries, a lover of the King's English seldom feels any such urge!

Over against all these negations let us put the saying of a teacher who inspired countless students to do their own thinking and speaking. This beloved dean has in view the meaning of days in college, but his

[5] *The Hope of the World,* pp. 131-32.

THE ETHICS OF QUOTING MATERIALS

words embody an ideal for the pastor in his study, where he can transform drudgery into delight:

What has it all been for? For the knowledge that makes life richer; for the friendship that makes life sweeter; for the training that brings power to the task which is hard and high; for the wisdom that suffers and triumphs and is strong; for the vision that shall light your path like a pillar of fire; for the truth that shall make you free.[6]

Suggested Readings

Articles on "Copyright" and "Plagiarism" in *Encyclopaedia Britannica*.
Harmon, Nolan B., Jr. *Ministerial Ethics and Etiquette*. Nashville: Abingdon-Cokesbury Press, 1928.
Turnbull, Ralph G. *The Minister's Obstacles*. New York: F. H. Revell Co., 1946.

[6] L. B. R. Briggs, *Routine and Ideals* (Boston: Houghton Mifflin Co., 1904), p. 135.

CHAPTER XXIII

The Sermon as an Act of Worship

FOR THE SAKE OF SIMPLICITY we have been looking at the sermon by itself, as though it were "a star, and dwelt apart." Now we must take a broader view, and think of the message from the pulpit as an act of public worship. By public worship we understand God's revelation of Himself through grace and our response through faith. In terms of the Old Testament, the angels keep ascending and descending, rising to the throne of God with the praises and prayers of His children, and returning to men with blessings from the Father of mercies. These blessings from God come partly through the reading of the Scriptures and the preaching of the Word. So the hour of worship calls for the interworking of the divine and the human, or else the human and the divine.

Any such account makes the twofold movement of thought and feeling appear more simple than the facts warrant. The public worship of God must ever remain a mystery, though "a mystery of light." When we delve into the theory of worship we may begin to falter, but when we approach it as a matter of Christian experience, we find God waiting to bless. All the while we ought to remember that in every stage of public worship someone must lead. Part of the time, in a sort of priestly ministry, the minister stands before God on behalf of men, pleading for mercy and for grace. In other parts of this hour, notably in the sermon, the leader serves more as a prophet who appears before men in the name of his God. So that the minister engages in public worship as truly when he preaches as when he prays.

THE IMPORTANCE OF THE SERMON

This way of looking at the facts ought to heighten our appreciation of the sermon, and of everything else we do in public worship. Sometimes we carelessly refer to other parts as "preliminaries," or "the setting of the sermon." On the other hand, a person of a different

THE SERMON AS AN ACT OF WORSHIP

school may exalt other parts of public worship so as to overshadow the sermon. Over in London, at St. Martin's-in-the-Fields, according to a rumor half of the people used to put up with the service for the sake of the sermon, whereas the other half endured the sermon for the sake of the service. But why make such a distinction? Why not enjoy both? Surely all of the parts in Christian worship belong together! "What therefore God hath joined together, let not man put asunder" (Matt. 19:6b).

Why then do we debate about the relative importance of preaching and worship? Should we not think of preaching as a part of worship, and of the whole as more important than any of the parts? Why do we ever let the sermon dominate the hour of worship? On such a special day as Easter or Pentecost the theme of the hour ought to control all the worship, including the message. At regular services, however, the praises and prayers of the sanctuary may range over wider areas of thought and feeling, though never without unity and progress like that of Handel's *Messiah*. In making the plans for any hour of public worship be sure, therefore, to let the sermon form an integral part of the whole.[1]

Some of us think of the reading from the Scriptures as the most important part of public worship except for the sacraments. We regard the prayers as all-important, and we highly esteem the music, especially the songs by the people. Amid all these holy concerns, how can the leader maintain the correct proportion? By thinking much about the glory of God and the needs of people! At present we must focus attention on the sermon, but we ought to remember that its effectiveness depends largely on what has gone before and on what will come after. So we must face the question of how to make the most out of the sermon as an act of worship.

Think of the leader as a guide. If he knows how to do his part during the first twenty-five or thirty minutes, he can guide the people stage by stage onto the mountaintop where they will come face to face with the Lord Jesus in the glory of His transfiguration. Just

[1] See A. W. Blackwood, *The Fine Art of Public Worship* (New York and Nashville: Abingdon-Cokesbury, 1939), chap. X.

before the sermon he may have them rise to sing "Spirit of God, Descend upon My Heart," or "Love Divine, All Loves Excelling." If the traditions of the church permit, he may lead in an expression of their common faith. Then, as the people look to him for a message from God, he may imagine that he hears them saying: "Now therefore we are all here present in the sight of God, to hear all that you have been commanded by the Lord" (Acts 10:33b, R.S.V.). When the minister starts to preach, what should he do? Let him continue to lead in the public worship of God!

If the sermon in church is what it ought to be—if it is not an exhibition of the preacher, but of Jesus—there should be nothing in it even conceivably in contrast with worship, but the very reverse. What can be more truly described as worship than hearing the Word of God as it ought to be heard, hearing it with penitence, with contrition, with faith and self-consecration, with vows of new obedience? If this is not worship in spirit and in truth, what is? [2]

After the sermon the leader may do little more ere he pronounces the benediction, but he should do that little with distinction. If he has preached well, he knows that the friend in the pew wishes to act, and to do so now. Hence the sermon may lead up to a word of prayer, voicing the spirit of dedication to God. Then may follow a hymn of enlistment on the part of the worshipers one by one or by the group as a whole. After the man in the pew has stood up to sing "Jesus, I My Cross Have Taken" or "The Son of God Goes Forth to War," he should feel ready to bow down and receive the benediction of the Triune God.

In the Lutheran Church, as elsewhere, the latter part of public worship takes a different form, still more climactic. After the sermon and a hymn the officers receive the gifts of the people. Then the minister takes these offerings, lays them on the altar, and leads the congregation in the pastoral prayer full of thanksgivings and supplications. Such an order places the sermon almost in the center

[2] Frank Cairns, *The Prophet of the Heart* (London: Hodder & Stoughton, 1934), p. 64; see also pp. 46-92.

of the service, and encourages everyone present to look on the message as an act of worship.

On a special day in another body, the sermon may lead up to a memorable act of corporate worship. For example, think about the baptism of new converts, the ordination of elders-elect, or the public recognition of workers in the church school. What an opportunity for the minister to vary the program, using the sermon as a preparation for the special act of worship! But sometimes the man in charge arranges to have the climactic feature before the sermon. If he looked forward to the Holy Communion, he would plan for the meditation to come before. Why should he not do the same with the other sacrament, Holy Baptism, and with any other ceremony that deserves a place of distinction in the public worship of God?

This whole matter of blending the sermon with the other parts of public worship calls for time and thought, in the spirit of humility and prayer. From the beginning to the end of every service, the tone color ought to harmonize. Neither before nor after the sermon ought anyone to sense a loss of connection. Why permit any rift or crevice, not to speak of a gulf, between any two main parts of corporate worship? What an ideal! Actually the worshiper may feel a sense of uplift during the early part of the hour, and he may derive much help from the sermon. But on the way home he may wonder why the two halves did not hang together. Some other day he may ask himself why the minister did not put as much of the Christian religion into his sermon as into the other parts of public worship.

THE INFLUENCE OF THIS CONCEPTION

If every minister looked on the sermon as an act of worship, many a pulpit would gain dignity and power. The one who stands there ought to serve as an ambassador of the Most High. Every preacher should look on himself as an interpreter of the Book, in which God makes known His will for the people. In the Protestant Episcopal Church, as in the Methodist, every candidate for ordination to the ministry receives from the officiating bishop a copy of the Scriptures. Ever afterwards the preacher ought to regard his messages from the Book as holy acts of corporate worship. Whenever he approaches the truth or the duty in hand, he should look on it through light that streams from above.

This ideal ought to influence the spirit of the preacher, making him as reverent when he speaks from the sacred desk as when he engages in corporate prayer. In the pulpit now and again he should bring the people face to face with their sins, and in doing so he needs to speak with humility, yet with "holy boldness." Both in praying and in preaching the ideal pastor thinks of himself as a minister of reconciliation. In other days a minister such as Richard Baxter often referred to his preaching as "a dying man to dying men." In a sense that still holds true, but many a pastor today prefers to think of himself as a living man with words of hope for living men.

In the public worship of God the leader ought to bring every hearer into right relations with God, and then show him how to be happy in the Lord. For an example of such a "happy" preacher take Brooks or Jowett. Does this theory of pulpit work afford a place for humor? The answers differ widely. Spurgeon would say yes, whereas Gossip insists that most preachers ought to abstain from humor in the pulpit. But he would allow an exception for such a "happy" preacher as the "Scottish Spurgeon," John McNeill. Brooks, too, loved all sorts of harmless jollity, but still he warned young ministers not to become known as "clerical jesters":

[The clerical jester] appears in and out of the pulpit. He lays hands on the most sacred things, and leaves defilement upon all he touches. He is full of Bible jokes. He talks about the Church's sacred symbols in the language of stale jests that have come down from generations of feeble clerical jesters. . . . There are passages in the Bible which are soiled forever by the touches which the hands of ministers who delight in cheap and easy jokes have left upon them. . . . The buffoonery which merely tries me when I hear it from a gang of laborers digging a ditch beside my door angers me and frightens me when it comes from the lips of the captain who holds the helm or the surgeon on whose skill my life depends.

Humor . . . is one of the most helpful qualities that the preacher can possess. . . . The truest humor is the bloom of the highest life. . . . But humor is something very different from frivolity. People sometimes ask whether it is right to make people laugh in church by something you say from the pulpit,—as if laughter were always one invariable thing; as if there were not a smile which swept across a great congregation like the breath of a May morning, making it fruitful for whatever good thing might be sowed in it, and another laughter that was like the crackling of thorns under a pot.[3]

When a man looks on the sermon as an act of worship, he can preach with authority not his own. "Thus saith the Lord!" The authority comes from God, who has spoken through the prophets and the apostles, and supremely through His Son. In our own day also, through the Holy Spirit, God speaks to waiting hearts through the preaching of His Word. He stands ready to bless whatever the ministering servant utters in His name. "In His Name!" According to Gossip, whenever a man preaches or prays he stands before the people "in Christ's stead." Hence the interpreter ought to say and do only what pleases the King. Where on earth does He make Himself known so clearly today as in the sanctuary? Where does the King speak more strongly than through His ministering servant? This way of looking on the sermon influences a man's attitude towards the hearers. He ought to know:

> Congregations desire their preachers to take high ground, and to speak with authority. There is no more fatal habit than the not uncommon one of punctuating one's message with the modest word "perhaps." It is not incumbent upon us to soften down the word of God to suit the taste of a refined audience. We used to be warned . . . not to preach that "he who, so to speak, believeth not shall, as it were, be damned." Arm your personality with the armour of certainty, and let it go free, strenuous, and unhesitating. Let it be the personality of an athlete of the spirit, who has wrestled in meditation and made up his mind in the sweat of his brow. Such a personality will be well worth sending forth.[4]

As an act of public worship every sermon calls for a man's best. If anyone needs a motto by way of reminder, he may choose the words

[3] *Lectures on Preaching*, pp. 55-57.
[4] John Kelman, *The War and Preaching* (New Haven: Yale University Press, 1919), pp. 211-12.

of David about the purchase of a site for an altar: "Neither will I offer burnt offerings unto the Lord my God of that which doth cost me nothing" (II Sam. 24:24). As an artist G. F. Watts expressed much the same feeling: "The Utmost for the Highest!" With such an ideal the man in the study can toil day after day as though everything depended upon him and his sermon; in the pulpit he can speak with assurance because everything depends upon God and His grace.

Suggested Readings

Calkins, Raymond. *The Romance of the Ministry*. Boston and Chicago: The Pilgrim Press, 1944. Chap. XIII.

Forsyth, P.T. *Positive Preaching and the Modern Mind*. New York: Hodder & Stoughton, 1907. Chap. III.

CHAPTER XXIV

The Round of the Christian Year

AS AN ACT OF WORSHIP what has the sermon to do with the
Christian Year? The answer depends in part on the church to
which a minister belongs. If he serves God as a Lutheran or an
Episcopalian, he does well to follow the Church Year [1] as a guide
in preaching. In nonliturgical bodies, too, many of us have learned
to value the Christian Year as a help in preparing for the pulpit. As
for other aspects of public worship, we need not think of them now.
For the sake of clarity we shall deal only with the morning service.

In most of its varied forms the Christian Year begins with Advent,
a period that includes the four Sundays prior to Christmas. After
Advent the successive seasons have to do with stages in the earthly
career of our Lord. From the beginning of Advent until after Easter,
for almost six months, the Christian Year points repeatedly to Christ.
During these six months, despite the worst weather in the year,
people throng our churches as at no other season. But when skies
become balmy, and attention shifts away from Christ, attendance
begins to wane. Partly for this reason wise men have been insisting
that we continue to stress the living Christ, the work of the Spirit, and
the coming of the Kingdom. Somehow or other we must claim for
the King both halves of the Christian Year.

In almost every form the Christian Year calls for a lectionary—a
list of Bible passages for reading from the pulpit. In a liturgical body
the pastor must use some of these lessons in public worship, though
not in preaching. In another branch of the Church ecumenical the
minster can adopt a lectionary, or else make one of his own, and if
he does that, he may compile a new one every year. As a preacher
he can use the lectionary for a guide in all his planning for the pulpit.

[1] The "Church Year" means an order of worship prescribed by an ecclesiastical
body; the "Christian Year" is an order suggested rather than prescribed. The two terms
often appear interchangeably.

However, he must not follow the lectionary slavishly, lest he become so obsessed with a system as to ignore human needs and divine grace.

THE EFFECT ON PREACHING

The wise use of the Christian Year encourages a man to preach from the Bible. Instead of living from hand to mouth he can plan the work of the pulpit so as to secure continuity and progress. During the period before Advent he can preach often from the Old Testament, showing how God revealed Himself to one man after another, and thus prepared for the coming of Christ. During the harvest season of the Christian Year—between the middle of December and the coming of Easter—the pulpit interpreter can bring forth riches from one of the Gospels. If he keeps to only one, he can guide the lay friends in reading it as the unfolding of truth in the life and death of our Lord. Especially at Christmas, Easter, and Pentecost he can find climactic stages in the onward sweep of redemption. So he may begin to transform the tasks of the study into adventures of faith.

In the right sort of hands the Christian Year goes far to insure a well-rounded succession of sermons. This way of planning enables a minister every twelve months to deal with all the central truths and cardinal duties of Christianity. Every year he can approach these basic truths and duties from a different point of view. If he did not think in terms of more than a week or two, he might ignore certain truths and duties so as to stress others out of all proportion. At times almost every pastor finds himself falling into a sermonic rut of his own making. Where can anyone discover a better way to keep out of such a rut than by preaching the round of the Christian Year?

This way of planning encourages a minister to prepare an occasional series, or a course. In a series the pastor announces a group of sermons as a whole, and in preparing them he works as in writing a book with that many chapters, all about the subject in the title. In a course a man proceeds without any such announcement, so that week after week, at the same service each Lord's Day, he can lead the flock through hills and valleys full of pasture. In a downtown church with a shifting procession of hearers a minister can offer one series after another. Elsewhere a pastor may have only three or four series a year, one of them during Holy Week; but he can run as many courses as he desires, the more the better. As for the benefits, listen to the B. H. Streeter, of Oxford. When he uses the term "series," he may refer also to what some of us know as a "course":

A connected series on any subject by a man of quite moderate ability will make far more permanent impression than an equal number of isolated sermons by a brilliant speaker. The congregation recall what was said last time, they look forward expectantly to what will be said next time. . . . The congregation knows that the preacher is taking his duties seriously. The uncharitable can no longer surmise that the subject of his exhortation is determined by the text that happened to come into his head on Saturday morning while shaving. . . . No man can give the best that he has it in him to give in a single sermon. In a course of sermons he has some chance of making a definite and permanent impression.[2]

The use of the Christian Year in preaching tends to fix the hearer's attention on Christ. Sunday after Sunday, at least for six months, the man who attends church feels sure of coming face to face with truth or duty as it has to do with the Lord Jesus. Strange as it may seem, many a regular churchgoer reports that he seldom hears a sermon directly about Christ as Saviour and Lord. Without intending to do so, the man in the pulpit may let causes and movements crowd out Christ and the Kingdom. If he discussed all the subjects outsiders keep suggesting he would have few opportunities to say a good word for his Lord.

THE CALL FOR PULPIT DRAMA

The man who follows the Christian Year in his pulpit work needs to cultivate a sense of drama. Otherwise he may turn out sermons all alike, and all "duds." Drama calls for a person, or persons, in action, with struggle, conflict, and suspense, after which comes the dénouement. Where can anyone find all this more surely than in the drama of

[2] B. H. Streeter, *Concerning Prayer* (New York: The Macmillan Co., 1916), pp. 275-76.

redemption? In the Old Testament see how the Lord God prepared for the coming of the Redeemer by raising up one man after another who "climbed the steep ascent of heaven through peril, toil, and pain." Preach about those heroes of faith, one at a time, and look at each of them in the light that streams from the New Testament. Herein lies no small part of the drama in our redemption. Let the laymen sense more and more of its onward sweep and wonder. When you can preach according to a forward-looking plan, do not play hop, skip, and jump. Follow the course of the Christian Year!

Especially do the records about the Lord Jesus provide materials for pulpit drama. Instead of man-centered messages or hearer-centered sermons, every discourse for six months and longer may center in Christ. As for variety from week to week, that will come to the man who shares with his friends what he finds in the Book. Especially when the sermons draw near to Palm Sunday, the beginning of Passion Week, they ought to show more and more intensity. In the pulpit here at home, as in the Passion play at Oberammergau, every new scene in the drama of redemption should open up a vista of the grace that appeared in Jesus Christ, supremely in His Cross and in His Resurrection.

After Easter the drama of redemption ought still to go on; ideally it should soar to still loftier heights. "He who believes in me will also do the works that I do; and greater works than these will he do, because I go to the Father" (John 14:12, R.S.V.). After the Ascension our Lord fulfilled that promise through the Holy Spirit, thus leading the Apostolic Church from triumph to triumph. Today He wishes to guide the Church in a conquest of the world, and that largely through preaching the gospel. Now, as in other times, He waits to bless the good news as it rings out through the Christian Year. But all the while He wishes the man in the pulpit to stress the gospel message, and not any preaching method. God forbid that anyone should try to substitute a method for a message!

In view of these ideals, why has the use of the Christian Year not resulted in better preaching? In other days men like Brooks and Robertson, Newman and Taylor, with the French orators of the

THE ROUND OF THE CHRISTIAN YEAR

seventeenth century, showed the possibilities of the pulpit in a liturgical Church. Of course no one of them followed such a plan blindly, but somehow every one of them kept the hearts of people moving onward toward the mountain-top experiences of the Christian life on earth. If such pulpit work has seemed uncommon of late, one reason may be that ministers follow the Christian Year in other parts of public worship more than in preparing to preach. If so, why do they not "possess their possessions"?

Let no one construe this chapter as a plea for the adoption of liturgical forms in public worship, or as an argument for not doing so. That issue looms large among more than a few churches today, and may become still more pressing tomorrow, but the matter does not concern us here. Many of us have inherited other traditions, and have held to other ideals. In public worship we feel free to use historic forms or not to use them, within certain limits, as the Spirit of God may direct.

Our Christian liberty applies even more to the use of the Christian Year as a guide in preaching. Here too many of us rejoice in our freedom and our opportunity. More and more we have gone in this direction, and we can testify that this way of working tends to give a man's pulpit ministry stability and power. But we do not look on this method, or any other, as a panacea for the ills of church and state. No way of working in study and pulpit can begin to heal the deep hurt of humanity. For all that we must look to the grace of God: "Is there no balm in Gilead; is there no physician there? why then is not the health of the daughter of my people recovered?" (Jer. 8:22).

In the present time of *Weltschmerz* the Spirit of God has quickened concern about our public prayers and our pulpit work. He has led us to hope for a revival of preaching, so that the Christian Church will awake to the importance of proclaiming the evangel. Many of us rejoice to believe that this awakening has started, for more than a few of our younger ministers have begun to get their bearings. So have countless others still young in heart. These men have tasted the joys of meeting the needs of men by preaching the truths of God. Hence they have determined to put the work of the pulpit first in all their ministry for God and men. By His grace they have set themselves to make the future of the Christian pulpit more than worthy of its past. Who follows in their train?

Anoint them priests! Strong intercessors they
For pardon, and for charity and peace!
O that with them might pass the world, astray,
Into the dear Christ's life of sacrifice!

Make them apostles! Heralds of Thy cross,
Forth may they go to tell all realms Thy grace;
Inspired of Thee, may they count all but loss,
And stand at last with joy before Thy face.

Suggested Readings

Adams, Fred W. *The Christian Year*, pamphlet. New York: Federal Council of Churches of Christ in America, 1940.

Blackwood, Andrew W. *Planning a Year's Pulpit Work.*

———. *This Year of Our Lord.* Philadelphia: Westminster Press, 1943.

Brooks, Phillips. *Sermons for the Principal Festivals and Fasts of the Church Year.* New York: E. P. Dutton & Co., 1910.

Davis, Ozora S. *Preaching on Church and Community Occasions.* Chicago: University of Chicago Press, 1928.

Gibson, George M. *The Story of the Christian Year.* New York and Nashville: Abingdon-Cokesbury Press, 1945.

Hedley, George P. *A Christian Year.* Toronto: The Macmillan Co., 1934.

Keble, John. *The Christian Year: Thoughts in Verse.* New York: D. Appleton & Co., 1848.

Strodach, Paul Z. *The Church Year.* Philadelphia: United Lutheran Publishing House, 1924.

Wilson, Frank E. *An Outline of the Christian Year*, a booklet. New York: Morehouse-Gorham Co., 1941.

Index of Passages

Index of Persons

267

Index of Subjects

INDEX OF SUBJECTS

271

251
B63pr

71279